The Intrinsic Worth of Persons
Contractarianism in Moral and Political Philosophy

Contractarianism in some form has been at the center of recent debates in moral and political philosophy. Jean Hampton was one of the most gifted philosophers involved in these debates and provided both important criticisms of prominent contractarian theories and powerful defenses and applications of the core ideas of contractarianism. In these essays, she brought her distinctive approach, animated by concern for the intrinsic worth of persons, to bear on topics such as guilt, punishment, self-respect, family relations, and the maintenance and justification of the state. Edited by Daniel Farnham, this collection is an essential contribution to understanding the problems and prospects of contractarianism in moral, legal, and political philosophy.

Jean Hampton completed her Ph.D. under the direction of John Rawls at Harvard University. She was a Harvard Knox Fellow at Cambridge University; a Pew Evangelical Scholar; and a distinguished visiting lecturer at Dalhousie University, University of Notre Dame, Pomona College, and Bristol University. She taught at several American institutions, most recently the University of Arizona, where she was a professor of philosophy at the time of her death in 1996. Her last book, *The Authority of Reason*, was published posthumously in 1998.

Daniel Farnham is a Franklin Fellow in Philosophy at the University of Georgia.

The Intrinsic Worth of Persons

Contractarianism in Moral and Political Philosophy

JEAN HAMPTON

Edited by
DANIEL FARNHAM
University of Georgia

CAMBRIDGE
UNIVERSITY PRESS

CAMBRIDGE
UNIVERSITY PRESS

University Printing House, Cambridge CB2 8BS, United Kingdom

One Liberty Plaza, 20th Floor, New York, NY 10006, USA

477 Williamstown Road, Port Melbourne, VIC 3207, Australia

314-321, 3rd Floor, Plot 3, Splendor Forum, Jasola District Centre, New Delhi - 110025, India

79 Anson Road, #06-04/06, Singapore 079906

Cambridge University Press is part of the University of Cambridge.

It furthers the University's mission by disseminating knowledge in the pursuit of education, learning and research at the highest international levels of excellence.

www.cambridge.org
Information on this title: www.cambridge.org/9780521673259

© Cambridge University Press 2007

First published 2007

A catalogue record for this publication is available from the British Library

Library of Congress Cataloging in Publication data
Hampton, Jean.
The intrinsic worth of persons : contractarianism in moral and political philosophy / Jean Hampton.
p. cm.
Includes bibliographical references and index.
ISBN 0-521-85686-8 (hardback) – ISBN 0-521-67325-9 (pbk.)
1. Contractarianism (Ethics) I. Title.
BJ1500.C65H36   2006
171´.7–dc22   2006005044

ISBN 978-0-521-85686-7 Hardback
ISBN 978-0-521-67325-9 Paperback

Contents

Preface and Acknowledgments

Jean Hampton wrote on an astonishing variety of topics. A small collection cannot hope to convey the full power and breadth of her thought. But it can suggest its richness, and it can push our own thinking further on issues she cared about. I have chosen essays on some of her central concerns in moral, legal, and political philosophy – concerns she returned to repeatedly to improve her view. Fortunately, much of Jean's work on other topics – in particular, her book on reason – remains in print. I have appended a selected bibliography to help guide the reader looking for further engagement with Jean's philosophy.

I would like to thank Tom Christiano, Richard Healey, Christopher Morris, David Schmidtz, and three anonymous referees from Cambridge University Press for their guidance. I am especially grateful to David Gauthier for his foreword and remembrance. The late Terry Moore helped to initiate the project at Cambridge, and Beatrice Rehl and Stephanie Sakson patiently saw it through to its completion. Work on this collection was supported by the Jean Hampton Memorial Fund at the University of Arizona.

These chapters originally appeared in the publications listed below. Permission to reprint them is gratefully acknowledged. Chapter 1, "Feminist Contractarianism," previously appeared in *A Mind of One's Own: Feminist Essays on Reason and Objectivity*, ed. L. Anthony and C. Witt. Copyright © 1992 by Westview Press. Reprinted by permission of Westview Press, a member of Perseus Books, LLC. Chapter 2, "Selflessness and Loss of Self," previously appeared in *Social Philosophy and Policy* 10, no. 1 (1993): 135–65. Chapter 3, "*Mens Rea*," previously appeared in *Social*

Philosophy and Policy 7, no. 2 (1990): 1–28. Chapter 4, "Correcting Harms versus Righting Wrongs: The Goal of Retribution," previously appeared in *UCLA Law Review* 39 (1992): 1659–1702. Chapter 5, "The Common Faith of Liberalism," previously appeared in *Pacific Philosophical Quarterly* 775 (1994): 186–216. Chapter 6, "The Contractarian Explanation of the State," previously appeared in *Midwest Studies in Philosophy* 15 (1990): 344–71.

Foreword

For Jean – Some Opening Words

David Gauthier

To be invited to introduce a selection of Jean Hampton's writings is a great honor. Would though that neither I nor anyone else were to receive it, and that Jean herself were still among us, able to write her own introduction. And if still among us, then still contributing striking ideas and challenging arguments to the never-ending conversation that we call philosophy. I miss Jean. But I am glad to have known her, and because to know Jean was to argue with her, glad to have crossed swords with her in mutually fruitful, constructive confrontation.

Like many moral philosophers of her generation, Jean received the core of her training from John Rawls – an experience that encouraged the development of a Kantian perspective. Kant was certainly one of Jean's philosophical progenitors, but so was Hobbes, and at times one can sense the opposing tugs of each on her thought. And we should not overlook the presence of a third influence, for Jean belonged to the distinct minority of analytic philosophers who are firmly committed Christians. Not that her faith replaces argument in her writings, but it is, I think, easier to appreciate the focus of some of her thinking, especially in one of the finest pieces in this volume, "*Mens Rea*," if one is aware of her religious background.

As a philosopher Jean was unusually forthcoming. Too many of us – at least in my experience – are reluctant to let our views into the public sphere until we believe we can meet all objections to them – a futile hope! – and once publicly committed, we are even more reluctant to

Emeritus Distinguished Professor of Philosophy, University of Pittsburgh.

change our positions, disguising shifts in thought as elaborations of what we of course meant all along. Jean didn't express views casually, but being rightly suspicious of final truths in philosophy, she willingly shared her views with her fellows and, while she defended them vigorously, was ready to alter or even abandon them in the light of what seemed to her the better argument. Tenacious in debate, she was flexible in her thought – an uncommon but welcome combination.

Were Jean still with us, she would be ready and eager to continue the debates that the chapters in this collection invite. Instead, we must carry on alone, absent the protagonist. Not being able to provoke her to respond, I will play a tamer role, raising, in this introduction, my questions and worries that the reader may, if he or she wishes, try either to answer on Jean's behalf or to incorporate into developing a more convincing alternative. Or the reader may prefer to ignore my comments, as distracting him or her from the encounter with Jean. What matters most is that the reader find, or find again, how fertile it is to read Jean and enter with her into some of the most challenging questions of moral, political, and legal philosophy.

In discussing Jean's papers that are reprinted here, I shall follow my own thread through her ideas, rather than proceeding in the order the editor has chosen for them. I begin with "*Mens Rea*," in which Jean offers an original account of culpability, taking defiance as her key. Genuine culpability, whether rational, moral, or legal, requires a defiant mind. The culpable lawbreaker knows, or should know, the law; he or she recognizes its authority but believes that authority can be defied, replaced by a different authority more to his or her liking. I am reminded of Milton's Satan, who expresses his (futile) defiance of God's law in his cry, "Evil, be thou my good!"

Essential to Jean's account is the idea that defiance is, and must be, deeply futile, in that the authority defied, be it reason, morality, or law, cannot be dethroned. Jean gives us an account of rational authority that establishes this. But moral and legal authority, as she recognizes, are deeply problematic. So what Jean offers us seems to me to be an account of legal culpability that needs impregnable authority as its basis. And the reader must ask him- or herself if such authority is to be had.

Before leaving this profoundly original chapter, one word of advice as to how to read it. Read the conclusion only after you have assimilated the body of the chapter. For the conclusion should come as an unexpected twist in Jean's argument – and, as it happens, one that reveals more about her character than any other single passage in this collection.

"Selflessness and the Loss of Self" is also a deeply illuminating chapter, both for its argument and for what it reveals about its author. Moral philosophers are all too ready to come down on the side of altruism and to consider self-sacrifice, if not always a moral demand, yet a mark of moral sainthood. Jean is rightly suspicious; not all self-sacrifice, she tells us, deserves our respect or approval. Selflessness may be a loss of the self that we should be guarding against those whom we might call moral imperialists (my term, not hers) – those who would use their fellows in the name of morality.

Of course Jean would not have us embrace egoism and selfishness in our effort not to be stifled by altruism and selflessness. There is a balance to be struck – and it is the need for balance that made contractarian thinking appealing to Jean, since the contractarian seeks principles and practices that afford fair mutual benefit, rejecting one-sided sacrifice but forbidding unconstrained self-assertion.

Two of the chapters in this collection focus on contractarian themes. In "The Contractarian Explanation of the State" Jean boldly attempts to use the social contract argument to answer not normative or justificatory but causal questions about the state, its origins, and its maintenance. Most contemporary contract theorists would cast a dubious eye on the explanatory use of the social contract, but Jean, with her usual disregard for conventional wisdom, is undaunted.

But Jean recognizes that her claim is deceptive, in that the procedure by which she supposes a state might be generated is coordinative rather than contractual, in that it does not involve the promises that characterize contractual agreement. (We in North America follow a convention in driving on the right; common sense, and not any contract or promise, ensures that we follow the convention.)

The interest of the chapter, however, does not turn on a terminological point. Jean proposes what she calls the convention model, and the questions for the reader should concern the merit of the model. And here one should, I think, applaud Jean for recognizing that any explanation of a democratic state must account for two directions of control: the rulers by the people and the people by the rulers. She deploys her model to try to show how these seemingly opposed directions may be fitted together. If she succeeds, we can readily forgive her for replacing the idea of a contract with that of a self-interested convention.

But we may be less ready to forgive her departure from the idea of a contract in "Feminist Contractarianism." This chapter plays a valuable philosophical role, making clear the difference between Hobbesian and

Kantian ideas of the social contract and showing how contractarian modes of thought are the ally, rather than the enemy, of the feminist moral theorist. And before raising my concern with Jean's approach, I want to comment briefly on the divide between Hobbes and Kant. The former treats the contract as a deal that each person finds reasonable to accept in order better to advance his or her own interests. The latter treats the contract rather as guaranteeing proper respect for him- or herself as an end. One can readily appreciate, in the latter, the connection with Jean's insistence that we not be morally used. The contract ensures that everyone receives due moral recognition. And it is a short step from this to seeing the contract as a device appealing to feminists who seek to eradicate male dominance in morality as elsewhere.

But now my worry. In "Feminist Contractarianism" Jean insists that "every contract theory . . . has used the idea of a contract as a heuristic tool that points us toward the correct form of moral reasoning and has not relied on the notion of contract in any literal way to do any justificatory work." This seems to me to sell contractarianism short. For at least on my view, the contract is intended to do real work.* Only by determining what rational persons would agree to in a suitable pre-moral situation can we give content to and a rationale for moral principles. Proposed or alleged moral principles can be put to the contractarian test – might they be agreed to by rational persons seeking principles to govern their interactions? I leave to the reader the question whether this role is merely a "heuristic tool." Would that I could argue the issue with Jean herself!

"The Common Faith of Liberalism" pits Jean once more against her mentor, John Rawls. Here the issue is whether a pluralist society can be unified by "Enlightenment liberalism," a rationally grounded political conception that provides social justice and stability. Rawls dismisses such a conception as partisan and tries to replace it by a conception of political liberalism freed from the bias of the Enlightenment. Jean – rightly to my mind – argues that Rawls is unable to avoid the faith that, she believes, all liberals share: faith in the possibility of "a social and political structure that is reliant on reason and respectful of all individuals' dignity and autonomy." In a world increasingly hostile to the idea of the Enlightenment, Rawls has sought to maintain the vestiges of liberalism without

---

* *Editor's note*: Hampton discusses Gauthier's view at length in "Two Faces of Contractarian Thought," in Peter Vallentyne, ed., *Contractarianism and Rational Choice: Essays on David Gauthier's Morals by Agreement* (Cambridge: Cambridge University Press, 1991), pp. 31–55.

its traditional commitments. Jean's chapter is a salutary reminder that without those commitments, liberalism would be defenseless.

One chapter remains to be mentioned: "Righting Wrongs: The Goal of Retribution." Jean sees retribution as expressive, as asserting the claim of the moral order in the face of one who denies it. (Is this another case of defiance?) More specifically, moral wrongdoing consists in diminishing human value; retribution reasserts that value. But what is it to *diminish* value? It cannot be literally to degrade someone, for as a Kantian Jean denies that persons can be degraded. The attempt to degrade is futile. (But, to refer back to another of Jean's papers, what is loss of self if not degradation?) Diminishment is "the appearance of degradation" – treating someone as if he or she lacked the inalienable value he or she possesses. And retribution treats the wrongdoer in a way that repudiates his or her attempt to degrade and reasserts the value that he or she diminishes.

I find this doctrine puzzling. If we cannot be degraded, how can we appear to be degraded – how can we be diminished? Jean is aware of this question – objections to her views rarely escape her notice. And of course she grapples with it – how successful she is will have to be judged by the reader.

So these are the ideas awaiting the reader of this book. I have tried to suggest some of the treats in store – and some of what to me are the hard questions to be faced. Jean would want us to pursue those – and other – questions. She was never one to shy away from controversy. The best way we can honor her is to accept the challenges of the papers she has left us, and seek to carry forward their arguments.

1

Feminist Contractarianism

Like any good theory, [a woman's moral theory] will need not to ignore the partial truth of previous theories. So it must accommodate both the insights men have more easily than women, and those women have more easily than men. It should swallow up its predecessor theories. Women moral theorists, if any, will have this very great advantage over the men whose theories theirs supplant, that they can stand on the shoulders of men moral theorists, as no man has yet been able to stand on the shoulders of any woman moral theorist. There can be advantages, as well as handicaps, in being latecomers.

Annette C. Baier[1]

Is it possible to be simultaneously a feminist and a partisan of the contractarian approach to moral and political theory? The prospects for a successful marriage of these two positions look dubious if one has read recent feminist criticisms of contemporary contractarian theories. Moreover, this brand of moral theory has been suffused with the technical machinery of game theory, logic, and economics of the sort often thought to attract male philosophers and repel female ones, making such theorizing, in the words of one feminist philosopher, a "big boys' game" and a "male locker room" that few female philosophers have "dared enter."[2]

But this seemingly inhospitable philosophical terrain has been my intellectual home for some years now. And I have been persistently attracted to contractarian modes of theorizing not merely because such

---

[1] Annette C. Baier, "What Do Women Want in a Moral Theory?," *Nous* 19, no. 1 (March 1985): 56.

[2] Ibid., p. 54. And see Ian Hacking, "Winner Take Less: A Review *of The Evolution of Cooperation* by Robert Axelrod," in *New York Review of Books,* June 28, 1984.

theorizing offers "good clean intellectual fun"[3] but also because it holds out the promise of delivering a moral theory that will answer to my political – and in particular my feminist – commitments. This is not to say that particular contractarian moral theories don't deserve much of the feminist criticism they have received. In this chapter, I will explore and acknowledge the legitimacy of these feminist challenges. Nonetheless I want to argue that one version of this method of moral theorizing offers us what may be the keystone of any truly adequate moral theory.

In a nutshell I will be contending that contractarianism illuminates distributive justice, and this form of justice is required not only in relationships between strangers but also in relationships between intimates, including husbands and wives, parents and children, friend and friend. In making this argument I am opposing conventional philosophical wisdom going back as far as Aristotle, who writes, "If people are friends, they have no need of justice."[4] Among contemporary theorists, David Hume's claim that justice is necessary only in circumstances in which people have limited feelings of benevolence or friendship toward one another has been accepted by virtually every political philosopher since then, including Karl Marx and John Rawls. But I will contend that distributive justice, understood in its deepest sense, is inherent in any relationship that we regard as morally healthy and respectable – particularly in a friendship. Indeed, Aristotle himself hinted at this idea immediately after the passage just quoted – he says not only that those who are just also require friendship but also that "the justice that is most just seems to belong to friendship."[5] The reflection in this chapter might be taken as a way of exploring this enigmatic passage.

I. Hearing Voices

Recent work by Carol Gilligan has reinforced the general tendency of philosophers to see the concerns of justice and friendship as distinct from one another. Using interviews with older children and adults that address real or hypothetical moral problems, Gilligan attempts to display two different "moral voices" – voices she calls the "ethic of justice"

---

[3] Baier, "What Do Women Want in a Moral Theory?," p. 55.

[4] Aristotle, *Nicomachean Ethics,* trans. by T. E. Irwin (Indianapolis: Hackett, 1985), 1155a22 (p. 208).

[5] See 1155a27 (Irwin translation, p. 208). It may be, however, that Aristotle is primarily arguing that if one is just, one is also friendly (as part of his concept of civic friendship), whereas I want to emphasize that if one is friendly, one is also just.

and the "ethic of care" – and finds some evidence (albeit controversial) associating the first with men and the second with women.[6]

Two of her interviews with older children have always struck me as highly interesting. Eleven-year-old Jake, whose answers to the interviewers earned him high marks on Lawrence Kohlberg's moral maturity scale, gave the following answer when asked, "When responsibility to oneself and responsibility to others conflict, how should one choose?" He replied with great self-assurance, "You go about one-fourth to the others and three-fourths to yourself."[7] Contrast the following answer to the same question given by eleven-year-old Amy, whose answers to the interviewers earned poorer marks on Kohlberg's scale:

Well, it really depends on the situation. If you have a responsibility with somebody else [*sic*], then you should keep it to a certain extent, but to the extent that it is really going to hurt you or stop you from doing something that you really, really want, then I think maybe you should put yourself first. But if it is your responsibility to somebody really close to you, you've just got to decide in that situation which is more important, yourself or that person, and like I said, it really depends on what kind of person you are and how you feel about the other person or persons involved.[8]

This rather tortured reply indicates considerable sensitivity and beneficent concern for others. Unsurprisingly, Amy's discussion of other moral problems reveals an interest in maintaining the well-being of others and in keeping relationships intact, which, according to Gilligan, shows that Amy values care. In contrast, Jake's remarks take for granted the importance of following rules that preclude interference in other people's pursuit of their interests, which, according to Gilligan, shows that Jake values justice. When asked to explain his answer to the question about responsibility to himself and others, Jake replies, "Because the most important thing in your decision should be yourself, don't let yourself be guided totally by other people, but you have to take them into consideration. So, if what you want to do is blow yourself up with an atom bomb, you should

---

[6] Carol Gilligan's classic work is *In a Different Voice: Psychological Theory and Women's Development* (Cambridge, Mass.: Harvard University Press, 1982). She has revised and expanded her ideas since then. See a variety of articles about Gilligan's recent work in *Mapping the Moral Domain*, ed. Carol Gilligan, Victoria Ward, and Jill McLean, with Betty Bandige (Cambridge, Mass.: Center for the Study of Gender, Education, and Human Development, 1988). See also Carol Gilligan, "Moral Orientation and Moral Development," in *Women and Moral Theory*, ed. Eva Feder Kittay and Diana T. Meyers (Totowa, N.J.: Rowman and Littlefield, 1987), pp. 19–33.

[7] Gilligan, *In a Different Voice*, pp. 35–36.

[8] Ibid.

maybe blow yourself up with a hand grenade because you are thinking about your neighbors who would die also."[9]

As Jake's remarkable example shows, he regards "being moral" as pursuing one's own interests without damaging the interests of others, and he takes it as a matter of moral strength not to allow the interests of others to dictate to him what he ought or ought not to do. ("Don't let yourself be guided totally by other people," he warns.) In contrast, "being moral" for Amy means being responsive to the needs of others who are close to you or to whom you have made a commitment. Each child therefore makes a different assumption about the extent to which any of us is self-sufficient. Jake assumes that we are and ought to be interested in and capable of caring for ourselves, so that interaction with others is likely to be perceived either as interference or as an attempt to compromise one's independence. In contrast, Amy takes it for granted that we are not self-sufficient and that service to others will be welcomed as a sign of care and commendable concern.

Many feminist theorists maintain that the kind of moral voice that Amy exemplifies is clearly preferable to that of Jake. Annette Baier, for example, writes,

Gilligan's girls and women saw morality as a matter of preserving valued ties to others, of preserving the conditions for that care and mutual care without which human life becomes bleak, lonely, and after a while, as the mature men in her study found, not self affirming, however successful in achieving the egoistic goals which had been set. The boys and men saw morality as a matter of finding workable traffic rules for self assertors, so that they do not needlessly frustrate one another, and so that they could, should they so choose, cooperate in more positive ways to mutual advantage.[10]

Certainly Baier is right that a "traffic rule" perspective on morality is neither a sophisticated nor a mature moral perspective. It appears to derive from the mistaken assumption that each of us is self-sufficient, able, and desirous of "going it alone." Amy is surely right that this is false. In contrast, a perspective on morality that emphasizes caring for and fostering the well-being of others appears to be not only a richer, sounder theory of what genuine moral behavior is all about but also a better guide to behavior that enables one to live a life full of friendship and love. Such a perspective is one that women (and especially mothers) are frequently thought to exhibit more than men. Baier concludes, "It

---

9 Ibid., p. 36.
10 Baier, "What Do Women Want in a Moral Theory?," p. 62.

would not be much of an exaggeration to call the Gilligan 'different voice' the voice of the potential parent."[11]

Baier's way of responding to Jake's answer makes him into an archetype for a (commonly male) brand of moral immaturity. But one can respond to Amy's answer in a way that makes her an archetype for a quite different (and commonly female) brand of moral immaturity. Consider that Jake's answer is 13 words; Amy's is 109 words, and it is neither clear nor self-assured. *Maybe* she can put herself first, she says, if not doing so would mean losing out on something that she "really, really" wants. But only maybe. Jake is convinced not only that his interests count, but that they count far more than other people's (three-quarters to one-quarter). Amy appears to be having trouble figuring out whether or not her interests count at all. Consider her answer to the responsibility question:

Some people put themselves and things for themselves before they put other people, and some people really care about other people. Like, I don't think your job is as important as somebody that you really love, like your husband or your parents or a very close friend. Somebody that you really care for – or if it's just your responsibility to your job or somebody that you barely know, then maybe you go first.[12]

Again, note her "maybe." Even in a situation in which she takes her responsibility to others to be minimal, she is having trouble asserting the priority of her own interests. Here is a child who appears very much guided by the interests of other people and takes that guidance to be what "being moral" means. One worries that she will find it difficult to plan a life that takes into consideration what she alone wants, because she is highly susceptible to being at the beck and call of others.

These interpretations are harsh and are probably not fair to the real children. But the fact that they are not only possible but natural shows the immature directions in which each child's thinking tends. Jack is susceptible to a brand of moral immaturity that manifests itself in an insensitivity to the needs of others and a failure to see himself as a fellow caretaker in a relationship. His remarks define a morality only in the most minimal sense. There is too much distance between him and others to enable him to be aware of and responsive to the needs or interests of others. In contrast, Amy is susceptible to a moral perspective that makes her too sensitive to other people, and her concern to meet their needs borders on

---

[11] Annette Baier, "The Need for More Than Justice," in *Science, Morality, and Feminist Theory*, ed. Marsha Hanen and Kai Nielsen (Calgary: University of Calgary Press, 1987), p. 54.
[12] Gilligan, *In a Different Voice*, p. 36.

outright servility. Whereas the authority and importance of others' needs are clear for her, the authority and importance of her own needs appear not to be. Indeed, unlike Jake she can offer no principle upon which to adjudicate the conflict between her claims and the claims of others, presumably because she has difficulty seeing herself as entitled to make any claim at all. And because she is so readily able to appreciate and be responsive to the needs of others, she is potentially a highly exploitable person. Thus if we interpret Amy's remarks as typifying a brand of moral immaturity quite different from that of Jake, they define an "ethic of care" that is really just a mimicry of genuine morality insofar as "caring" actions are generated out of the assumption that the agent is worth less than (and hence the servant of) the people she serves. Such caring cannot be moral because it is born of self-abnegation rather than self-worth.[13]

Although she respects Amy's concern for care, Gilligan herself admits the immaturity of Amy's response (while also stressing the immaturity of Jake's perspective). Moreover, that this brand of caring is an imitation of a genuinely moral response to others has also been noticed by other feminist writers,[14] and it is a surprisingly common theme in literature by women. For example, Charlotte Bronte's heroine in *Shirley* begins the journey to genuine maturity when she comes to question her own propensity to offer to care for others:

"What was I created for, I wonder? Where is my place in the world?" She mused again. "Ah! I see," she pursued presently, "that is the question which most old maids are puzzled to solve: other people solve it for them by saying, 'Your place is to do good to others, to be helpful whenever help is wanted.' That is right in some measure, and a very convenient doctrine for the people who hold it; but I perceive that certain sets of human beings are very apt to maintain that other sets should give up their lives to them and their service, and then they requite them by praise: they call them devoted and virtuous. Is this enough? Is it to live? Is there not a terrible hollowness, mockery, want, craving, in that existence which is given away to others, for want of something of your own to bestow it on? I suspect there is. Does virtue lie in abnegation of self? I do not believe it. Undue humility makes tyranny: weak concession creates selfishness. . . . Each human being has his share of rights. I suspect it would conduce to the happiness and welfare of all, if each knew his allotment and held to it as tenaciously as a martyr to his creed."[15]

[13] See Marcia Homiak's "Feminism and Aristotle's Rational Ideal," in L. Antony and C. Witt, ed., *A Mind of One's Own*, 2nd ed. (Boulder: Westview Press, 2001), which discusses the degenerate form of kindness that emerges when one lacks self-love.

[14] See, for example, L. Blum, M. Homiak, J. Housman, and N. Scheman, "Altruism and Women's Oppression," in *Women and Philosophy*, ed. Carol Gould and Marx Wartofsky (New York: G. P. Putnam's Sons, 1976), pp. 222–47.

[15] Charlotte Bronte, *Shirley*, quotation taken from edition of Andrew Hook and Judith Hook (Harmondsworth: Penguin, 1987), p. 190.

And there is Virginia Woolf's well-known description of "the angel in the house" who threatens to take over and destroy a woman's soul:

She was intensely sympathetic. She was immensely charming. She was utterly unselfish. She excelled in the difficult art of family life. She sacrificed herself daily. If there was chicken, she took the leg: if there was a draught she sat in it – in short she was so constituted that she never had a mind or a wish of her own, but preferred to sympathize always with the minds and wishes of others. Above all – I need not say it – she was pure. . . . I turned upon her and caught her by the throat. I did my best to kill her. My excuse, if I were to be had up in a court of law would be that I acted in self-defence. Had I not killed her she would have killed me.[16]

Both novelists believe that a genuine moral agent has to have a good sense of her own moral claims if she is going to be a person at all and thus a real partner in a morally sound relationship.[17] She must also have some sense of what it is to make a legitimate claim if she is to understand and respond to the legitimate claims of others and resist attempts to involve herself in relationships that will make her the mere servant of others' desires. Both philosophical and commonsense understandings of morality have been so fixated on the other-regardingness of moral life that they have encouraged us to mistake archetypal Amy's response for a moral response.[18]

What happens when archetypal Jake and archetypal Amy grow up? If they were to marry, wouldn't Amy take it upon herself to meet the needs of Jake and do the work to maintain their relationship (giving up her career

[16] From "Professions for Women" in *The Virginia Woolf Reader*, ed. Mitchell A. Leaska (San Diego: Harcourt Brace, 1984), pp. 278–79.

[17] See Blum et al., "Altruism and Women's Oppression," for a discussion of the way altruism must be accompanied by autonomy if it is going to be a morally healthy response.

[18] I take this to be an idea suggested by Susan Wolf in her "Moral Saints," *Journal of Philosophy* 79, no. 8 (August 1982): 419–39. Ironically, this fixation has been more the product of theories developed by males (e.g., Immanuel Kant and Jeremy Bentham) than by females. Perhaps such a fixation is the natural result of male dissatisfaction with a Jake-like moral perspective and an attempt to redirect the largely self-regarding focus of that perspective. But theorists, such as Kant, who stress the other-regarding nature of morality, invariably start from an assumption of self-worth and personal autonomy. In a paper that celebrates interdependence and connection, Baier notes that Kant thought women were incapable of full autonomy and then remarks, "It is ironic that Gilligan's original findings in a way confirm Kant's views – it seems that autonomy really may not be for women. Many of them reject that ideal" ("Need for More Than Justice," p. 50). But such a rejection may actually be evidence of these women's development into servile and dependent beings rather than free, self-respecting, and claim-making persons. For discussions on this general topic, see the contributions by DuBois, Dunlap, Carol Gilligan, Catharine MacKinnon, and Menkel-Meadow in "Feminist Discourse, Moral Values, and the Law," *Buffalo Law Review* 34 (1985): 11ff.

if necessary, insofar as she thinks that a job isn't as important as "someone you really love")? And wouldn't Jake naturally take it for granted that his interests should predominate (three-fourths to one-fourth) and be ignorant of many of the needs of others around him that might prompt a caring response? I find it striking that these children's answers betray perspectives that seem to fit them perfectly for the kind of gendered roles that prevail in our society. In their archetypal forms, I hear the voice of a child who is preparing to be a member of a dominating group and the voice of another who is preparing to be a member of the group that is dominated. Neither of these voices should be allowed to inform our moral theorizing if such theorizing is going to be successful at formulating ways of interacting that are not only morally acceptable but also attack the oppressive relationships that now hold in our society.

II. Two Forms of Contractarian Theory

So how do we set about defining an acceptable formulation of morality? The idea that the essence not only of human rationality but also of human morality is embodied in the notion of contract is the heart of what is called the "contractarian" approach to moral thinking. Advocates of this approach ask us to imagine a group of people sitting around a bargaining table; each person is interested only in himself. This group is to decide answers to moral or political questions by determining what they can all agree to or what they would all be unreasonable to reject.

However, both proponents and opponents of this style of argument have failed to appreciate just how many argumentative uses of the contract idea have appeared over the centuries. Arguments that self-consciously invoke a social contract can differ in what they aim to justify or explain (for example, the state, conceptions of justice, morality), what they take the problem of justification to be, and whether or not they presuppose a moral theory or purport to be a moral theory. Thus, even though theorists who call themselves "contractarians" have all supposedly begun from the same reflective starting point – namely, what people could "agree to" – these differences and disagreements among people who are supposedly in the same philosophical camp show that contractarians are united not by a common philosophical theory but by a common *image*. Philosophers hate to admit it, but sometimes they work from pictures rather than ideas. And in an attempt to get a handle on the nature of the state, the reasons for its justification, and the legitimate moral claims each of us can make on our behalf against others, the contract imagery has struck many as enormously promising. But how that image has been translated into argument has varied considerably, and philosophers have disagreed about what political or moral issue that image can profitably illuminate.

A number of feminist theorists reject out of hand the idea that this could be an acceptable approach to defining morality precisely because of what they take to be the unattractiveness of the contract image.[19] Virginia Held, for example, insists:

> To see contractual relations between self-interested or mutually disinterested individuals as constituting a paradigm of human relations is to take a certain historically specific conception of 'economic man' as representative of humanity. And it is, many feminists are beginning to agree, to overlook or to discount in very fundamental ways the experience of women.[20]

And at first glance this way of thinking about morality does seem rather Jake-like. People are postulated to be self-regarding rather than other-regarding and their project is to define rules that enable them to live in harmony – which sounds a great deal like constructing (to quote Baier again) "traffic rules for self assertors."[21] Moreover, their distance from one another seems to prevent them from feeling emotional bonds of attachment or concern that would prompt care without the promise of pay.

I will be arguing that this type of attack on contractarian theory is importantly misguided. But before I can begin that argument, I want to clarify in this section exactly what kind of contractarian argument I will be defending in the rest of the chapter. There are two kinds of moral argument that one contract image has spawned in modern times – the first has its roots in Thomas Hobbes and is exemplified in the work of David Gauthier, James Buchanan, Gilbert Harman, and John Mackie; the second has its roots in Immanuel Kant and is exemplified in the work of John Rawls and T. M. Scanlon. I will review these two forms of contractarian theory and the criticisms to which each is subject before I go on, in the next section, to locate my own contractarian approach in this conceptual space.

Hobbesian Contractarianism

Although Hobbes himself never repudiated a divine origin for moral laws, he and the moral philosophers who followed him have attempted

[19] Virginia Held, "Noncontractual Society: A Feminist View," in Hanen and Nielsen, eds., *Science, Morality, and Feminist Theory*, p. 111.
[20] Ibid., p. 113. For similar criticisms, see Carole Pateman, *The Sexual Contract* (Palo Alto, Calif.: Polity/Stanford University Press, 1988).
[21] Baier, "What Do Women Want in a Moral Theory?," p. 62.

to develop an entirely *human* justification of morality.[22] Hobbesians start by insisting that what is valuable is what a person desires or prefers, not what he ought to desire (for no such prescriptively powerful object exists); and rational action is action that achieves or maximizes the satisfaction of desires or preferences. They then go on to insist that moral action is rational for a person to perform if and only if such action advances the satisfaction of his desires or preferences. And usually, they argue, for most of us the moral action will be rational. Because moral actions lead to peaceful and harmonious living conducive to the satisfaction of almost everyone's desires or preferences, moral actions are rational for almost everyone and thus "mutually agreeable." But in order to ensure that no cooperative person becomes the prey of immoral aggressors, Hobbesians believe that moral actions must be the conventional norms in a community, so that each person can expect that if she behaves cooperatively, others will do so too, and vice versa. These conventions constitute the institution of morality in a society.

So the Hobbesian moral theory is committed to the idea that morality is a human-made institution that is justified only to the extent that it effectively furthers human interests. Hobbesians explain the existence of morality in society by appealing to the convention-creating activities of human beings; they also argue that the justification of morality in any human society depends upon how well its moral conventions serve individuals' desires or preferences. So Hobbesians do not assume that existing conventions are, in and of themselves, justified. By considering "what we *could* agree to" if we had the chance to reappraise and redo the cooperative conventions in our society, we are able to determine the extent to which our present conventions are mutually agreeable and thus rational for us to accept and act on. Consequently, Hobbesians invoke both actual agreements (or rather, conventions) and hypothetical agreements (which involve considering what conventions would be mutually agreeable) at different points in their theory. The former are what they believe our moral life consists in; the latter are what they believe our moral life *should* consist in – that is, what our actual moral life should model.[23]

---

[22] Hobbes believed that moral imperatives were also justified by virtue of being commanded by God. However, his contractarian justification seeks to define the nature and authority of moral imperatives solely by reference to the desires and reasoning abilities of human beings, so that regardless of their religious commitments, all people will see that they have reason to act morally.

[23] Hobbes believes he performed the latter project in chapters 14 and 15 of *Leviathan*, ed. C. B. MacPherson (Hammondsworth: Penguin, 1968).

This means the notion of contract does not do justificational work *by itself* in the Hobbesian moral theory – this term is used only metaphorically. What we "could agree to" has moral force for the Hobbesians not because make-believe promises in hypothetical worlds have any binding force but because this sort of agreement is a device that (merely) reveals the way in which the agreed-upon outcome is rational for all of us. In particular, thinking about "what we could all agree to" allows us to construct a deduction of practical reason to determine what politics are mutually advantageous. Thus the justificational force of this kind of contract theory is carried within but is derived from sources other than the contractor agreement in the theory.

As I've noted, many theorists are attracted to this theory because of its sensible metaphysics: It doesn't base morality on strange, nonnatural properties or objects; nor does it credit human beings with what Mackie calls "magical" powers capable of discerning the moral truth "out there."[24] Instead it sees morality as a human invention that we commend to the extent that it is mutually advantageous for those who would use it. But such a metaphysical foundation is attractive only if what is built upon it counts as a genuine morality. And there are good reasons for complaining that Hobbesian contractarianism yields considerably less than the real thing. When *Leviathan* was originally published in 1651, some readers sympathetic to Aristotelian ideas were shocked by the idea that the nature of our ties to others was interest-based and contended that Hobbes's theory went too far in trying to represent us as radically separate from others. Their worries are also the worries of many twentieth-century critics, including feminists, who insist that any adequate moral theory must take into account our emotion-based connections with others and the fact that we are socially defined beings.[25]

But I would argue that what disqualifies it at a more fundamental level as an acceptable moral theory is its failure to incorporate the idea that individuals have what I will call "intrinsic value." It has not been sufficiently appreciated, I believe, that by answering the "Why be moral?" question by invoking self-interest in the way that Hobbesians do, one makes not only cooperative action but also the human beings with whom

---

[24] However, I have argued elsewhere that Hobbesian contractarians implicitly assume the kind of problematic metaphysical ideas they criticize in the theories of others. See "Naturalism and Moral Reasons," in *On the Relevance of Metaethics*, ed. J. Couture and K. Nielsen, *Canadian Journal of Philosophy*, supplementary volume 21: 107–33.

[25] Gauthier himself has been moved by these kinds of worries, inspired, he says, by Hegel. See his "Social Contract as Ideology," *Philosophy and Public Affairs* (1977): 130–64.

one will cooperate merely of *instrumental value.* That is, if you ask me why I should treat you morally, and I respond by saying that it is in my interest to do so, I am telling you that my regard for you is something that is merely instrumentally valuable to me; I do not give you that regard because there is something about you yourself that merits it, regardless of the usefulness of that regard to me. Now Hobbes is unembarrassed by the fact that on his view, "the *Value,* or WORTH of a man, is as of all other things, his Price; that is to say, so much as would be given for the use of his Power: and therefore is not absolute; but a thing dependent on the need and judgment of another."[26]

But this way of viewing people is not something that we, or even some Hobbesians, can take with equanimity. In the final two chapters of his book, Gauthier openly worries about the fact that the reason why we value moral imperatives on this Hobbesian view is that they are instrumentally valuable to us in our pursuit of what we value. But why are they instrumentally valuable? Because, in virtue of our physical and intellectual weaknesses that make it impossible for us to be self-sufficient, we need the cooperation of others to prosper. If there were some way that we could remedy our weaknesses and become self-sufficient – for example, by becoming a superman or a superwoman, or by using a Ring of Gyges to make ourselves invisible and so steal from the stores of others with impunity – then it seems we would no longer value or respect moral constraints because they would no longer be useful to us – unless we happened to like the idea. But in this case, sentiment rather than reason would motivate kind treatment. And without such sentiment, it would be rational for us to take other people as "prey."

Even in a world in which we are not self-sufficient, the Hobbesian moral theory gives us no reason outside of contingent emotional sentiment to respect those with whom we have no need of cooperating or those whom we are strong enough to dominate, such as the elderly, the physically handicapped, mentally disabled children whom we do not want to rear, or people from other societies with whom we have no interest in trading. And I would argue that this shows that Hobbesian moral contractarianism fails in a serious way to capture the nature of morality. Regardless of whether or not one can engage in beneficial cooperative interactions with another, our moral intuitions push us to assent to the idea that one owes that person respectful treatment simply in virtue of the fact that she is a *person.* It seems to be a feature of our moral life that we regard

---

[26] Hobbes, *Leviathan,* chapter 10, paragraph 16 (p. 42 in MacPherson edition).

a human being, whether or not she is instrumentally valuable, as always intrinsically valuable. Indeed, to the extent that the results of a Hobbesian theory are acceptable, this is because one's concern to cooperate with someone whom one cannot dominate leads one to behave in ways that mimic the respect one ought to show her simply in virtue of her worth as a human being.

Kantian Contractarianism

To abandon the idea that the only value human beings have is instrumental is to abandon the Hobbesian approach to morality and to move in the direction of what I will call "Kantian contractarianism." In his later writings Immanuel Kant proposed that the "ideal" of the "Original Contract" could be used to determine just political policies:

Yet this contract, which we call *contractus originarius* or *pactum sociale*, as the coalition of every particular and private will within a people into a common public will for purposes of purely legal legislation, need by no means be presupposed as a fact. . . . It is rather a *mere idea* of reason, albeit one with indubitable practical reality, obligating every lawmaker to frame his laws so that they *might* have come from the united will of an entire people, and to regard any subject who would be a citizen as if he had joined in voting for such a will. For this is the touchstone of the legitimacy of public law. If a law is so framed that all the people *could not possibly* give their consent – as, for example, a law granting the hereditary *privilege* of *master status* to a certain class of subjects – the law is unjust.[27]

As I interpret this passage, when Kant asks us to think about what people could agree to, he is not trying to justify actions or policies by invoking, in any literal sense, the consent of the people. Only the consent of *real* people can be legitimating, and Kant talks about hypothetical agreements made by hypothetical people. But he does believe these make-believe agreements have moral force for us, not because we are under any illusion that the make-believe consent of make-believe people is obliging for us, but because the process by which these people reach agreement is morally revealing.

Kant's contracting process has been further developed by subsequent philosophers, such as John Rawls and T. M. Scanlon, convinced of its moral promise. Rawls, in particular, concentrates on defining the hypothetical people who are supposed to make this agreement to ensure

[27] Immanuel Kant, "On the Common Saying: 'This May Be True in Theory, But It Doesn't Apply in Practice,'" in *Kant's Political Writings*, ed. Hans Reiss (Cambridge: Cambridge University Press, 1970), p. 63. Emphasis in original.

that their reasoning will not be tarnished by immorality, injustice, or prejudice and thus that the outcome of their joint deliberations will be morally sound (although not all contractarians have agreed with his way of defining the parties to get this result). The Kantians' social contract is therefore a device used in their theorizing to reveal what is just or what is moral. So like the Hobbesians, their contract talk is really just a way of reasoning that allows us to work out conceptual answers to moral problems. But whereas the Hobbesians' use of contract language expresses the fact that, on their view, morality is a human invention that (if it is well invented) ought to be mutually advantageous, the Kantians' use of the contract language is meant to show that moral principles and conceptions are provable theorems derived from a morally revealing and authoritative contractarian reasoning process or "moral proof procedure."[28]

There is a prominent feminist criticism of Rawls's version of this form of contractarianism. These feminists charge (along with certain Hegelian critics) that Rawls's stripping people of their socially defined identities and sending them off to an "Archimedean point" to choose among or between moral conceptions asks us to do the impossible – namely, to abstract from our socially defined identities in order to reveal some sort of transcultural truth.[29] Because we are socially defined, these critics contend that any intuitions remaining after people are supposedly stripped

---

[28] Rawls, for example, explicitly compares his original position procedure to Kant's Categorical Imperative procedure (see Rawls, *A Theory of Justice* (Cambridge, Mass.: Harvard University Press, 1971), section 40). And Scanlon suggests that the contractarian form of argument is a kind of proof procedure for ethics that is analogous to proof procedures in mathematics; its basis is in human reason, and we use it to construct moral laws in a way that gives them objectivity. See Scanlon's "Contractualism and Utilitarianism," in *Utilitarianism and Beyond*, ed. A. Sen and B. Williams (Cambridge: Cambridge University Press, 1982).

[29] Sarah Ruddick, for example, writes, "Especially masculine men (and sometimes women), fearful of physicality and needs of care, develop a transcendence based on a 'tradition of freeing the thinking brain from the depths of the most pressing situations and sending it off to some (fictive) summit for a panoramic overview.' From this perch they promulgate views that are inimical to the values of caring labor. They imagine a truth abstracted from bodies and a self detached from feelings. When faced with concrete seriousness, they measure and quantify. Only partially protected by veils of ignorance that never quite hide frightening differences and dependencies, they forge agreements of reason and regiment dissent by rules and fair fights." From Ruddick, *Maternal Thinking: Toward a Politics of Peace* (Boston: Beacon, 1989); quotation in passage taken from Klaus Thewelweit, *Male Fantasies* (Minneapolis: University of Minnesota Press, 1987), p. 364. Ruddick's criticism is similar to those made by Rawls's Hegel-inspired communitarian critics (e.g., Michael Sandel).

to their bare essentials will still be permeated with the assumptions of a sexist society, producing (not surprisingly) "patriarchal outcomes."[30]

There is good reason to think that this feminist complaint is importantly misguided, particularly in view of the feminists' own political commitments (and at least one feminist has already argued this point).[31] Although feminists often insist that our natures are to a high degree socially defined – which means that, on their view, theorizing about what we are "really like" will tend to be informed by intuitions that reflect the society that forms us – it is part of the feminist challenge to our society that some ways in which our society forms us are wrong – producing human beings whose development is stunted or distorted and whose connection with other human beings is problematic (because they are either too inclined to want to master others or too likely to wind up being mastered). So although many feminists call themselves "pluralists" who advocate the recognition of many points of view and the legitimacy of many kinds of theorizing about the world, in fact there are some points of view that they reject outright, including sexist and racist views and inegalitarian conceptions of human treatment. Whether or not they explicitly recognize it, this rejection is motivated by an implicit appeal to objective ideals of human interaction and optimal socialization of men and women. The pluralists' vision of a better world, in which the oppression of women does not exist, is a vision of human beings developing in the right – that is, objectively right – way, such that they can flourish and interact well with one another rather than in ways that precipitate oppression or abuse. Accordingly, it is ironic that a Rawlsian Archimedean point is exactly what feminists require to carry out their form of social criticism.

Some feminists will insist that although they do attack some of the practices and points of view in their society, nonetheless the values they use in their criticisms are still authored by their society. Hence, they argue, their society is sufficiently pluralistic to produce mutually inconsistent value schemes. But even if that is so, what bearing does this sociological fact have on what ought to happen in the sociopolitical arena? In particular, what justifies the feminists in thinking that their values should come to predominate? Merely appealing to consistency or social stability isn't sufficient to justify that predominance, because these reasons could just as easily justify the predominance of racist/sexist values. Feminists not only

---

[30] See Kathryn Morgan, "Women and Moral Madness," in Hanen and Nielsen, eds., *Science, Morality, and Feminist Theory*, pp. 201–26.

[31] Susan Moller Okin, *Justice, Gender, and the Family* (New York: Basic Books, 1989).

want their values to predominate, they want them to do so because they are the right values. Hence to argue for their values, they must have an Archimedean point from which to survey and critically assess the value schemes in their societies. The Rawlsian Archimedean point "forces one to question and consider traditions, customs, and institutions from all points of view"[32] and thus attempts to go beyond mere shared understandings, common beliefs, or social practices that may be oppressive or exploitative. Hence, it seems to offer feminists the perspective they need to be able to identify and attack unjust social practices.[33]

Feminists, however, have an important counterresponse to this defense of the Rawlsian method. They can grant that an Archimedean point would be highly desirable for them given their political agenda, but go on to complain that no Kantian contractarian, including Rawls, has convincingly demonstrated that his contractarian theory provides one, because no contractarian has specified his theory sufficiently such that we can be sure it relies only upon "morally pure" starting points and not the sort of "biased" (for example, sexist or racist) ideas or intuitions that an unjust society can encourage in its citizens. There are two ways in which feminists could charge that these morally suspect intuitions might be intruding into Rawls's theory. First, these intuitions may be covertly motivating the particular constraints, assumptions, or features that are supposed to apply in the contract situation. Feminists are implicitly criticizing Rawls's theory on this basis when they charge that his assumption that parties in the original position are self-interested is motivated by intuitions about what counts as a plausibly "weak" psychology, intuitions that actually derive from a discredited Hobbesian view of human nature. According to these

---

[32] Ibid., p. 101.

[33] Indeed, as I have reflected on Archimedean thinking in the literature, it has struck me that it is interestingly akin to a certain kind of thinking of mothers as they raise their children. In the words of one novelist, mothers are "Conscious Makers of People" who strive to develop an environment for their children that will allow them to grow up well (i.e., confident rather than fearful, fulfilled rather than miserable, capable rather than dependent) and try to ensure that the institutions with which their children come into contact will operate in a way that fosters that end. The Rawlsian contractarian also wants us to play a role in shaping the people of our society by asking us to formulate principles that will animate the social institutions that make any of us who we are. Members of a Rawlslike Archimedean position have as their primary concern the development of an environment in which future members of the society can grow up well, and insofar as they are aware of the powerful effect society and its institutions have on shaping the kind of people any of us become, they are just as interested as any mother in constructing or changing social institutions to foster the development of mature and morally healthy human beings. Far from being antithetical to the perspective of mothering, Rawls's Archimedean point is a way to encourage mothering-like concerns in a political context.

critics, this Jake-like component of Rawls's thinking drives out of his theory
both our emotion-based attachments to others' well-being and our other-
regarding, duty-based commitments to them, demonstrating the extent
to which even this high-minded Kantian appears heavily in the grip of
outmoded and distorting individualistic intuitions. Second, suspect intuitions may be illicitly operating within the original-position reasoning
procedure and thereby playing a direct role in the justification of Rawls's
political conclusions. Critics who charge that Rawls's reliance on the maximin rule cannot be justified will note that if the rule is removed from
the argument, only vague intuitive appeals could explain how the parties
would reach the political conclusions Rawls recommends, appeals that
might not withstand sustained moral scrutiny if they were better understood.[34]

Although Scanlon does not presume that his contract approach
defines an Archimedean point, his approach is even more susceptible
to the charge that it is covertly relying on ill-defined or ill-defended intuitions. Scanlon argues that (what he calls) the "contractualist" account of
the nature of moral wrongdoing goes as follows: "An act is wrong if its performance under the circumstances would be disallowed by any system of
rules for the general regulation of behavior which no one could reasonably reject as a basis for informed, unforced general agreement."[35] This
definition is intended as "a characterization of the kind of property which
moral wrongness is."[36] In this statement of contractualism, the reader is
inevitably drawn to the word 'reasonably,' yet Scanlon never explicitly
cashes out the term. He claims, for example, that a policy A that would
pass an average utilitarian test but that would cause some to fare badly is,
prima facie, a policy that the "losers" would be reasonable to reject.[37] He
goes on to say, however, that ultimately the reasonableness of the losers'
objection to A is not established simply by the fact that they are worse off
under A than they would be under some alternative policy E in which no
one's situation is as bad. Instead, says Scanlon, the complaint against A by
the A losers must be weighed against the complaints made by those who
would do worse under E than under A. "The question to be asked is, is it

---

[34] For a review of the problems with Rawls's maximin rule, see John Harsanyi, "Can the
Maximin Principle Serve as a Basis for Morality? A Critique of John Rawls's *A Theory
of Justice*," *American Political Science Review* 69 (1975): 594–606. And for a discussion of
these problems from a philosophical standpoint, see D. Clayton Hubin, "Minimizing
Maximin," *Philosophical Studies* 37 (1980): 363–72.
[35] Scanlon, "Contractualism and Utilitarianism," p. 110.
[36] Ibid.
[37] Ibid., pp. 123–24.

unreasonable for someone to refuse to put up with the Losers' situation under A in order that someone else should be able to enjoy the benefits which he would have to give up under E?"[38]

But on what grounds, or using what criteria, can we provide the right answer to this question? Scanlon gives us no directions for adjudicating the complaints of the two groups in this situation, and one begins to worry that his appeal to "reasonableness" as a way of determining the solution is an appeal to inchoate intuitions. Occasionally, he seems to link the term to the purported desire that people in the hypothetical contract are supposed to have to reach an agreement with one another: "The only relevant pressure for agreement comes from the desire to find and agree on principles which no one who had this desire could reasonably reject."[39] But what is this desire? It seems to be more than just the desire to reach an agreement, for Scanlon says later that the desire is one to "find principles which none could reasonably reject."[40] So, because the desire is defined in terms of reasonableness, it cannot be taken to explicate it. And if reasonableness is defined using moral notions such as fairness (as in, "It is only reasonable for me to reject proposals that are unfair"), Scanlon's moral project is circular, because on his view moral properties are supposed to be defined by the contract test, thereby precluding a central component of that test that presupposes one or more moral properties.[41]

---

[38] Ibid., p. 123.

[39] Ibid., p. 111.

[40] Ibid., p. 127.

[41] In "Contractualism and Utilitarianism," Scanlon seems to vacillate between regarding the test as defining moral properties and regarding it as a test that presupposes and uses those properties. He begins the essay by pushing the first position, arguing that we should follow Mackie in being suspicious of moral properties that are supposed to be instances of "intrinsic 'to-be-doneness' and 'not-to-be-doneness'" (p. 118), and he proposes instead that moral properties be defined via a reasoning procedure (and in particular, a contractualist procedure) that would define rather than presuppose such properties (making the view the moral equivalent of mathematical intuitionism). But later Scanlon cannot help but appeal to properties that are right- and wrong-making independent of the contractualist agreement test, properties that he relies upon in order to define that reasoning procedure. "There are also right- and wrong-making properties which are themselves independent of the contractualist notion of agreement. I take the property of being an act of killing for the pleasure of doing so to be a wrong-making property of this kind" (p. 118). But immediately after stating this, Scanlon writes, "Such properties are wrong-making because it would be unreasonable to reject any set of principles which permitted the acts they characterise" (ibid.). But now it sounds as if their wrong-making character is *derived from* the contractualist test, such that it cannot be independent of the test after all.

So we don't know what is really doing the work in Scanlon's test, and this generates at least three problems for his theory. First, we can't be sure that everyone who uses Scanlon's test will rely on the same conception of reasonableness to arrive at the same answer. Second, unless his conception of reasonableness is fully (and acceptably) explicated, feminists have good reason to worry about what might seem reasonable to people raised in a sexist patriarchal society. And third, unless this conception is fully explicated, those of us loyal to contractarianism as a distinctive form of moral argument have reason to worry that there is so much reliance on intuition in the operation of Scanlon's test that his approach ultimately reduces to some other ethical theory. For example, if these intuitions are understood as foundational, his theory would seem to amount to nothing more than a version of ethical intuitionism. Or if they are understood to be generated by some other moral theory, such as utilitarianism, the contract method would appear to be merely a way of marshaling ideas generated by that other theory. Thus a utilitarian might argue that "reasonable rejection" should be understood as rejection on the grounds that what is being proposed is not utility-maximizing for the group. But Scanlon wants to be able to draw upon and generate anti-utilitarian ideas in his contractarian argument through argument rather than through an appeal to intuition alone.[42] Because neither he nor, for that matter, any Kantian contractarian has given us any sense of what these ideas are, or why they are appropriate to rely upon, or how they work together to form a nonintuitionistic moral reasoning procedure, we begin to wonder whether or not this or indeed any Kantian's appeal to "what we could agree to" is just a way to fabricate a defense for moral or political conceptions that these Kantian theorists happen to like but for which they cannot provide a valid argument resting on plausible and well-explicated premises.

III. A Feminist Form of Kantian Contractarian Theory

In view of these criticisms against both Hobbesian and Kantian contractarianism, it might seem that the whole approach is a theoretical dead end not only for feminists but also for *any* philosopher interested in

---

[42] Scanlon is prepared to allow that contractarian reasoning might endorse the utilitarian principle, but he would have to insist that it would do so in a "contractarian way" – i.e., a way that was not itself a form of utilitarian reasoning. Hence, he needs to give us the structure of this uniquely contractarian way of reasoning.

developing a successful theory of our moral life. But I want to try to reha-
bilitate this approach in the eyes of its critics by outlining what might be
called a "Hobbesian" brand of Kantian contractarianism that is responsible both to the meta-ethical and to the feminist criticisms I have outlined
and that holds the promise of being at least part (but only part) of a
complete theory outlining a mature morality.

"Private" Relationships and the Contractarian Test

As I tried over the years to determine the source of my own support for the
contractarian approach, I found myself increasingly convinced that the
contract test was highly appropriate for the evaluation of exactly the kinds
of relationships feminists assumed they could not illuminate: personal,
intimate ones. It is a testament to the powerful control that the public–
private distinction has over even its most ardent feminist critics that they
resist the appropriateness of what they take to be a "public" metaphor to
evaluate the morality of a "private" relationship. I want to propose that
by invoking the idea of a contract we can make a moral evaluation of
any relationship, whether it is in the family, the marketplace, the political
society, or the workplace[43] – namely, an evaluation of the extent to which
that relationship is just ("just" in a sense I shall define below).

A necessary condition of a relationship's being just is that no party in
that relationship or system is exploited by another. But exploitation is
possible even in the most intimate relationship if one party relies upon
the affection or duty felt by another party to use that other party to her
detriment. In Gauthier's words, our sociality

> becomes a source of exploitation if it induces persons to acquiesce in institutions
> and practices that but for their fellow-feeling would be costly to them. Feminist
> thought has surely made this, perhaps the core form of exploitation, clear to
> us. Thus the contractarian insists that a society could not command the willing
> allegiance of a rational person if, without appealing to her feelings for others, it
> afforded her no expectation of benefit.[44]

As I understand Gauthier's remarks, he is not suggesting that one should
never give gifts out of love or duty without insisting on being paid for
them; rather, he is suggesting that one's propensity to give gifts out of

---

[43] See also Marilyn Friedman, "Beyond Caring: The Demoralization of Gender," in Hanen
and Nielsen, eds., *Science, Morality, and Feminist Theory*, p. 100. I am in substantial agreement with Friedman's arguments that the "justice perspective" properly understood is
just as concerned with and relevant to the health of a variety of human relationships –
including intimate ones – as is the "care perspective."

[44] David Gauthier, *Morals by Agreement* (Oxford: Oxford University Press, 1986), p. 11.

love or duty *should not become the lever that another party who is capable of reciprocating relies upon to get one to maintain a relationship to one's cost.*

Perhaps this is most deeply true within the family. A woman whose devotion to her family causes her to serve them despite the fact that they do little in return is in an exploitative relationship. Of course, infants cannot assume any of her burdens; fairness cannot exist between individuals whose powers and capacities are so unequal. (Note that this relationship is not unfair either; the infant does not use the mother's love in order to exploit her.) But older children can. Indeed, as children become able to benefit those who have cared for them, it becomes increasingly unacceptable to see them failing to return these benefits. Unless they are encouraged to reciprocate the care they have received as they become able to do so, they are being allowed to exploit other human beings by taking advantage of their love for them.

So our ties (for example, of friendship or marriage) to those who are able to reciprocate what we give to them (as opposed to victims of serious diseases, impoverished people, or infants) are morally acceptable, healthy, and worthy of praise only insofar as they do not involve, on either side, the infliction of costs or the confiscation of benefits over a significant period that implicitly reveals disregard rather than respect for that person.

In order to test for the presence of such disregard, I want to argue that we should apply a version of a contractarian test to the relationship by asking: "Given the fact that we are in this relationship, could both of us reasonably accept the distribution of costs and benefits (that is, the costs and benefits that are not themselves side effects of any affective or duty-based tie between us) if it were the subject of an informed, unforced agreement in which we think of ourselves as motivated solely by self-interest?" Note, first, that the self-interested motivation is assumed for purposes of testing the moral health of the relationship; one is essentially trying to put aside the potentially blinding influence of affection or duty to see whether costs and benefits are distributed such that one is losing out to the other party. Second, note that the costs and benefits that the test inquires about are not ones that come from the affection or duty holding the parties together in the relationship – for among other things, these cannot be distributed and are outside the province of justice. One cannot distribute the pain that a parent feels when her teenage child gets into trouble, the happiness felt by someone because of the accomplishments of her friend, the suffering of a woman because of the illness of a parent. But one can distribute the burdens of caring for an infant or running a household, the costs of correspondence, the work involved in a project jointly undertaken by two friends. These nonaffective costs and benefits that the relationship itself creates or makes possible must be distributed fairly if the relationship is to be just.

But how does this test actually work? In particular, how do we give content to the word 'reasonable' such that it is not just a covert appeal to our (perhaps morally suspect) intuitions?

A simple appeal to equality won't do. Exploitation doesn't loom every time a person gets a present from a friend and then forgets her friend's birthday, or when she pays less in long-distance phone calls than her friend does. Nor would the test be reliable if it relied only upon feelings of "being used"; such feelings are all too likely to be wrong, or exaggerated, or inappropriately weak for us to put full moral faith in them. So I shall now argue that the test must be informed by a set of normative concepts that, taken together, enable us to define exploitation and recognize it when it occurs.

The Concept behind the Test

I claim that at the base of the Kantian contract theory is not a collection of inchoate and perhaps morally suspect intuitions that might vary among human beings; rather, it is a particular set of defensible concepts composing what I will call, after Rawls, a "conception of the person." As I understand it, in a successful contractarian theory the contract is a (mere) device that, if used in the right circumstances, will call to mind and organize these concepts in a way that will enable us to apply them to diagnose successfully the presence of injustice in a relationship. The contractarian conception of the person includes a list of characteristics of personhood. But it is more than just a list. It also includes two normative conceptions that are central to understanding how we are to respond to a person: namely, a conception of human worth and a conception of a person's legitimate interests.

A conception of human worth tells one what sort of treatment is appropriate or required or prohibited for certain types of individuals on the basis of an assessment of how valuable these individuals are. Some philosophers follow Hobbes in thinking that any assessments of our value as individuals can only be instrumental, whereas other philosophers such as Kant believe that, regardless of our price, our worth is noninstrumental, objective, and equal. Kant also has opponents who, while agreeing that our value is noninstrumental and objective, reject the idea that all humans are of equal value – for example, those who think human beings of a certain gender or race or caste are higher in value (and so deserving of better treatment) than those of a different gender, race, or caste.

I want to argue that animating the contract test is a certain very Kantian conception of human worth. To say that a policy must be "agreed to" by all is to say that in formulating a just policy, we must recognize that none of us can take only herself to "matter" such that she can dictate the solution alone, and also that none of us is allowed to ignore or disregard her own importance in the formulation of the right policy. Therefore, the self-interested perspective each person takes when she uses the test to assess a relationship shouldn't be seen as arrogant selfishness but as a way of symbolizing (as Jake would wish) the proper self-regard each of us should have in view of our worth, in view of the fact that, as Kant would put it, we are "ends in ourselves." However, by requiring that a policy be one that we could all agree to, the contractarian doesn't merely ask each of us to insist on our own worth; he also asks us (as Amy would wish) to recognize and come to terms with the fact that others are just as valuable as we ourselves. So without being an explicit theory of how we are valuable relative to one another, the contract device nonetheless "pictures" that relative value.

It was because the contractarian image implicitly calls forth a certain conception of relative human worth that Rawls was drawn to it as a way of combating the sacrificial tendencies of utilitarianism. The Amy-like insistence of the utilitarian that we should put the group first and accommodate ourselves to the well-being of others even if it would mean substantial and serious sacrifices either on our part or on the part of others has been the central reason why so many have rejected it as an adequate moral theory. If, on the other hand, we evaluate policies, actions, or treatments in any relationship by asking whether each individual, from a self-interested point of view, could reasonably reject them, we are letting each person "count" in a certain way. And I am proposing that we can give content to a Scanlon-like contract test as long as we develop the conception of how human beings ought to count – that is, the conception of human worth that implicitly informs the contract image.[45]

Because the contract image is ultimately animated by this conception of worth, a contractarian doesn't even need to appeal to "what we

---

[45] Moreover, to make a meta-ethical point, although I am understanding this notion of dignity or worth to be the source of moral rightness and wrongness, it may not itself be a moral notion. So if "reasonableness" is cashed out using this notion, we may be able to interpret the contractarian test as Scanlon wished – i.e., as that which defines moral rightness and moral wrongness while being informed by something nonmoral.

could agree to" if she has another device that is animated by the same conception. In this regard, it is important to note that although Rawls is called a contractarian, he makes minimal use of the contract device in A *Theory of Justice* and relies on another method of accomplishing the morally revealing representation of relative worth.[46] Although he says that each party to the original position must agree with all the rest on which available alternative is the best conception of justice, in fact that agreement is otiose because each party in his original position follows the same reasoning procedure and reaches the same conclusion – namely, that the Rawlsian conception of justice is preferable to all others. This reasoning procedure requires those who use it to appraise policies, rules, or principles without knowing which person she will become in the society that will be subject to these policies, rules, or principles. But note that, as with the contract device, this "I could be anybody" device requires that I reason in such a way that each person matters, so that I will be reluctant to permit any one of them (who might turn out to be *me)* to be sacrificed for the benefit of the group. So although Rawls relies on a noncontractarian device in A *Theory of Justice*, he is nonetheless a "real" contractarian because the device he uses taps into the same conception of worth as the contract device.[47] And this shows that it isn't the contract device that is the substance of a contractarian theory but the conception of worth that informs that device.

But, the reader may ask, if the conception of the person you're developing is the *real* moral theory and the contract talk only a heuristic device useful for picturing or suggesting this conception, are you really a contractarian?

In a way I don't care about the answer to this question: I am ultimately uninterested in labels, and if my insistence that the substantive roots of my theory are not found in the idea of a contract convinces readers that the label 'contractarian' is inappropriate for that theory, then so be it. But, as I've discussed, every contract theory, whether Hobbesian or Kantian,

---

[46] See Jean Hampton, "Contracts and Choices: Does Rawls Have a Social Contract Theory?," *Journal of Philosophy* 77, no. 6 (June 1980).

[47] Thus I disagree with Scanlon ("Contractualism and Utilitarianism," pp. 124–28), who argues that Rawls is not a real contractarian because of his reliance on the "I could be anyone" device. Both devices aim to bring others' needs to bear on your deliberations such that your choice takes them into account in the right way. Whether the others are there "in person" around an agreement table in your thought experiment, or whether they are there in virtue of the fact that you are forced to choose as if you were any one of them, does not seem to matter at all in the final result.

has used the idea of a contract as a heuristic tool that points us toward the correct form of moral reasoning and has not relied on the idea of contract in any literal way to do any justificatory work. Moreover, there is not enough in the notion of a contract to constitute an adequate moral reasoning procedure in and of itself, as the discussion of Scanlon's theory shows. Hence, in my theory (and, I would argue, in Kant's), the idea of a contract serves as a device that points to, or suggests, the concepts (in particular, the concept of human worth) at the substantive heart of morality. And I would argue that it is because of its suggestiveness that philosophers like me have been persistently attracted to talk of contract and have used the term to label their theories.

Clarifying the Concept

On my view, the way to develop a successful Kantian contractarian argument so that it is not worryingly "intuitive" is to understand and make precise the conception of the person, and particularly the conception of human worth, implicitly underlying the contract image. I regard this as a tough, lengthy, and long-term project. Nonetheless, I can at least make a few preliminary remarks here to show how I believe we can read off from the contract image aspects of the conception of human worth that animates it.

The most important idea invoked by the image is the Kantian idea that people have *intrinsic, noninstrumental value* (which is why I take it that Kant himself invoked the image in his political writings). But some readers may wonder why the contract image doesn't imply, instead, the idea that the people involved in the contract, or the services they would provide, are mere commodities. This is the assumption of many Marxists and some feminists: Carol Pateman, for example, has argued that the logic of contractual thinking would effect a morally offensive "universal market in bodies and services" in which people would contract for the services they desired (many of which they now get "for free" in a marriage – for example, sex, surrogate parenting, selling human eggs, renting wombs, and so on).[48]

But my understanding of the contract image suggests nothing of the sort. This is because, first, the contract image I invoke is deliberately

---

[48] Carol Pateman, *The Sexual Contract* (Stanford, Calif.: Stanford University Press, 1988), p. 184; see also p. 187. Patemen lays out the peculiarities of the marriage contract on pp. 163–67. Feminist advocates of contractualization include Marjorie Schultz, "Contractual Ordering of Marriage: A New Model for State Policy," *California Law Review* 70 (1982): 207–334.

meant to be an *ideal* agreement between equals. I do not regard the contract test as a morally neutral device (as Rawls, for example, suggests); rather, I see it as an image fed by normative ideas that one is ultimately relying on when using the test to make moral evaluations. And it is not true that in an ideal contract each party responds to the other solely as instrumentally valuable. Think literally about what one means when one says a person is instrumentally valuable: One is saying that the person is valuable in the way that a pen or typewriter or a hammer is valuable. That person has the value *and the status* of a tool. But in an ideal contract among relative strangers, neither party responds to the other only in that way. I don't get you to paint my house simply by whistling and pointing to the paint, as if you were some kind of automated paint machine. I believe that to get you to paint my house I must get your *consent* to do so, and I also believe (if I think our contractual relationship is ideal and hence just) that I can get your consent only if you are sure that I am not asking you to bear the costs of doing so without any reciprocating benefit from me to you. But note that this attitude implicitly rejects the view that the other person has only instrumental standing. In an ideal contract between equals, each person must respect the wishes of the other in order to achieve the agreement; hence, requiring mutual consent under these circumstances means requiring respect.

So understood, the contract test could be successfully used to disallow the commodization of certain aspects of our person. It could be used, for example, to preclude the commodization of a womb: Before a group of people could even consider the question, "What terms could we reasonably accept for our surrogacy contract?" they would have to ask the question, "Is the very idea of a surrogacy contract something that each of us could reasonably accept?" And it is plausible to suppose that people equally situated and motivated to secure their legitimate interests could not all agree to such a contract (in particular, the prospective surrogate mother could not). Remember that both Kant and Rawls have argued that the contract idea, when invoked, precludes certain institutional structures and social practices (for example, aristocratic social orders or slavery) that are degrading; similarly, I argue for an understanding of the contract test that forbids a variety of social arrangements that are demeaning – that is, inconsistent with the worth of all the parties involved.

As these remarks show, the conception of worth informing the contract device, understood ideally, is an *egalitarian* conception: Contractarians aim to idealize parties in a relationship so that each of them not only is an equal participant in the agreement process but also possesses equal bargaining power. And this is a way of expressing the idea that no person's intrinsic worth is greater than any other's. Finally, it is a *nonaggregative* conception. Although utilitarians grant people value, and can even be called "egalitarians" about value insofar as they allow each person to count equally in the utilitarian calculation, this way of "counting" still isn't good enough for the contractarian, who would note that each person appears in the utilitarian calculation as a number representing how much he contributes to the total good. This means that it is not really the individual so much as the summable units of good that he contributes (and, in the final analysis, represents in the calculation) that the utilitarian takes seriously. Each individual is therefore valued by that theory (only) to the extent that he will respond to any resources by contributing units of good to the total. In contrast, the contractarian gives each person the ability to veto an arrangement that he believes will unreasonably disadvantage him relative to the others, and this reflects the contractarian's view that each of us has a value that resists aggregation and that makes demands on us regardless of how advantageous a group might find it to ignore those demands.

The other component of the conception of the person informing the contract device is the conception of a person's legitimate interests. If one has something of great value, that value requires that one, for example, preserve it, treat it carefully so as not to hurt it, and, if it is sentient, minimize its experience of pain. That is, its value requires that one care for it in view of its importance. These responses presuppose a theory of what a valued object requires such that its value can be both preserved and respected. Human beings' unique and considerable value requires that they be properly cared for. But what does such care involve? I believe that the answer to such a question would involve detailing who we are and what interests of ours are urgent given our nature. These interests would include not only having enough to eat but also have the psychological conditions that allow us to function well and the liberty that, as autonomous beings, we need. To put it in Aristotelian terms, the answer involves constructing a normative theory formulating what is good for human beings (both as a species and as distinctive individuals).[49] This normative theory is, however, connected to the contractarian's theory of human worth. If we regard a certain set of sentient creatures as relatively unimportant,

---

[49] Such an Aristotelian theory needn't say that all of us have the same legitimate interests. This theory could ascribe to us a certain set of interests but insist that the different psychological and physiological natures of each of us generate different needs.

what we take to be their legitimate interests will differ sharply from what we take to be the legitimate interests of those to whom we attribute great worth. Of course, a conception of human good will also be informed by a host of physiological and psychological facts about human beings, but how we respond to those facts is fundamentally dependent upon how we understand human beings to be valuable.

To the extent that we can pin down what our legitimate interests are, we can also pin down some of the ideas to which we are implicitly appealing in the contract test. When we ask, "Could all of us reasonably accept this if it were proposed as the subject of unforced, informed agreement?" we must assume that each of us is consulting interests that we are legitimately entitled to have respected. Rawls's theory is famous for trying to define these interests in a political context, and many critics have noted that despite his demurrers to the contrary, his is a normatively loaded conception. But of course it must be, because not all of our interests are good ones and thus count as grounds for "reasonable rejections." Contractarians have thus far been unable to get philosophical control over the concept of legitimate interests to which they must appeal if their test is going to have real bite; I am proposing that to do so, they must not rely upon vaguely defined intuitions called forth by the contract device but must instead develop and defend in its own right the concept of legitimate interests generating these intuitions.

Contractarianism and Feminist Politics
The development of this theory depends upon the development and defense of the conception of the person informing the contract test. I believe feminist theorizing can be a highly useful resource for this development and defense. Feminist writings have a lot to say about questions surrounding worth, status, and honor. They also have a lot to say about the pain and damage human beings experience when they are considered second-class and subject to discrimination and prejudice, or when they are denied not only economic opportunities but decent housing and food. Implicit in these writings, on my view, is a conception of how people can go wrong not only in how they treat others but also in how they regard these others such that this treatment is permitted (and even, at times, encouraged). So both contractarians and many feminists are concerned to clarify the right kind of regard that any human being, in any human relationship, must be paid by others. Once that regard, and the treatment associated with it, are better understood, we will be able

to clarify what each party to the contract wants when she is motivated to secure "what is best for her." Feminist theorizing can therefore do much to help the development and analytical precision of Kantian contractarian theory.

But contractarian theory can also help the feminist cause, and it can do so because it unabashedly insists on the worth of each of us. The reliance on self-interest in my formulation of the contract test is not an unfortunate remnant of Hobbes's moral theory; rather, it is a deliberate attempt to preserve what may be the only rightheaded aspect of Hobbes's thought – namely, *the idea that morality should not be understood to require that we make ourselves the prey of others.* The self-interested concern that each party to a Kantian social contract brings to the agreement process symbolizes her morally legitimate concern to prevent her exploitation and have the value of her interests and her person respected. My insistence that each party to a relationship take a self-concerned perspective in his or her evaluation of its moral health is really the insistence that each of us is right to value ourselves, our interests, and our projects and right to insist that we not become the prey of other parties in the pursuit of their projects. The contractarian method grants us what Charlotte Brontë in the passage quoted earlier seems to want: a way to be tenacious advocates of ourselves. What has attracted so many to this form of argument and what makes it worthy of further pursuit is precisely the fact that by granting to each individual the ability to be his or her own advocate, this method enables us to conceive of both public and private relationships without exploitative servitude.

Nonetheless, a philosopher's call for all of us to insist that our interests be accorded proper weight in a relationship will sound foolish indeed to a mother caring for three kids alone after her husband has left her and who ends up taking in an aging mother too ill to take care of herself. Women in this society are in trouble largely because society has defined roles for them to play in a variety of relationships that involve them bearing a disproportionately larger share of the costs and receiving a disproportionately smaller share of the benefits than others.

The strength and downright bravery many women display as they endure their burdens is considerable and impressive, but such strength is, in the eyes of one feminist, also a roadblock to ending the abuse: "Certain values described as feminine virtues may get some women through but they do not seem to offer most women the resources for fighting the enemy – for genuine resistance. They do not, that is, push one to 'cripple' or 'damage' or stop the enemy... or at least to try."[50] However impressive the heroic service women have traditionally provided – to the extent that it is soul-destroying for them and for the women who will follow them – they must develop forms of thinking and acting that prevent their propensity to care from being the source of their abuse and exploitation. Thus it is precisely because its self-interested perspective is so alien to their other-regarding modes of thinking that feminist critics of contractarianism should welcome it as they pursue changes not merely in intimate relationships but in society at large. It is a form of thinking about moral relationships that not only encourages individuals to insist on the acknowledgment of their own interests and concerns but also (as a Rawlsian would wish) encourages them to attack societal and political sources of the exploitative roles in which women find themselves.

IV. The Uses and Limits of Contractarian Moral Theory

I have been arguing that if we understand the structure and role of the contractarian device in our moral thinking, the contract idea isn't in any sense foundational, or even necessary, for effective moral reasoning. It is merely a test that is heuristically valuable for the moral agent in virtue of the fact that it is informed by ideas that are the real source of moral reasoning. In particular, *the contract device is effective at illuminating the nature of distributive justice, which I understand to be the 'distribution of benefits and burdens in a relationship consistent with the contractarian conception of the person.'* Thus exploitation, or distributive injustice, is a distribution inconsistent with that conception. So understood, the concern to realize distributive justice is a species of moral concern generally, which I define as *treating people consistent with the contractarian conception of the person.* In this section I shall explore how and when the contract test works and when it is not appropriate to use it.

There are three different ways exploitation can exist and thus three ways that the contract test can be used to search for it. First, as I've emphasized, exploitation can exist within a relationship when it evolves such that the distribution of nonaffective costs and benefits is unfair. In this situation, there is nothing inherent in the relationship itself that creates the

[50] Joan Ringelheim, "Women and the Holocaust: A Reconsideration of Research," *Signs* *10*, no. 4 (1985): 741–61; quoted by Barbara Houston, "Rescuing Womanly Virtues: Some Dangers of Moral Reclamation," in Hanen and Nielsen, eds., *Science, Morality, and Feminist Theory*, p. 248.

exploitation; instead, the behavior of the parties involved precipitates it. Consider a relationship held together by bonds of affection. Although the contract test is misapplied if someone were to try to use it to evaluate directly those affective bonds (such as love or sympathetic concern), it might nonetheless be instrumental to preserving these affective bonds by enabling the parties to locate and correct ways in which they have been behaving unfairly toward one another. In a good friendship, for example, each friend naturally accords the other noninstrumental value. In response to this value, each is prepared to give gifts to the other. A "pay for service" mentality exists between business partners; but between genuine friends, there is a concern to serve the other insofar as she is (each believes) the sort of valuable being for whom such service or such gift-giving is appropriate. Note, however, that when both friends take this kind of interest in the other, the gift-giving will be roughly reciprocal, and each will be loathe even to appear to use the other as a means.

In contrast, when a friendship starts to get corrupted, one of the parties begins to enjoy the gifts being given more than he does the giver of those gifts, thereby evaluating the one who is giving the gifts as a gift-giver, as a servant of his desires, as the one who ministers to his needs or desires. And if her affection for him is sufficiently strong to motivate her to continue to give the gifts without being paid, why should he reciprocate? He gets what he wants "for free" (or perhaps with minimal cost on his part). This is an example of the kind of exploitation that, as Gauthier notes, can exist in the context of an affective relationship. One party uses the other party's affection to get her to serve him, according her mere instrumental worth. This is not only unjust; it is also a sign that the love in the relationship has been corrupted.

So although philosophers have generally believed that distributive justice has little to do with friendship or love, in fact a concern to locate and eradicate this kind of exploitation can be understood to derive not only from an interest in securing justice between the parties but also from an interest in preserving a genuinely caring relationship. Or to put it another way, insofar as I am arguing that "being just" in a distributive sense means "distributing benefits and burdens in a relationship such that each person's worth is properly respected," then love and distributive justice so understood are not opposing responses because the former is possible only if the latter prevails.

Second, the contract test can function as a test, not of the operation of a relationship, but of the relationship itself, to determine whether exploitation is inherent in the design of some of the roles played by those involved in it. The master–slave relationship is an example of a relationship that would fail the test, "Could all of us reasonably accept the idea of entering into or remaining in any of the roles in this relationship if doing so were the subject of an informed, unforced agreement in which we think of ourselves as motivated solely by self-interest?" Yet another example is given by Charlotte Brontë's account of society's role for spinster women: "Your place is to do good to others, to be helpful whenever help is wanted." As she notes, this is "a very convenient doctrine for the people who hold it," but one that results in "a terrible hollowness, mockery, want, craving, in that existence which is given away to others, for want of something of your own to bestow it on." It is a good example of a social role that could not be agreed upon by those called upon to assume it were they freed of social pressures and imagined obligations and encouraged instead to consult (and regard as legitimate) their own wishes and aspirations.

Third, even if no injustice would occur within a relationship, it might occur as a result of one's decision to enter into it. A relationship can be nonexploitative in its nature and in its operation but still precipitate exploitation if one's decision to participate in it will result in someone (for example, oneself or a third party) getting less than her due. So the contract test can be used to explore whether everyone involved could agree to one's participation in that relationship. Suppose, for example, that you were considering whether to become a parent, teacher, doctor, or minister. The contract test would evaluate whether, if you took on one of these roles and, as a result, developed obligations and affective connections toward others, you could remain fair to yourself and/or to others toward whom you already had obligations or affection. ("If I have this child, can I still do what I need to do for myself?" "If I adopt this profession, will I be able to give to my family what I owe them?") There may be nothing unjust in, say, a parent–child relationship in and of itself, but there may be injustice in the adult's decision to become a parent in the first place.

There are also times, however, when the contract test is not appropriate to use. In particular, it is not appropriate for morally evaluating relationships between people radically unequal in capacity.[51] There is

---

[51] Annette Baier writes: "It is a typical feature of the dominant moral theories and traditions, since Kant, or perhaps since Hobbes, that relationships between equals or those who are deemed equal in some important sense, have been the relations that morality is concerned primarily to regulate.... This pretence of an equality that is in fact absent may often lead to desirable protection of the weaker, or more dependent. But it somewhat masks the question of what our moral relationships are to those who are our superiors or

something absurd about inquiring into the morality of the relationship between, say, a mother and her newborn infant by asking, "What services could each agree to? What would they be unreasonable to reject?" For, so long as this radical inequality prevails, such a relationship is outside the province of distributive justice – in part because an infant or anyone severely infirm is incapable of reciprocating the benefit, making it ridiculous for any moral theory to require it, and in part because such people are not manipulating the situation to extract "free care" from others.[52] The contract test is not useful in helping to determine the obligations parties have to one another in these relationships because there are no issues of distributive justice involved in them. However, the conception of the person animating that device is directly relevant to defining those duties.

As I have discussed, it is part of what it means to respect someone's worth that one attend to her legitimate interests. So a traveler who, like the Samaritan, sees someone bleeding to death on the roadside and refuses to help him is failing to honor that person's worth, and a society that fails to define or develop institutional or social responses to those who are in serious need is failing to respond to the worth of its own citizens effectively. In such "Good Samaritan" cases, we commend the care givers precisely because they unselfishly provide care for the needy person, without thinking of any benefits for themselves. It is not only permissible but also appropriate to give one's services as a gift to those who are in trouble. But note that what we are concerned about when we test relationships for their justice – namely, that each party's worth is properly acknowledged – is never compromised in these sorts of relationships. We are able to commend the service provided by the Good Samaritan because the person being benefited receives the aid without ever taking advantage of

---

our inferiors in power. A more realistic acceptance of the fact that we begin, as helpless children, that at almost every point of our lives we deal with both the more and the less helpless, that equality of power and interdependency, between two persons or groups, is rare and hard to recognize when it does occur, might lead us to a more direct approach to questions concerning the design of institutions structuring these relationships between unequals (families, schools, hospitals, armies) and of the morality of our dealings with the more and the less powerful" ("Need for More Than Justice," pp. 52–53).

[52] See also Will Kymlicka, "Two Theories of Justice," *Inquiry* 33, no. 1 (1990): 109–10: "In an important sense, the 'ethic of care' advanced by recent feminists does reverse these questions, replacing the contractual relationship between adults with the mother-child relationship as their paradigm of a morally responsible relationship. But the conclusion they reach is that our responsibilities to dependents can only be met if we replace the appeal to impartiality with attention to particularity, and replace justice with care."

the benefactor's affection for or feeling of duty toward him in order to receive the service. He has a great need to which the Samaritan responds insofar as she is respectful of his value as a human being.

Suppose the incapacitated person regains (or develops) his capacities. Once that happens, the use of the contract test becomes appropriate to determine the response he ought to make toward his benefactor. Normally we say that such a person should feel "gratitude" toward his benefactor and take steps to benefit her in some way in order to thank her for his care. I would argue that gratitude is at least partly generated by a concern to be just: Gratitude contains within it the appreciation of the worth of the person who would provide such care, engendering in the genuinely moral person the desire to give benefits in return as a way of showing that he desires to honor, rather than take advantage of, his benefactor's services. An ungrateful recipient of a Good Samaritan's care is therefore unjust, not because he did anything to manipulate the situation such that he received care for which he did not have to pay, but because he is now acquiescing in the uneven distribution of benefits and burdens that could not have been agreed to by self-interested parties had such agreement been possible before the care. This acquiescence may not be as bad as actions that have manipulated the exploitation, but it is still an unjust reaction to the benefactor – a way of responding to his benefactor solely as instrumentally valuable to his needs and interests.[53]

But let me stress once again that the return needn't be equal to the gift received in order for justice to be realized. Even after one gains capacities roughly equal to those of one's benefactor, an equal return might be impossible. The impoverished widow who gave her mite to the Lord in gratitude surely indicates by her actions that she honors the one who benefited her and does not view him merely as a means. Even a bare "thank you" from one who can give little else may be sufficient to show this person's desire to honor rather than take advantage of the one who helped him.[54] The bottom line for those who use the contract test

---

[53] Of course, a person is grateful for what the benefactor did, not for his worth. Gratitude is a reaction to the beneficial deed; but the benefited one feels it to the extent that he appreciates that his benefactor's services came about not because the benefactor was a servant or tool of his desires, but because the benefactor freely chose to bestow these services upon him. So an acknowledgment of that choice – and thus of the noninstrumental standing of the benefactor – is implicit in the emotion of gratitude.

[54] There is a reason why those benefited by Good Samaritans may want to benefit their benefactors in return – they desire to preserve their own worth. Those who are in extreme need, although equal in worth to those who help them, are nonetheless not equal in circumstance or capacity, and in this sense they do not have the equal standing necessary

is not whether the distribution of costs and benefits between them has been equal, but whether the distribution is such that either of them is exploiting the other. Given the complexities of human circumstances, there is no formula applicable in all situations to decide the answer to this question. It is for this reason that Scanlon's imprecise word *reasonable* may be a good one to use to characterize what we are looking for in an acceptable distribution of costs and benefits – assuming, of course, that it is nonetheless given content by the conception of the person defined earlier – because *reasonable* implies both that there is no set of rules we can invoke that decisively determines how to distribute costs and benefits and that there are still right and wrong answers as to how to do it.

V. Communitarian Concerns

Suppose the conception of the person required by the contract test can be developed successfully. Nonetheless, is this the sort of theory upon which our moral and political theorizing should rest? There are two interesting reasons why certain communitarian political theorists might argue it should not.

Consider, first, Michael Sandel's criticism of Rawls's contract theory as one that presupposes an implausible metaphysical conception of the person. In his recent work, Rawls has tried to back away from grounding his argument in any metaphysical claims at all. So a communitarian might argue that my theory takes on the sort of metaphysical baggage other contractarians don't (and shouldn't) want. I would insist, however, that the metaphysical claims made in my theory are the strength of that theory and not an embarrassment to it. There is nothing in the contractarian conception of the person as I understand it that would deny our deep sociality as a species; indeed, like Rawls, who stressed our sociality as a reason for beginning moral philosophy at the level of the basic structure of society, I agree that it is this structure that plays a primary role in forming

for justice to demand that they make a return. But many find this inequality a painful and humiliating experience. They wish to be in a position to return the favor in order to establish themselves as equal in capacity and circumstance to those who benefited them. Thus they want to respond as justice would require in order to show that they have the standing that the demands of justice presuppose. I am told by a family counselor that this attitude of wishing to return the benefits to parents who have freely given their care is frequent among teenagers desiring to manifest equal status with their parents (sometimes even leading them to insist that all future benefits and burdens in the family be the subject of contracts).

us. But I would also insist that, regardless of the society we develop in, we are autonomous beings possessing a worth that is noninstrumental and equal, with certain needs that ought to be met. So on this view, a society that teaches its members to believe that some of them are inherently more valuable than others by virtue of their birth, or gender, or race is importantly *wrong*. I will not dispute that this metaphysical claim requires a defense, and in a forthcoming work I aim to propose one; but I will insist that there is nothing "unattractive" about this metaphysics. Indeed, a communitarian who is ready to embrace whatever views about relative value his culture communicates to him will have to swallow views (for example, about women or people of color) that many of us believe are unacceptable. The driving force behind the contractarian theory is what might be called a "socially responsible metaphysics" that insists on the equal intrinsic worth of all people. I would argue that we owe this idea our allegiance, even as we strive to construct philosophical arguments that develop and defend it.

Which brings us to the communitarian's second concern: Isn't a contract test likely to generate a liberal political theory hostile to the interests of a community? In answering this concern I admit – and welcome – the idea that it would do so, although I do not have time to spell out in detail the structure of the political liberalism it would generate. Nonetheless, it is not a morally neutral form of political liberalism but rather (and quite deliberately) a morally loaded liberalism informed by a conception of the person prescribing the creation and sustenance of institutions that respect the worth and legitimate interests of persons. Thus a society that has an unregulated market economy, or wholesale allegiance to the doctrine of freedom of contract, or patriarchal institutions, or racist practices will not function so that each gets what she is due as a person; accordingly, it would be criticized as unjust by this theory. Of course, individuals, not groups, are the fundamental concern of this theory; in this sense, the theory might be thought anti-communitarian. But insofar as our legitimate needs include the need to function as part of a collective, the interests of a collective will be recognized insofar as they are instrumental to the aims of (intrinsically worthy) individuals. (So, on this view, collectives are protected only to the extent that they have instrumental value for the individuals who compose them.) And the operation of these collectives – the roles they define for people and the institutions they adopt – are the appropriate subjects of a contract test concerned with locating the presence of exploitative injustice, subjects ranging from the monogamous nuclear family to market society, from democratic polities to social practices defining gender. It is a fundamental (and liberal) tenet of this view that a community's practices must answer to the worth of individuals and not the other way around.

VI. Beyond Morality

Let me conclude on a note sympathetic to some of the feminist criticisms I reviewed earlier. Suppose we had a complete moral theory founded on the contractarian's conception of the person and, as part of this theory, a conception of distributive justice effectively revealed by the contract test. Would we have arrived at a fully mature or (perhaps better) genuinely wise perspective regarding how we should live our lives with one another?

I think not, because we would still not understand certain important reasons why individuals forge relationships or the full nature of the affective or duty-based connections holding our relationships together. Contra the beliefs of Hobbesians, in our various relationships with others we are not simply concerned with gaining the advantages of cooperation from people we take to be instrumentally valuable to the pursuit of our own interests. Moreover, even if our relationships are subject to the demands of justice, most of them are not undertaken in order to realize justice. A person doesn't become a parent so that she can be just toward her children. None of us fosters a friendship with another out of a concern to be fair. Joining a church or a charity organization, volunteering in one's community, organizing charities for people in other countries, committing oneself in the manner of Mother Theresa to the needs of the desperately poor, are ways of creating a role for oneself that are prompted by interests that may have a good deal to do with honoring the worth of these individuals but perhaps have much more to do with the love one feels toward others.

I believe that if we begin to theorize in a more complete way about the values inherent in human relationships, we will find that the concepts of justice as well as morality are too limp to help us understand many of the responses we commend when we praise human beings. Consider, for example, the response of a Texas farm woman to a tornado that destroyed her family's home. As the destruction was occurring she sat in a shelter with her family and worked on a quilt, explaining, "I made my quilt to keep my family warm. I made it beautiful so my heart would not break."[55]

---

55 Sara Ruddick, "Maternal Thinking," in *Women and Values*, ed. M. Pearsall (Belmont, Calif.: Wadsworth, 1986), p. 344 and note 8.

To describe this woman as "moral" seems evaluatively inept. In fact, there is no traditional ethical theory (except perhaps Aristotle's) that could shed much light on what this woman was aiming at by her actions with respect to her family or herself. Yet here is someone whose response to herself and those around her is impressive and important; the story surely brings to mind memories of what our families and friends have done for themselves and for us, not merely because they were "moral" and concerned to respect us as persons, but because they loved us, and themselves, and those aspects of the world around us that are worth loving. The intrinsic value morality tells us to respect in our dealings with other persons is probably not the only kind of value each of us has, and to love someone may be to appreciate them in a quite special way – to accord them a particular non-moral value (think of how parents cherish their children, or how people take delight in their friends' company).

Nonetheless, real love can exist only if there is also moral respect. The contract device therefore gives us a way to evaluate one moral component of any human relationship. It helps us to understand what to protect in our relationships with others, but it doesn't tell us all the ways we should respond to human beings in order to build a fine friendship, a loving marriage, a bond with our children. It tells us the harmful emotional responses we must control in order to accord people their worth; it does not tell us the emotions we ought to cultivate if we wish to develop enriching ties to others. And outside of explaining their instrumental value, it can never tell us what our lives, and our relationships with others, are *for.*

So contractarian theorizing is the beginning of wisdom about how we should relate to our fellow human beings – but it is only the beginning.[56]

[56] Portions of this chapter were read at Texas Technical University, Yale Law School, and the 1991 Pacific Division Meeting of the American Philosophical Association, and I wish to thank those audiences. I also wish to thank the members of the Los Angeles Law and Philosophy Group; the members of my graduate seminar at the University of California, Davis, in the fall of 1990; and Marcia Homiak, for their help during the writing of this chapter.

2

Selflessness and Loss of Self

The biggest danger, that of losing oneself, can pass off in the world as quietly as if it were nothing; every other loss, an arm, a leg, five dollars, a wife, etc. is bound to be noticed.

Søren Kierkegaard, *The Sickness unto Death*[1]

Sacrificing one's own interests in order to serve another is, in general, supposed to be a good thing, an example of altruism, the hallmark of morality, and something we should commend to (but not always require of) the entirely-too-selfish human beings of our society. But let me recount a story that I hope will persuade the reader to start questioning this conventional philosophical wisdom. Last year, a friend of mine was talking with me about a mutual acquaintance whose two sons were in the same nursery school as our sons. This woman, whom I will call Terry, had been pregnant with twins, but one of the twins had died during the fourth month of pregnancy, and the other twin had just been born prematurely at six months with a host of medical problems. We were discussing how stressful this woman's life had been while she was pregnant: she was a housewife, and her two boys, aged three and five, were lively, challenging, often unruly – a real handful to raise. Her husband worked long hours in a law firm, so the vast majority of the child-care and household chores fell on her shoulders. "You could see that she was exhausted by the end of the first trimester," I maintained, "because her eyes were tired, and her cheeks were sunken – she looked almost like a cadaver." My friend

---

[1] Søren Kierkegaard, *The Sickness unto Death*, trans. Alastair Hannay (Harmondsworth: Penguin, 1989), pp. 62–63.

agreed. I went on to blame her exhaustion on the fact that she had to do too much during a pregnancy that anyone would have found difficult. "I don't understand her husband," I maintained. "Surely he could see how badly she looked. If he had concern for his future children, why didn't he do something to help her so that the pregnancy had a chance of going better? And if he loved *her*, why didn't he cut down his hours so that he could help out at home? Surely he could see just by looking at her that she was in trouble." My friend said nothing at the time, but after a week she called me, and told me that my criticism of this woman's husband had bothered her all week. "You're wrong about Terry's husband not caring enough about her. They have a good marriage," she insisted, and then she continued: "You know, you're not like us. We accept the fact that we should do most of the child care and housework. Terry's husband wasn't doing anything wrong expecting her to take responsibility for that side of things."

What troubled me most about my friend's remarks was her assumption that it was not only permissible but appropriate for "her kind" to care for other people, even to the point where they were endangering their own health (and in this case, also the health of those they were responsible for nurturing). And I realized that Terry herself bore some of the responsibility for these events: not only had she harmed those fetuses by insisting on carrying the entire burden of care in the family, but she had also harmed herself by putting enormous stress on her body, in a way that had bad physical and, one suspects, bad psychological repercussions.

Often philosophers who commend altruism assume that someone who cares for another even at the expense of her own welfare is an impressive and highly moral figure. But surely the story I have just told indicates that the truth is much more complicated: not all self-sacrifice is worthy of our respect or moral commendation, and not all such sacrifice really benefits those at whom it is aimed. Often men and women who give to others at their own expense are called "selfless," and I find that to be a revealing term, because "selfless" people such as Terry are in danger of losing the self they ought to be developing, and as a result, may be indirectly harming the very people for whom they care.

This essay attempts to explore the sort of "selfless" act that is bad, and the sort of "selfish" conduct that is good. I am using the terms 'good' and 'bad' in the preceding sentence as moral terms, so my understanding of what counts as 'moral' is unconventional. The adjective 'moral' is normally understood to be a term referring to traits of character or actions that are, in either a direct or indirect way, other-regarding. But this chapter attempts to pursue what might be called the "self-regarding" component of morality, a component which has been curiously neglected over the years.

I. Two Conceptions of Morality

I want to begin by exploring traditional conceptions of what morality is, and how they tell us to evaluate altruistic action. By the term 'conception of morality' I do not mean any particular theory (such as Kantianism or utilitarianism) justifying or attempting to define moral conduct. I mean the deeper understanding of morality which moral theories are *about* – our intuitive sense of what morality is, which we use to recognize moral actions and about which we develop moral theories to defend or precisely define it. There are two conceptions of morality that have undergirded moral theories in modern times, both of which, I shall argue, are problematic.

In order to flesh out these conceptions, I will make use of Carol Gilligan's interviews with two children – interviews that address real or hypothetical moral problems, which she has presented in a number of forums, most prominently in her book *In a Different Voice.* On the basis of interviews such as these, Gilligan argues that in our society there are currently two different "moral voices," which she calls the "ethic of justice" and the "ethic of care," and she finds some evidence (albeit controversial) associating the first with men and the second with women.[2] Now Gilligan's work is that of a psychologist, and thus she is not concerned to be very clear about what a "voice" is, nor does she attempt to use the resources of moral philosophy to clarify or define any theoretical details involved in these voices. But as a philosopher I have found her work valuable because it takes seriously the moral views and perspectives of everyday people, and thus offers us a way to uncover what I am calling "conceptions of morality" by exposing the deep-seated assumptions people in our society have about what morality is, what it requires of us, and the nature of its authority over our lives. And (as I shall show at length in

---

[2] See Carol Gilligan, *In a Different Voice* (Cambridge: Harvard University Press, 1982). She has revised and expanded her ideas since then. See a variety of articles about Gilligan's recent work in *Mapping the Moral Domain*, ed. Carol Gilligan, Victoria Ward, and Jill McLean, with Betty Bandige (Cambridge: Center for the Study of Gender, Education, and Human Development, 1988). And see Carol Gilligan, "Moral Orientation and Moral Development," in *Women and Moral Theory*, ed. Eva Feder Kittay and Diana T. Meyers (Totowa, N. J.: Rowman and Littlefield, 1987), pp. 19–33.

a discussion of the work of one philosopher below) such conceptions are an important source of the intuitions upon which we philosophers are subtly relying when we generate moral theories. Hence, in this section I want to present Gilligan's two voices, and then go on to discuss how they can be understood as (in my sense) two different moral conceptions.

As I have noted elsewhere,[3] two of Gilligan's interviews with older children clarify these two "voices" nicely. Gilligan originally initiated these interviews in order to test Lawrence Kohlberg's theory of moral development, which Gilligan believed did not adequately describe the moral development of many females. Eleven-year-old Jake, whose answers to the interviewers earned him high marks on Kohlberg's moral-maturity scale, gave the following answer when asked: "When responsibility to oneself and responsibility to others conflict, how should one choose?" He replied with great self-assurance: "You go about one-fourth to the others and three-fourths to yourself."[4] When asked to explain his answer to the question about responsibility to himself and others, Jake replies:

Because the most important thing in your decision should be yourself, don't let yourself be guided totally by other people, but you have to take them into consideration. So, if what you want to do is blow yourself up with an atom bomb, you should maybe blow yourself up with a hand grenade because you are thinking about your neighbors who would die also.[5]

As this remarkable example shows, he regards "being moral" as pursuing one's own interests without damaging the interests of others, and he takes it as a matter of moral strength not to allow the interests of others to dictate to him what he ought or ought not to do. For Jake, morality defines the rules governing noninterference.

Contrast the following answer to the same question given by eleven-year-old Amy, whose answers to the interviewers earned poorer marks on Kohlberg's scale:

Well, it really depends on the situation. If you have a responsibility with somebody else [sic], then you should keep it to a certain extent, but to the extent that it is really going to hurt you or stop you from doing something that you really, really, want, then I think maybe you should put yourself first. But if it is your responsibility to somebody really close to you, you've just got to decide in that

[3] The discussion of Jake and Amy is partly drawn from my paper "Feminist Contractarianism," in *A Mind of One's Own*, ed. L. Antony and C. Witt (Boulder: Westview Press, 1992).
[4] Gilligan, *In a Different Voice*, pp. 35–36.
[5] Ibid., p. 36.

situation which is more important, yourself or that person, and like I said, it really depends on what kind of person you are and how you feel about the other person or persons involved.[6]

When asked to explain this answer, Amy replies:

...some people put themselves and things for themselves before they put other people, and some people really care about other people. Like, I don't think your job is as important as somebody that you really love, like your husband or your parents or a very close friend. Somebody that you really care for – or if it's just your responsibility to your job or somebody that you barely know, then maybe you go first.... [7]

Whereas Jake's remarks take for granted the idea that being moral means following rules that preclude interference in other people's pursuit of their interests, Amy's remarks make clear that for her, moral conduct is beneficent involvement that may require, at times, self-sacrifice. And her discussion of other moral problems reveals the assumption that being moral means actively pursuing the well-being of others. Whereas Jake sees others' interests as constraints on the pursuit of his own ends, Amy believes others' ends are ones that morality obliges her to help pursue.[8]

Many feminist theorists maintain that, in contrast to the ranking Kohlberg would assign to them, the kind of moral voice Amy exemplifies is clearly "higher" or more advanced than Jake's.[9] On Jake's view, morality is seen as – to use Annette Baier's term – "traffic rules for self-assertors,"[10] and Baier argues plausibly that such a perspective on morality is neither a sophisticated nor a mature moral perspective. It appears to derive from the mistaken assumption that each of us is self-sufficient, able, and desirous of "going it alone." Amy is surely right that this is false. Her perspective on morality, which emphasizes caring for and fostering the well-being of others, appears to be a richer, sounder theory of what genuine moral behavior is all about. Such a perspective is one which women (and especially mothers) are frequently thought to exhibit more than men.

However, Amy's conception of her moral role is certainly not beyond criticism. *Maybe* she can put herself first, she says, if not doing so would

---

[6] Ibid., pp. 35–36.

[7] Ibid., p. 36.

[8] I am indebted to Elizabeth Willott and David Schmidtz for this way of contrasting the children's moral outlooks.

[9] Annette Baier, "What Do Women Want in a Moral Theory?" *Nous* 19, no. 1 (March 1985): 62.

[10] Ibid.

mean losing out on something that she "really, really" wants. But only maybe. Jake is convinced not only that his interests count, but that they count far more than other people's (three-quarters to one-quarter). Amy appears to be having trouble figuring out whether or not her interests count at all. Even in a situation where she takes her responsibility to others to be minimal, she finds it difficult to assert the priority of her own interests.

On the basis of these children's observations and remarks, we can outline two conceptions of morality which they are assuming as they answer the interviewers' questions; and we will see that neither of the conceptions is fully acceptable. First, although they disagree in many ways, both children accept the following tenet:

(1) Moral behavior is almost exclusively concerned with the well-being of others and not with the well-being of oneself.

In his discussion of Marx's criticism of morality, Allen Wood argues that something along the lines of tenet (1) must be included in any adequate understanding of what morality is. Although he admits that the word 'morality' can be used to include certain forms of self-regarding behavior, nonetheless he writes that

there is a narrower and I think more proper sense of 'moral' in which we distinguish *moral* goods and evils from *nonmoral* ones. We all know the difference between valuing or doing something because conscience or the 'moral law' tells us we 'ought' to, and valuing or doing something because it satisfies our needs, our wants or our conceptions of what is good for us (or for someone else whose welfare we want to promote – desires for nonmoral goods are not necessarily selfish desires).[11]

Both children seem to agree with Wood that "nonmoral goods" include most of what we want for ourselves, goods whose pursuit often competes with activities that we "ought" to do for others – activities that most of us tend to find less compelling precisely because they do not lead to self-benefiting goods.

However, although they both accept tenet (1), Amy and Jake have very different conceptions of what it means to be "other-regarding." Amy assumes it means caring for others, and accepts the following tenet:

(2A) A perfectly moral person is one who actively seeks out ways of benefiting others, and offers her services and/or her resources in order to meet others' needs.

[11] Allen Wood, *Karl Marx* (London: Routledge & Kegan Paul, 1981), pp. 126–27.

In contrast, Jake assumes that "being moral" primarily involves not hurting others. Although he is prepared to choose to be responsible toward others "one-quarter" of the time, when he gives an example of moral behavior, it is a "noninterference" example: that is, do not interfere with others when you are engaged in your pursuits (in his example, the pursuit is "blowing yourself up"!). So for Jake, being moral is primarily perceived as a negative activity; he accepts the following tenet:

(2J) A perfectly moral person does not do anything to interfere with or injure other people or their (noninjurious) activities.

Now Amy would certainly agree that (2J) is part of being moral, but only because it is implied by (2A). However, Jake would likely reject (2A) as being *too* responsive to other people; after all, he insists, we are permitted to put ourselves ahead of others "three-quarters" of the time.

Because they have different conceptions of how moral behavior benefits others, Jake and Amy have different understandings of what altruistic behavior is, and how it should be commended. Because Jake believes that morality generally only requires him to refrain from hurting people, he is convinced that this is a realizable ideal, allowing him plenty of room for his own activities. Now he is prepared to go beyond this and offer help (giving other people one-quarter of his attention, and reserving for himself three-quarters), but I would suspect, if he did so, that he would often perceive this help to be something over and above the demands of morality – analogous to "moral extra credit." The tone of his remarks makes it clear that he would not feel terribly bad about refraining from performing costly care, since such care is not, strictly speaking, morally required in any case (morality is primarily about not hurting others), and thus an "extra" that any of us can forego with a fairly easy conscience. Therefore, someone with Jake's conception of morality accepts the possibility that there are what philosophers call "supererogatory acts." To put it precisely, such people believe:

(3J) There are acts that benefit other people which are morally commendable but not morally obligatory (i.e., supererogatory acts).

However, for people such as Amy, foregoing beneficial activity is not so easy. *Any* beneficent involvement in another's life is mandated by morality, and because so many people are in need in our world, Amy is the sort of person who will constantly feel the tug of conscience, chastising her for not doing more to care for others. Of course, many of these obligations may be defeasible, given other obligations she is under; but the point is that they would still be *obligations*, as opposed to mere "moral recommendations." This means that Amy accepts:

(3A) Any act that could benefit another person is *a prima facie* moral obligation.

One who accepts (3A) believes that there is no such thing as a morally supererogatory act (or "moral extra credit").

Although Gilligan's research suggests that people divide on gender lines in their advocacy of either of these conceptions, in fact it is interesting to note that over the centuries there have been entirely male-developed moral theories that have drawn from both conceptions. Consider, for example, that for the utilitarian, the fundamental business of the moral person is the pursuit of the happiness of the community, which is a difficult and demanding task. And while this pursuit may allow or even require one to serve one's own interests on occasion, it may also require considerable self-sacrifice. Moreover, at least one utilitarian has recently championed something like (3A), recognizing that the beneficence required of the utilitarian leaves no room for moral extra credit.[12]

On the other hand, there are also plenty of Jake-like theories. Consider, for example, Locke's formulation of what he takes to be the fundamental law of nature:

Every one as he is *bound to preserve himself,* and not to quit his Station wilfully; so by the like reason when his own Preservation comes not in competition, ought he, as much as he can, *to preserve the rest of Mankind,* and may not unless it be to do Justice on an Offender, take away or impair the life, or what tends to the Preservation of the Life, Liberty, Health, Limb or Goods of another.[13]

At first, it seems Locke perceives morality as an active and beneficent activity when he calls on people to do as much as they can to preserve others; but when he gives instances of moral activity later on, each prescribes a form of noninterference. In general, he tells us, do not "take away or impair" others' ability to preserve themselves, and this seems to be what he means by the phrase "preserve the rest of Mankind." Finally, note that he gives permission to behave in ways that can be damaging to others' lives if one's own preservation requires it ("when his own Preservation comes not in competition"). So while Locke, like Jake, perceives morality as an other-oriented activity, he does not perceive it to be so demanding that it would require one always – or even usually – to choose to serve

---

[12] See Shelly Kagan, *The Limits of Morality* (Oxford: Oxford University Press, 1988).
[13] The quote is drawn from section 6 of the Second Treatise in *Two Treatises of Government,* ed. Peter Laslett (Cambridge: Cambridge University Press, 1960), p. 311.

others' needs over one's own. He even seems prepared to sanction behavior that is destructive of others' interests if one's own preservation requires it.

Let us return, then, to the topic of altruism: on one conception, there are altruistic behaviors that are recommended but not required; on the other conception, all altruistic behaviors are prima facie moral obligations, to be performed unless there is a higher altruistic obligation in place. But note one interesting fact: *both* conceptions assume that if one has a choice between doing something self-regarding or doing something that is *genuinely* beneficial for others, the beneficent act can never be immoral. This is most obviously true for the utilitarian – assuming, of course, that the community would benefit more from your service to others than it would from your service to yourself: and any action that would further the happiness of the community, according to the utilitarian calculation, is a moral action, and thus an action to be morally commended, no matter what it might do to you. Moreover, while Locke gives his readers moral permission to choose themselves over others when their own self-preservation is at stake, he never considers the possibility that someone who did the reverse might be an immoral person. And this is probably because he assumed that such a person would be even more moral "than normal" insofar as he would be choosing to serve others even when permitted not to do so.

II. Morality's Hegemony

Which conception of morality is right? Although philosophers have tended to line up on both sides, and have rigorously debated this issue, we should consider how we react to the two children's articulation, in crude but pure terms, of the moral conception each accepts: we think each conception is wrong and, indeed, immature. But if we criticize both conceptions of morality, shouldn't we also criticize any moral theories that are based upon the assumptions of either of these conceptions?

We should. I have already alluded to Annette Baier's attack on Jake-like moral theories, which I will discuss later in this section. But we can just as easily criticize Amy-like moral theories; in fact, without realizing it, Susan Wolf develops such a criticism in her "Moral Saints."[14] In a nutshell, Wolf argues that two leading moral theories, utilitarianism and Kantianism, along with the "common-sense" morality accepted by nonphilosophers,

[14] Susan Wolf, "Moral Saints," *Journal of Philosophy* 79, no. 8 (August 1982): 419–39.

all regard moral activity as almost exclusively other-regarding and beneficent, so that were a person to become perfectly moral (i.e., a moral saint)
as defined by any of these approaches, he would be so focused on pursuing the well-being of others that he would have neither the time nor
the "moral permission" to develop a variety of the talents, skills, traits
of personality, and vocations that make each of us an interesting and
well-rounded person:

> If the moral saint is devoting all his time to feeding the hungry or healing the sick
> or raising money for Oxfam, then necessarily he is not reading Victorian novels,
> playing the oboe, or improving his backhand. . . .
>   There are, in addition, a class of nonmoral characteristics that a saint cannot
> encourage in himself for reasons that are not just practical. There is a more sub-
> stantial tension between having any of these qualities unashamedly and being
> a moral saint. . . . For example, a cynical or sarcastic wit, or a sense of humor
> that appreciates this kind of wit in others, requires that one take an attitude
> of resignation and pessimism toward the flaws and vices to be found in the
> world. . . . [A]lthough a moral saint might well enjoy a good episode of *Father
> Knows Best*, he may not in good conscience be able to laugh at a Marx Brothers
> movie or enjoy a play by George Bernard Shaw.[15]

Wolf goes on to argue that human institutions such as *haute cuisine*, high
fashion, interior design, and perhaps even fine art could not be said to
be worth as many resources as we standardly put into them, given how
these resources could be used in many morally superior ways. Hence,
she concludes that although morality is a highly valuable and important
human activity, it cannot be said to be always authoritative over all non-
moral options: in particular, there are, she insists, judgments that are
neither moral nor egoistic, about what would be good for a person to
do or be, which are made from a point of view outside the limits set by
the moral values, interests, and desires that the person might actually
have. These judgments arise from what she calls the "point of view of
individual perfection," and are governed by ideals and values that have
nothing to do with morality. She argues that, like moral judgments, these
perfectionist judgments claim for themselves a kind of objectivity and a
grounding in a perspective which any rational and perceptive being can
take up. Unlike moral judgments, however, the good with which these
judgments are concerned is not the good of anyone or any group other
than the individual himself.[16] She insists that we are sometimes (perhaps
even often) permitted to choose this perfectionist good over the values

---

[15] Ibid., pp. 420–21.
[16] Ibid., p. 436.

and dictates of morality. So, Wolf's conclusion in "Moral Saints" is that the unrelenting pursuit of morality is a bad thing, where 'bad' must be understood in some sense other than 'immoral.'

Now Wolf claims that *all* contemporary moral theories fall prey to her criticisms, and her attack on the currently popular moral approaches is supposed to reveal the mistake that pervades all contemporary approaches to morality. But the analysis in the preceding section of the two divergent conceptions of morality in our society should make it clear that Wolf is actually criticizing only *one* "common-sense" conception, namely, the "Amy-like" one. To see this, consider that Wolf takes it for granted that all three conceptions she criticizes have a highly active, "caring" conception of morality. Thus, she takes it for granted that, on any of these views, a perfectly moral person would be going out in the world looking for ways of benefiting others, offering her services, using her money for philanthropic gestures, constantly surveying her world to see how she could help, either by using her time and personal skills or by using her financial resources. Moreover, Wolf assumes, along with Amy, that this beneficent involvement is not only commendable but also morally required. It is not surprising that Wolf finds it easy to argue against such an exhausting and self-limiting ideal. Our intuitive rejection of the ideal of the moral saint she describes is not unlike our alarm at the kind of person Amy says she wants to become: Amy and the moral saint are so taken up with the needs of others that they seem to have no time to develop into interesting, distinctive (and not always "nice") human beings in their own right.

However, Wolf's criticisms do not seem to work against those moral theories and common-sense views that are more Jake-like. If you assume a Jake-like conception of morality, you view being moral as primarily a negative activity, requiring only that you refrain from hurting others, and not demanding that you do everything and anything you can in order to benefit them. So on this conception, the ideally moral person is both practically and logically able to pursue many nonmoral ideals. Admittedly, this conception would still preclude development of certain character traits or participation in certain activities that are harmful or interfering in the affairs of others, for example, the development of a caustic and wounding wit or a taste for clothing made by processes that injure workers. But many would insist – *contra* any claims to the contrary that Wolf might make – that this is not a drawback of this conception because such traits and activities are, in their view, correctly viewed as morally inappropriate.

Indeed, it is possible to interpret Kant's moral views so that they are more like Jake's than like Amy's, thereby allowing the Kantian theory to escape many of Wolf's criticisms. Consider that Kant seems to conceive of his moral law as that which merely *checks* the moral permissibility of one's behavior ("Could this action be a universal law of nature?" one is supposed to ask), and not something used to *uncover* beneficent, nurturing behaviors that might not otherwise occur to one without the help of the law. We are told that *after* we have consulted our (nonmorally defined) desires to formulate a maxim about what to do, we should use the law to find out if the maxim is morally permissible; we are not told to use morality in a more positive fashion, to formulate our maxims directly. So we could use Kant's law appropriately to evaluate our maxims for action and still be oblivious to a variety of ways that we could actively help others, if such ways of helping never occur to us. Indeed, why would they occur to us if desires are the source of all maxims and these ways of helping are opposed to the satisfaction of our desires?

So Kant's theory seems to leave plenty of room for the pursuit of individual perfection, but note that it does so only because, on this interpretation, it is a "reactive" rather than a "proactive" theory, unable to pick out and require the beneficent involvement in others' lives which might never be proposed by our desires, but which common sense tells us is nonetheless morally required.

However, just because Kant's theory, so interpreted, escapes Wolf's criticisms, does not mean that it is a successful portrayal of morality. To think of morality along Jake-like lines gives us *too much* room for self-development; such an approach assumes that we should look out for and respect others only insofar as they happen to be in the way of our own plans for self-gratification; it does not encourage us to see ourselves as having some responsibility for fostering others' plans for self-gratification apart from any impact those plans might have on us. Hence, it discourages us from recognizing and coming to the aid of those who are in need, and misleads us about the extent to which any of us can satisfy his or her own desires without the help and support of others. (Some of us may like to be so misled, finding it unpleasant to remember that each of us starts life as a helpless infant, and ends life "sans teeth, sans hair, sans taste, sans everything.") [17]

I regard this Jake-like way of reading Kant as disappointing, and I will develop an alternative way of using at least some of his moral views in

---

[17] From Shakespeare's *As You Like It*, Act III (in a speech by Jacques).

the next section. The challenge is to develop a conception of morality that recognizes the importance of beneficent involvement in other's lives, but which not only "leaves room" for the development of one's self, but also makes that development a moral requirement. In what follows, I will maintain that Wolf's moral saint is a failure not only from the standpoint of individual perfection but also from the standpoint of morality itself, properly understood.

III. Human Worth, Human Flourishing, and Human Self-Authorship

The ability of Jake-like people to incorporate room for themselves in a moral life is, I believe, the best part of their moral conception. On the other hand, as it stands, that conception fails (as I have noted above) to capture genuine morality. In what follows, I will contend that in order to understand what an ideally moral person would look like, we must define a new conception of morality which recognizes that any "altruistic" behavior is morally wrong when it prevents one from paying moral respect to oneself.

What does it mean to be a moral respecter of yourself? I want to argue that such respect involves having the following three characteristics:

1. a sense of your own intrinsic and equal value as a human being,
2. a sense of what you require, as a human being, to flourish, and
3. a sense of what you require, insofar as you are *a particular person*, to flourish as that particular person.

Let me explicate each of these in turn.

First, a person's conception of his own worth as a person is derived from his overall conception of human worth. Such a conception defines for this person how human beings are to be valued, and how to appraise each individual's value. Philosophers have varied in how they have understood the nature of human value; for example, Hobbes regards human value as no different from the value of any commodity: "the value of each person," he insists, "is his price."[18] So on his view our value is entirely instrumental: we are worth what anyone would give to make use of our skills, labor, or other characteristics. Naturally, such a position is going to accord people different values, depending upon the marketability of their various traits.

---

[18] See Thomas Hobbes, *Leviathan*, ed. C. B. Macpherson (Harmondsworth: Penguin, 1968), ch. 10, para. 16, p. 42.

There are a variety of noninstrumental conceptions which grant people inherent or intrinsic worth on the basis of one or more characteristics. Many such conceptions are inegalitarian, granting human beings (unequal) value depending upon their sex, or race, or caste, or alternatively, on the basis of how intelligent, or accomplished, or morally worthy they are. Others are egalitarian, insisting that people are equal in worth insofar as they all share certain critical, worth-defining characteristics. One popular egalitarian theory is that of Kant, who grants each of us equal worth insofar as we are all rational and autonomous. Now Kant does not deny that we can be evaluated in ways that make us unequal – noting, for example, that some of us are vastly better, and morally more worthy, than others. Nonetheless, he takes all such inegalitarian evaluations – including assessments of moral worth – as *irrelevant* to defining the kind of moral respect a person deserves. On his view, our moral obligations to people do not increase with, say, their moral virtue; instead, we are obliged to respect our fellow human beings equally, no matter the state of their moral character, insofar as each of us is an autonomous, rational being (although Kant would certainly maintain that how this respect should be demonstrated can vary depending upon the state of a person's moral character).[19] This "democratic" conception has been highly popular in the modern world (some arguing that it is the offspring of Judeo-Christian religious teaching).[20]

I want to propose that our conception of morality is properly understood to involve a Kantian conception of worth, that is, a conception of human beings as intrinsically and equally valuable, where that value is not straightforwardly capable of aggregation in the way that some utilitarian doctrines characterize it. If this conception of our value is adopted, one must respect the value not only of others but also of oneself, and must therefore reject any roles, projects, or occupations which would be

---

[19] For example, Kant maintains that those who are morally bad can deserve punishment, but he is also well known for insisting that punishment is a way of respecting a person's autonomy and represents neither a violation nor a suspension of that autonomy.

[20] See Jeffrie Murphy, "Afterword: Constitutionalism, Moral Skepticism, and Religious Belief," in *Constitutionalism: The Philosophical Dimension*, ed. H. Rosenbaum (New York: Greenwood Press, 1988), pp. 239–49. I was struck recently by how many people in American culture accept this view of worth when I read a letter written by parents of children in a Tucson-area elementary school, calling upon the school to foster the idea that "all people are equal." In attempting to explain this equality, the authors of the letter noted that although each of us is different, our differences do not affect our equality. As they put it: Just as 3 + 3 + 1 is different from but equal to 3 + 4, so too are we different from, but equal to, one another.

self-exploitative. So the first, and most important, way in which morality involves self-regard is that it demands of each of us that we take a certain kind of pride in ourselves – not the pride that, say, a white supremacist takes in his alleged superiority, but the pride that arises from a sense of our own inherent worthiness in a world of intrinsically valuable equals. Henceforth, I shall say that to call us "persons" is to accord us this kind of intrinsic and equal worth.

It is this sort of pride which people such as Terry in my earlier example do not have. They perceive themselves as subordinate, a different kind of human being whose role is to serve others. Unable to put their interests and concerns first, they struggle to feel satisfied as they care for others. And to those (especially their children) who observe them, they teach the permissibility of their own exploitation by submitting to, and even supporting, their subservient role. Often these beneficent "saints" are revered by those whom they serve because of their caring ways, but the appropriateness of their devotion to the service of others at their own expense is never questioned or challenged, probably because those who revere them unconsciously recognize that such people are highly useful to them, given their own self-interested concerns. What better way to promote this useful servitude than by continually commending such people as "moral," "saintly," "devoted," "virtuous"?

The second way in which morality involves self-regard concerns what I will call the conception of the legitimate needs of human beings. If you respect others' value, you make sure that they have what they need to thrive as human beings and as persons, where that includes air, water, food, shelter, clothing, and medical care to meet physical needs, along with a decent measure of freedom, self-control, and love to meet psychological needs. But those who respect their own value will be just as concerned that these needs be met in their own cases. Leaving aside conditions of severe scarcity where resource allocations are agonizing and highly controversial, the saint who devotes herself and virtually all the resources at her disposal to benefiting others is in danger of damaging herself, and in this way failing to respect her own needs as a human being. In Terry's case, her persistent service to her family left her little time to rest, to the point where her body became severely stressed. Rather than understanding that she should rightfully demand time off from her child-care and household duties given her physical problems, she continued her regimen of care. To those readers who, like Jake, find it easy to put themselves first, it may seem fantastic that a person could be so other-regarding that she would literally make herself sick rather than take time out to care for herself. But Terry's behavior is not unusual. As another example, consider that Virginia Woolf's life and the content of her novels (especially *To the Lighthouse*) were strongly influenced by the example of the early death of her mother, Julia Stephen, which, according to Woolf, resulted from exhaustion brought on by caring unceasingly for seven children and a demanding husband.[21] Woolf's novels strongly suggest that such behavior is connected to a conception of self as servant, which makes one a less important, second-class kind of person. Indeed, that self-conception would figure in a general explanation of why it does not seem more obvious to obsessive care givers that in order to be able to care for others properly, they must care for their own needs, since the importance of these needs is never clear to them.[22]

Of course, not all self-denying care givers are female. One colleague of mine told me about her father's insistence on helping his friends and relatives to the point of risking his health and well-being (for example, throwing out his back helping a neighbor repair her fence, or risking the severing of his fingers helping his daughter move a freezer into the basement). Indeed, his desire to help has been sufficiently extreme that he once locked his daughter out of the garage so that he could unload her luggage from the trunk of a car! How do we explain his obsessive, self-damaging, and (for the recipients) frequently suffocating interest in "helping"? Part of the explanation seems to be that he, and others like him, not only have a poor sense of self-worth and a poor grip on what they owe to themselves in order to meet their objective needs, but also a dearth of plans, projects, and goals that are uniquely their own. Thus, they decide to satisfy the ends of others because they have so few ends of their own to pursue.[23] This explanation accounts for why those of us who have received help from such obsessive care givers frequently resent and feel violated by the help: it is as if our own ends of action have been seized and taken away from us by these "helpers" when they insist on pursuing them for us.

---

[21] Woolf's account of her mother's life can be found in autobiographical fragments published as "A Sketch of the Past," in *The Virginia Woolf Reader*, ed. Mitchell Leaska (New York: Harcourt, Brace, Jovanovich, 1984).

[22] This obvious lesson is often missed. Consider that airlines find it necessary to teach parents that if oxygen masks are necessary during flight, they should place the masks over their own noses and mouths first, and only then help their children to secure *their* masks.

[23] I am indebted to Elizabeth Willott for this way of putting the point.

Such behavior illustrates a third way in which morality involves self-regard: namely, it requires us to ensure that we have the time, the resources, and the capacity to develop the characteristics, skills, plans, and projects that make us unique individual selves. One of the traits that mark us out as human beings is our capacity to develop distinctive personalities. Granted, some of the distinctiveness that differentiates us from one another is the product of the environments in which each of us grows up – our families, schools, religious organizations, political institutions, and so forth. And some of it is the product of biological characteristics, destined to develop in us because of our genetic makeup. But some of that distinctiveness is what I shall call "self-authored." There are many times in our lives when we choose what we will be. For example, when a young girl has the choice of entering into a harsh regimen of training to become an accomplished figure skater or refusing it and enjoying a more normal life with lots of time for play, she is being asked to choose or author whom she will be. When a graduate student decides which field of her discipline she will pursue, or when a person makes a decision about his future religious life, or when someone takes up a hobby – all of these choices are ways of determining one's traits, activities, and skills, and thus ways of shaping one's self, of determining one's self-identity. Nor are these self-determining choices always earth-shaking or major. In small ways we build up who we are: if we successfully forgive a friend a misdeed, we thereby become a little more generous, or if we give way to anger and hit a loved one, we do a little bit more to build an abusive personality. Just as a sculptor creates a form out of a slab of rock, so too do people (in concert with their environment and their biology) create a distinctive way of interacting with, thinking about, and reacting to the world. It is this distinctiveness, which each individual plays a major role in creating, that I am calling the "self." Whereas we say that we respect one another as "persons," we say that we love or hate, approve or condemn, appreciate or dislike, others' selves.

This self-authorship is not only something that we do, but also something that it is deeply important for us to do; through self-authorship we express our autonomy and prosper as human beings. To be prevented from self-authorship is to undergo brutal psychological damage. Therefore, morality requires that others give each of us the opportunity to author ourselves, and it requires of each of us that we perform that self-authorship. But the objective requirement of self-authorship is satisfied by an individual when she *subjectively* defines who she is, what she wants, and what she will pursue in her life. Whereas the conception of legitimate needs is objectively defined, reflecting a theory of what it is that each of us requires, as a human being, to flourish (where this includes, among other things, the ability and opportunity to engage in self-authorship), the conception of "personal needs" sets out what one requires as a particular personality or self, and is subjectively defined, arising from a person's decision to be a certain way, to have certain aspirations, and to undertake certain projects – all of which are up to her to determine.

So who I am is partly "up to me." Nonetheless, to make sense of self-authorship each of us needs to understand when we are genuinely engaged in self-defining, as opposed to self-denying, activities. I shall now argue that in order to define what counts as genuine self-authorship, we require objective constraints. The subjectivity of preference formation only counts, from a moral point of view, as self-authorship if that preference formation occurs in a certain way, when a person is in a certain kind of state. In the discussion that follows, I will attempt to suggest the rough nature of these objective constraints, but this is theoretically difficult terrain, and as the reader will see, I will leave many questions unanswered.

IV. Understanding Self-Authorship

To determine the nature of self-authorship, we must answer a number of questions. First, we need to know what state a person must be in, such that *he*, and not some other person or thing, is doing the self-authoring. That is, we need to know when the plans and preferences are genuinely subjectively defined (i.e., defined by the subject), and not by something (some drug or other agent) other than the subject. Consider Ulysses before, during, and after his interaction with the Sirens. Before and after he heard their song, Ulysses preferred to stay on course with his ship, rather than steer toward the rocks where the Sirens sung. But while they were singing, his preference was reversed. Now it is natural to say[24] that Ulysses *really* preferred staying on course rather than steering toward the rocks, and presumably that judgment rests on the idea that the person who was in thrall to the Sirens was in some way "out of his mind" – not the *real* Ulysses, and thus not capable of forming a genuinely authentic preference. But making this evaluation requires developing objective criteria

---

[24] For a prominent discussion, see Jon Elster, *Ulysses and the Sirens* (Cambridge: Cambridge University Press, 1979); the fact that Elster takes for granted the idea that Ulysses' desire to steer the ship toward the rocks is not a genuine desire is noted, and criticized, by Don Hubin, "On Bindings and By-products: Elster on Rationality," *Philosophy and Public Affairs* 15, no. 1 (Winter 1986): 82–95.

for what counts as a real and satisfactorily operating person. I want to suggest that we use such criteria often, as when, for example, we discount the preferences of seriously ill people, or those whom we consider to be insane or in some way mentally defective (e.g., because they are on mind-altering drugs), or when we discount some (but certainly not all) of the preferences of very small children (who can get very confused, overtired, or over-emotional). Specifying what state a person has to be in, such that he or she can be considered capable (at that time) of generating authentic preferences, is highly difficult, and I will not attempt to elaborate such an account here. Suffice it to say that such an account is morally required if we are to understand what self-authorship is actually like, and would certainly involve specifying what we take to be at least a minimally rational person.

But once we have such an analysis, we are not done. To be self-authored, it is a necessary condition that a preference be subjectively defined, but it is not a sufficient condition. I want to propose that there are objective constraints on what can be the *content* of an authentic self-authored preference. This means that not everything that a self decides to pursue or prefer can count as a preference we are prepared to attribute to that self. This is *not* to say that morality should play any significant role in defining our vocations, or avocations, or skills, or personality traits (which is one point Susan Wolf certainly wants to make).[25] But morality does place constraints on what we can legitimately choose to pursue, and different moral theorists disagree both about how strong these constraints can be and about the role political institutions should play in enforcing them.

I shall argue that it is a necessary condition of a preference's being self-authored that its content not conflict with what is required to meet that person's objective needs as a human being. The following example illustrates this point: I once knew friends of a man who appeared to author the desire to be tied and beaten during sexual relations with young men. The violence in his desire makes it repulsive to most of us, and it is certainly in conflict with commonsense understandings of legitimate human needs. But it is at least arguably authentic insofar as it was a subjective preference of this human being (who was not obviously impaired or irrational). Nonetheless, most of his friends discounted the legitimacy of this desire, and attempted to interfere with his actions to satisfy it, partly because of what they saw as the reason he had the desire.

[25] See again her "Moral Saints."

According to them, this man was periodically filled with self-loathing (in virtue of a number of cruel deeds he had committed over the years), and it was during such a bout of self-loathing that he would solicit this kind of experience which, tragically, his friends concluded, only increased his self-loathing when it was finished. So in their view, he solicited the experience as a kind of self-punishment.

In what sense did this man "want" to undergo this experience? We are rightly uneasy in straightforwardly attributing to him a desire for it in the way that we might attribute to him, say, the desire to play chess. We want to discount it, in the same way that we want to discount the desire of, say, the addict for his drug. Why? I believe this is because, as Aristotle would say, we believe that subjectively defined preferences are authentic only if their content is consistent with what we take to be the objectively defined needs of human persons *qua* human persons. To the extent that one is renouncing or repudiating the meeting of these needs (as this masochist did), one will be incapable of authoring authentic preferences. Indeed, in an interesting passage in Book IX of the *Nicomachean Ethics*, Aristotle suggests that this is true of anyone whom we criticize as bad or evil:

And those who have done many terrible deeds and are hated for their wickedness even shrink from life and destroy themselves. And wicked men seek for people with whom to spend their days, and shun themselves; for they remember many a grievous deed, and anticipate others like them, when they are by themselves, but when they are with others they forget. And having nothing lovable in them they have no feeling of love to themselves. Therefore also such men do not rejoice or grieve with themselves; for their soul is rent by faction, and one element in it by reason of its wickedness grieves when it abstains from certain acts, while the other part is pleased, and one draws them this way and the other that, as if they were pulling them in pieces.[26]

If Aristotle is right, the harmful preferences of people not only toward themselves but also toward others cannot be considered authentic preferences of those selves, because they are the product of people in turmoil, who cannot author preferences satisfactorily. Because they are unable to understand or secure what it is they owe to themselves as human beings, they are unable to function effectively as human beings, and hence become impaired in their ability to develop preferences that accurately reflect who they are and what they require as persons. Or at least so

---

[26] Aristotle, *Nicomachean Ethics*, Book IX, 1166b22-24. The quote is drawn from the W. D. Ross translation in *The Basic Works of Aristotle*, ed. R. McKeon (New York: Random House, 1941).

I would like to argue. Actually developing such an account would involve developing Aristotelian-style criteria for what is objectively required for human flourishing – which is, to put it mildly, no easy task.

Note that to say a preference is not genuinely self-authored or "authentic" is *not* to say that one is not responsible for it. While it is "his" preference in the sense that he chose it, and thus must bear the consequences for having done so, it is not "his" preference in the sense that it is genuinely self-creating or self-expressing. This last remark assumes some kind of idealized conception not only of what a flourishing human being is like but also of what it is to be a particular, distinctive human person. Flourishing human beings will be different from one another, in their traits, activities, projects, and skills, in part because flourishing human beings are interested in and capable of defining themselves in distinctive and original ways.

The preceding remarks aim to disqualify the preferences of the wicked as self-authored. But I also believe they disqualify the preferences of people such as Terry as self-authored. Terry is certainly not what we would consider a wicked person, but like a wicked person or like the masochist in the example above, she has made choices about what to do and how to be that are personally destructive. "I love looking after my kids," Terry might insist, or "I love the domestic arts," or "I love helping out at the nursery school." But we would be suspicious of such enthusiasm for activities someone of her gender and class is "supposed" to like, and that suspicion would be confirmed if we found her life to have little in it that she "wants for herself." Her statements would therefore have all the hallmarks of inauthenticity. It is not so much that her preferences and activities are inauthentic because she has chosen to define herself by stepping into a (societally defined) role – after all, each of us must live life by choosing roles to some extent, for example, when we choose our careers or when we choose (or decline) to be married or to have children. Moreover, as I shall discuss in the next section, it is perfectly possible for a woman to make the *authentic* choice to be a housewife and mother. But in Terry's case, what primarily justifies our criticism of her choice as inauthentic is that her role, as she understands it, permits her to have very few ends other than those of her family, and thereby makes her, at virtually every turn, their servant. Although none of them wants to hurt her, they make use of her so thoroughly that she is not only unable to meet many of her objective needs as a human being, but also has very little room for engaging in self-expressing or self-defining activities outside that role.

There is something else that troubles us about Terry's choice. Many women make that choice in contemporary American society; whether or not these women work outside the home, they conceive of themselves as being responsible for most (and sometimes all) of the care giving in the family (and those who work sometimes suffer enormous guilt to the extent that their jobs preclude them from doing what they are convinced they ought to do). These women's choice of this role therefore seems to be, in part, a social phenomenon, one that they have made in order to avoid the disapproval of their friends, or family, or church, or colleagues, who expect them to make it. So even if Terry had redefined her role in the home so that her objective needs could be met, we would still reject the idea that the choice was authentic if we perceived it to be a choice she made in order to avoid such social disapproval.

Consider, in this regard, a male example of an inauthentic choice resulting from social pressure: in the spring of 1991, American newspapers recounted the story of an investment banker who, as a teenager, wanted to be a clown. His parents strongly discouraged it, regarding it as inappropriate for someone of his background and abilities, so he went to MIT and got a job working in Silicon Valley in computers. Still he was dissatisfied and decided things might go better if he had an MBA. With this degree he got a job on Wall Street making a lot of money in a high-powered investment bank. But one day, he claimed, he woke up realizing that if he kept working on Wall Street, he would end up close to death never having gone to clown school. So he quit his job, and did exactly that. This is a nice story of someone who struggled to author himself, while under pressure to be what people in his social group expected of him. Like Terry, he faced pressure to submit to a social role, to take on preferences, interests, and projects that he did not really want. He experienced understandable relief when he reclaimed himself.

These examples illustrate how people can choose *not* to author themselves. Self-authorship involves more than an autonomous choice: it involves a decision to develop the traits, interests, and projects that not only are consistent with meeting your objective human needs but are also ones *you* want, and not ones that others prefer that you want (and perhaps try to persuade you to want). When Terry and the MBA gave up the chance to author themselves early in their lives, they "sold out" to certain societal groups that believed they had the authority to determine who and what these individuals should become. Such "selling out" has been a common subject of story and legend in many cultures. Consider, for example, Stravinsky's *L'Histoire du soldat*, a work based on the story of a soldier who sells his violin, representing his soul, to the devil for money. Only when he reclaims that violin and gives away all his money – repudiating all that led him away from who he really was – does he reclaim his soul. It is perhaps hard for the MBA or for women such as Terry to see that they too have sold out by accepting the particular social role our society has created for them. And this may be particularly hard in Terry's case: how can embracing such a caring, beneficent role be a devilish act or be considered "selling out"? Yet is it so much better to give up the ability to define your own life in order to avoid sanctions from social groups you fear, than to give it up in order to secure money or power? And is it any easier for Terry or the MBA to reclaim themselves than it was for the soldier? Not only must they reconsider and redefine their goals and projects, but they must also reconsider and redefine their conception of who has the authority to determine or even criticize what they would pursue in life.[27]

These last remarks suggest that, like the MBA and the soldier, women such as Terry bear responsibility for succumbing to the temptations of embracing a self-denying social role. Many feminists may question how fair this is, given the societal assault on people such as Terry, and the high cost such women must pay if they do not succumb. The extent to which women must take responsibility for "selling out" is an issue discussed in novels, such as those by George Eliot and Jane Austen (think of Austen's Anne in *Persuasion* in contrast to Charlotte in *Pride and Prejudice*, or think of Maggie Tulliver in Eliot's *Mill on the Floss*). And the most striking discussion of this point by a philosopher is by Kierkegaard.[28] In *The Sickness unto Death* Kierkegaard argues that sin is a kind of despair, generated by the failure to be who we are, and he distinguishes masculine and feminine forms of sin. Whereas the masculine form is a kind of defiance – a failure to accept the limits of selfhood, the feminine form, he says, is a kind of *weakness*, a loss of self, which he links to the woman's service to others.[29] Such devotion he takes to be a kind of sinful self-abnegation: "the woman in proper womanly fashion throws herself, throws her self, into whatever she abandons herself to. If you take that away, then her self vanishes too, and her despair is: not wanting to be herself."[30]

---

[27] I am indebted to David Schmidtz for this last point.
[28] Catherine Keller discusses Kierkegaard's views in this context in her *From a Broken Web: Separation, Sexism, and Self* (Boston: Beacon Press, 1989), p. 12.
[29] See Søren Kierkegaard, *Sickness unto Death*, pp. 80–81n.
[30] Ibid., p. 81n.

To call this loss of self "sinful" is to suggest that the woman – a woman like Terry – is responsible for it, no matter how much she tries to excuse herself by appeal to "social pressure." But it is surely reasonable to wonder how far she, or indeed the MBA, can be blamed for making choices which her parents, teachers, and community members may be prepared to enforce with severe social sanctions (involving not only ridicule but also ostracism). Although I will not be able to pursue this point further, the possibility of self-authorship would seem to be as much the responsibility of society as it is of the individual; it would seem that society must not only be prepared to respect a variety of nonstandard choices, but must also provide what each person needs (e.g., educational opportunities and health care) in order that she be able to engage in self-authorship.

V. Altruism

Let us return to the issue of altruism. I have argued that service to others is morally acceptable only when it arises from an authentically defined preference, interest, or project undertaken by one who pursues her legitimate needs as a human being and who accepts a Kantian conception of human value. So one who lives up to these requirements accepts severe constraints not only on what she can do to others, but also on what she can do to herself. Such a person can certainly have authentically defined preferences leading her to serve others, but she will refrain from such service when it will lead her to become (to use a Hobbesian term) "prey" for those whom she serves. But can't there be people who authentically choose to help others at some cost to themselves, and whom we are right to praise for their unusual generosity and fellow feeling? For example, can't there be women who really want to stay home to care for their children, even while knowing that this will set back their career for years and mean a substantial loss of income, and whose choice we ought to value? Aren't there people (such as Mother Theresa) who are genuinely devoted to the poor at considerable cost to their own comfort, and who seem to be exceptionally fine people? Haven't major religions continually celebrated the martyrdom of saints and heroes who die for the benefit of others and their cause? Does my argument require that we cease our commendation of such people, and even criticize them for their self-sacrifice? It does not, as long as that sacrifice is authentic and done out of love, as I shall now explain.

I have a friend whom I consider to have made an authentic choice to be a housewife and mother and who lives a life very different from that of Terry. She stayed home to care for her children because she adored them, and she genuinely liked the control over her own time that the life of a housewife gave her. Moreover, she has been quite capable of limiting her care to her family over the years whenever she thought they were demanding too much, by using a kind of prickly sarcasm they have been loath to experience. Her life has always included all sorts of projects and plans (e.g., involvement in art organizations and women's organizations; self-study projects that have made her an expert in the flora and fauna of her region) that she greatly enjoys and that have helped to make her a fascinating individual to know. So she is a richly developed person, and her care of others is a natural result of what she has chosen to love in her life.

Nonetheless, I do not believe she deserves any special commendation for crafting this kind of care-giving life; those whose life choices do not include caring for children, or the aged, or the infirm are not thereby less impressive. We value genuine, richly developed persons, and that development can take all sorts of forms, only some of which involve extensive care giving. Susan Wolf assumes that when we value those people who are not care givers, our valuing must be nonmoral. But this is importantly wrong: we morally value *all* people with authentic lives, whether or not they are care givers, when we appreciate that each has had the strength to respond morally to herself, and thus has resisted pressure to make her life into something that is not authentic. It is abusive to demand of everyone (and in particular all females) that they lead a life with considerable service to others – and just as abusive to demand that no one, and in particular no female, should lead a life with *any* considerable service to others: such demands fail to recognize the diversity of talents and pleasures that make more or less care giving lives appropriate for different people. Those who yield to such demands can become disabled from developing an honest and authentic life.

Indeed, such demands may actually reflect the self-serving interests of the community. There is a doctor I know whose service to his community has been extraordinary: as a young man he became interested in drug addiction, and finally founded a free clinic in Northern California to treat addicts and provide medical service to the poor. What is striking about this doctor is that he will tell you that he has always *enjoyed* dealing with addiction problems, and has been very happy in his medical career. Thus, his service has always been authentically and happily given. Clearly he deserves our deep appreciation. But does he really deserve more praise than a doctor whose authentic choices are such that he intensely dislikes dealing with such problems, runs a medical practice that gives a decent share of free service to the poor but primarily serves the medical needs of the middle class, and who vastly prefers rock climbing to volunteering in Oakland drug clinics? Doesn't our community betray its *own* selfishness if it calls the first doctor "better" than the second, insofar as the services of the first are rarer and thus instrumentally more valuable to the community than those of the second? Many of our commendations of what look to be altruistic behavior may be more self-serving than we realize.

But what about people who devote their entire lives to serving the poor, or parents who risk their lives to save their children: don't these extraordinary acts of altruism spring from authentic preferences, and yet don't they involve great harm to self? Shouldn't we commend them as highly moral and hold up those who perform them for emulation, or at least consider the acts supererogatory and hence morally fine even if not morally required?

I am inclined to argue *against* doing either. Such behavior is morally commendable and *only morally permissible* when it is done authentically, out of a love that unifies the one who serves with the one who is being served. The love about which I am talking is not a feeling (although a feeling may often accompany it), but a point of view, a way of conceiving of oneself in connection to others, and it comes in more than one form. Those who experience such love are so unified with those whom their acts are attempting to benefit that what they regard as good for themselves is what will be good for those with whom they are unified.

From a moral point of view, the most important form of this love is that which connects us to our fellow human beings by virtue of our common humanity, such that we will naturally recoil at others' suffering and desire (authentically) to stop it. It may be that 'love' is not a particularly good word to use to describe this point of view (although it is commonly used for this purpose in Christian literature).[31] More particular and frequently more powerful forms of love are experienced by parents for their children, and by friends and spouses for each other; in these relationships there is an intimate connection between the parties – to the point where the pleasures of each are advanced when the other's needs and desires are satisfied. Contrast this kind of loving care to the self-sacrificing service of a reluctant benefactor who performs his caring deeds only because he believes it is his "duty" to do so: when we know that our benefactor believes he has brought (uncompensated) damage upon himself by serving us,

---

[31] Christian theology uses the Greek word *agape* to denote this form of love.

not only do we take no joy in that service, but we may also feel guilty and undeserving of help purchased at this cost, and we may be angry at how little our own good is a good for the reluctant benefactor, and thus regard his help with resentment. (There is nothing that kills the pleasure from a gift quite so much as the gift-giver's intimations that he has suffered a great deal too much in order to give it to you.) This sort of selfish and dishonest altruism deserves no commendation.[32]

However, those who feel *no* love for others, and thus (quite authentically) refuse to help them, are not thereby exempted from moral criticism. There are situations when moral criticism of them is appropriate, not because they did not help (their refusal is, after all, honest and authentic), but because they did not have the love – by which I mean the perception of connection with others, and not a mere feeling – from which such help would inevitably spring. (The appropriateness of such a connection is something that Amy can teach Jake.)[33] On my view, when we commend real altruists, we celebrate not only the authenticity of their choices, but also the point of view they have (authentically) adopted that has resulted in them wanting to make such choices. We commend their deeds *not* because these deeds are extraordinary acts of self-sacrifice; they *aren't* – real altruists do not understand their actions in this way. As Neera Kapur Badhwar makes clear in her essay "Altruism versus Self-Interest,"[34] most of the rescuers of the Jews in Europe during World War II told interviewers that it was "easy" to decide to help the Jews, because they felt a deep sense of union with them as fellow human beings. Hence, they refused to understand their deeds as self-sacrifices or acts of martyrdom. When we commend the acts of such altruists, we are actually commending *these people*, and the point of view they took toward their fellow human beings.

Does morality require that all of us take a loving point of view toward all of our fellows? This is a theoretically difficult question, for it is surely right

---

[32] But there may be times when a person serves reluctantly because he has a conflict between his love for others and his own self-regarding interests. I discuss such conflicts in the next section.

[33] So my position is not so anti-Kantian as it might initially appear. Like Kant, I agree that morality requires service to others, despite one's self-regarding interests. But I see that service as commendable only if it is connected in a certain way not only to that person's will but also to his conception of himself.

[34] See Neera Kapur Badhwar, "Altruism versus Self-Interest: Sometimes a False Dichotomy," in E. F. Paul, F. D. Miller, and J. Paul, eds., *Altruism* (Cambridge: Cambridge University Press, 1993). I am indebted to Badhwar for helping me to develop many of the ideas in this paragraph.

that *some* fellow feeling is morally required of all of us (which is the point Christianity tries to make), and yet the strength of the love the rescuers had for those whom they saved is extraordinary and unusual. To expect such love from everyone would seem to be unrealistic given the diversity of human personalities, and to socially pressure people to try to develop such love would likely result only in dishonest approximations of the real thing. Nonetheless, we are prepared to criticize severely those who aided the Nazis for their appalling lack of fellow feeling. Moreover, there are certain situations where we do think that morality demands that people develop *particular* forms of love. For example, a parent who risks his life to enter a burning building to save his children strikes us as animated by an appropriate love binding him to his children, whereas a parent who refuses to do so insofar as he takes himself to be removed from, and more important than, his children strikes us as (deeply) criticizable.

It is impossible in this chapter to explore when and how each of us is morally required to make various loving commitments to others (or when those commitments surpass such requirements), although our response to the examples of the rescuers and the parents risking their lives for their children illustrates that we believe such requirements exist,[35] constraining the territory over which morally acceptable authentic choices can be made. As I noted before, commendable authentic choices always operate subject to moral constraints. If Aristotle is right, we should not regard these constraints as unwelcome limits on what we can choose, but rather as directives which, when followed, will make our own lives better.

However, even love is not sufficient *by itself* to make such service worthy of our commendation. To be commendable, one's service to others must be performed in a way that fully recognizes one's own worth and distinctiveness. Terry may have thought that her self-sacrificing service to her children arose from her love for them, but since she was unable to bring a sense of herself and her own importance to her union with her family, she inflicted harm not only on herself but also on them. Commendable, effective love does not mean losing oneself in a union with others; instead, it presupposes that all parties to the union have a self,

---

[35] I cannot pursue here the difficult question of when (and in what way) human beings should establish connections of love with others. It cannot be morally required that we become friends with everyone, or that everyone become some kind of parent, although the kind of universal connection with fellow human beings experienced by the rescuers does seem to be morally required of us all. I have argued elsewhere that answering this question will involve, among other things, considering issues of justice (to oneself and others); see my "Feminist Contractarianism."

which they understand to be important, and which they share with one another.

It may even be that *real* love – and the sort of love that deserves moral commendation – exists only if this sense of self accompanies it. Consider, in this regard, the following Victorian poem about mothers – of the sort Terry is:

> There was a young man loved a maid
> Who taunted him, "Are you afraid,"
> She asked, "to bring me today
> Your mother's head upon a tray?"
>
> He went and slew his mother dead,
> Tore from her breast her heart so red,
> Then towards his lady love he raced,
> But tripped and fell in all his haste.
>
> As the heart rolled on the ground
> It gave forth a plaintive sound.
> And it spoke, in accents mild:
> "Did you hurt yourself, my child?"[36]

To love another deeply should not mean to lose all sense of oneself in another's personhood and to be unable to make any independent claims of one's own. Self-sacrifice cannot be commendable if it springs from self-abnegation. That Kierkegaard calls it a sin is rightly suggestive of the way it is immoral, a way of being deeply disrespectful to oneself. If we are so "altruistic" that we become unable to develop and express our selves properly, we become unable to give to others what they may want more than anything else.

Real care for others looks and feels much different from any socially encouraged, self-damaging imitation. We see the real thing in a story of a mother and her family who waited in a shelter in Texas while a tornado destroyed their home: as they waited, the mother sat and worked on a quilt, recalling later, "I made my quilt to keep my family warm. I made it beautiful so my heart would not break."[37] This mother's care for her family that day came from enormous strength and self-confidence, as she looked disaster in the eye and insisted that her family believe,

[36] Quoted by Sara Ruddick, "Maternal Thinking," in *Women and Values: Readings in Recent Feminist Philosophy*, ed. Marilyn Pearsall (Belmont, Calif.: Wadsworth, 1986), p. 340; from J. Echergaray, "Severed Heart," quoted by Jessie Bernard in *The Future of Motherhood* (New York: Dial, 1974), p. 4.

[37] Quoted by Sara Ruddick, "Maternal Thinking," p. 344; original story told to Ruddick by Miriam Schapiro.

despite the destruction, that something good would prevail. She used her talents and gifts as an individual to create a sign of that good. The service of such a mother is neither reluctant, nor soul-destroying, and may be extraordinarily important to those who receive it.

Real care may also come from human beings who do not in any way appear to be altruistic, saintly, or "good." A minister I know once told a story about a man named Doc that makes this point:[38]

Where I spent a good deal of my childhood in a small New England town, the meanest man in town owned the garage and fixed everything mechanical that went wrong. He was a foul mouthed, hostile fellow who had been brought up as a state boy. After going through numerous foster homes he had ended up as the foster child of the town's auto mechanic. He and his foster father got along badly, but he turned out to be an automotive Einstein, a total genius with any kind of machinery, and he learned everything in *this* line that his foster father had to teach him. When he got to be eighteen he was convicted of armed robbery and sent to prison for five years. By the time he got out, his foster father had died, but the foster father had left him the garage. The mythology of the town was that he had returned to arrange for its sale, but that he had decided suddenly and impulsively to stay and run the garage when he discovered that the townspeople greeted him warmly and even solicitously. And he had stayed, and he had run the garage. From the early 1930's to the middle 1950's you knew that if you lived in that town and ran out of gas late at night you could call Doc and he would arrive half drunk in his wrecker mumbling obscenities about anyone that idiotic, but Doc would arrive with a can of gas, or if your car had broken down, with the needed tow.

People, especially kids, were a little scared of Doc, but the farmers knew that if their equipment broke down during mowing or if they got into any kind of mechanical jam, Doc would stay up all night fixing what needed to be fixed. People were willing to put up with Doc's awful temper and acid remarks because he was utterly trustworthy.

As Doc grew older, his rages resolved into mischievous wit which, though not often kind, was always funny. The boys and young men of the town went back to hanging around the garage and many of them absorbed the mechanical skills which Doc possessed in such abundance. They also learned something about trustworthiness and dedication to service they might not have learned otherwise. Eventually Doc married, and he and his wife had two children. He even took to going to church occasionally.

This is hardly the portrait of an Aristotelian man of practical wisdom. But it *is* a portrait of a real altruist, someone who cared deeply about people in his community and who served them hard, long, and well – in large

---

[38] This story was told during a sermon by the Rev. John Snow, delivered at the Harvard University Chapel, in 1978. I am quoting from the text of that sermon.

part out of gratitude for their acceptance of and faith in him. In no way do we see his caring as self-destructive, but indeed as quite the opposite – a way of coming to terms with himself, his anger, his frustrations, and his losses as a child. This is certainly not a man who serves others in order to fulfill some kind of social role. His caring is the real thing.

VI. Authenticity and Conflict

There is a contemporary song by Tracy Chapman, which recounts the story of a young woman who faces a choice between living an authentic life of her choosing but abandoning her alcoholic father whom she loves, or serving the father but thereby accepting a life of poverty, drabness, and frustration. What ought she to do? If her love for her father is authentic and deep, she may choose to stay with him, and in those circumstances, that action would be self-authored. Indeed, to do anything else might mean she would be full of regret the rest of her life. Yet this decision will allow her few of the resources necessary to develop skills, talents, projects, and traits of character that are the mark of a well-developed self. Hers is a nasty choice, and in many respects, a deeply unfair one.[39] Compare it with the choice of the character that Jimmy Stewart plays in the movie *It's a Wonderful Life*, who has an authentic desire to help the poor of his town, but satisfying this desire requires such self-denial on his part that he comes close to suicide later in his life.

Note that both desires here are authentic – so authenticity alone does not help us to resolve how we ought to act in life in order to be respectful not only to others but to ourselves. The problem is that each of us has a *set* of authentic desires, and the other-regarding ones can require that we do things that preclude the self-regarding ones. So how do we choose? Conventional wisdom celebrates the other-regarding choice in these sorts of situations (although it may not always require it). But why should "being moral" always involve choosing in favor of others – why can't it sometimes involve choosing in favor of oneself?

---

[39] Life is filled with such unfairness, but we ought to blame our social systems for some of that unfairness if we live in a society that persistently puts people of a certain class, or gender, or race, or caste in the position of having to choose between caring for those whom they love and developing themselves as persons. Granted, it is hopelessly utopian to strive for a world in which individuals never have to compromise their own development in order to care for others whom they authentically love. But surely it is reasonable at least to strive for a world in which society is not persistently doing things that encourage such dilemmas for only some of its members.

In situations where self-development and service to others conflict, we have the familiar problem of balancing moral claims. Normally that problem is perceived as involving the conflicting moral claims of people other than yourself, all of whom have some call on you. In a conflict between your needs and others' needs, service to others has normally been considered the moral choice – either morally required, if you think as Amy does, or else merely recommended (but not required) if you think as Jake does. But I want to argue that in these situations, choosing in favor of yourself can be a morally permissible choice, and perhaps in some circumstances the morally required choice.[40]

Hence, I do not agree that all community-benefiting, other-regarding actions are morally required, and I believe that the advocates of the concept of supererogation are right to maintain that we are sometimes morally permitted not to choose an altruistic, self-sacrificing act but to act, instead, to benefit ourselves. However, this is true, on my view, (only) in situations where either choice is morally acceptable – that is, (only) in situations where duty to others and duty to self are opposed and we are morally permitted to choose either one. Moreover, I have also argued that in some situations in which duty to others and duty to self are opposed, the self-regarding choice is actually the morally superior and obligatory choice. To be "impartial" from a moral point of view does not always mean excluding oneself and one's own needs from moral deliberation. To treat all people equally does not mean giving everyone but oneself equal concern. Moral people do not put themselves to one side; they include themselves in the calculation and give themselves weight in the determination of the right action to take.

How much weight? To know the answer to that question is to have a moral theory that correctly adjudicates conflicting moral claims not only between others but also between oneself and others. I have no such theory (nor does any other philosopher!).[41] But surely Jake is wrong to

---

[40] Might this be a way to explain *why* many people regard as morally permissible Gauguin's choice to leave his family and go to Tahiti to develop as an artist? It strikes me as preferable to Bernard Williams's explanation that we commend the choice only because Gauguin prospered as an artist in Tahiti, and thus was "morally lucky." See Williams's discussion of this example in his "Moral Luck," in *Moral Luck* (Cambridge: Cambridge University Press, 1981).

[41] This is partly because contemporary moral philosophy has been fixated on other-regarding moral duties, to the serious neglect of self-regarding ones. What explains this fixation? A Marxist explanation (which was suggested to me by Christine Korsgaard) is that the call for equal rights by those who have been in lower class, "servant" groups (e.g., women and African Americans) has alarmed the rest of society sufficiently that *they* have

think that we can answer the question with some kind of easy formula; how that balance should be struck depends upon many things, including the circumstances and context of our lives (so, for example, that balance should rightly be struck one way if one is a student fighting to get a degree, and another way if one is the parent of a newborn infant). And it is just as easy for many of us to overestimate the weight our interests should get as it is to underestimate it. If, after all I have said in the name of self-authorship, it still seems unsettlingly wrong to spend $200 per person at a fancy New York restaurant in the name of individual self-expression when so many people in our society and around the world are unable to meet their most minimal human needs, then maybe that's because it really is wrong to do such a thing. I am arguing that we should not allow ourselves to be pressured – by society, by our religion, or by some philosopher's conception of our "moral duties" – to become the servant of others; but I do not want to deny that many of us who are privileged err in the other direction, and serve ourselves too much and others too little.[42] The art of living well is to know how to balance competing moral obligations – some of which are to yourself.[43]

encouraged servile conceptions of morality that would, if accepted by these people, keep them in their servile roles – and such conceptions have (wittingly or unwittingly) been accepted by moral philosophers (who have traditionally come from more powerful, non-servile social groups). An alternative explanation (which is potentially consistent with the first) is that moral philosophy, up until very recently, has been done almost exclusively by males, who commonly hold a Jake-like understanding of morality, and who are attracted to an other-regarding conception of morality as they become aware that their highly self-regarding conception of their connection to other people needs correction (not realizing that many people might need a very different kind of correction). Moreover, recent feminist celebrations of women's propensity to care have certainly encouraged this tendency to think of morality as almost exclusively other-regarding.

[42] Thus, I do not mean to be hostile to the currently popular celebration by feminists of women's persistent interest in caring. I only wish to put caring in its proper moral place. There are a number of women that have sounded similar themes recently; e.g., Susan Moller Okin, *Justice, Gender, and the Family* (New York: Basic Books, 1989); and Marilyn Friedman, "Beyond Caring: The Demoralization of Gender," in *Science, Morality, and Feminism*, ed. Marsha Hanen and Kai Nielsen (Calgary: University of Calgary Press, 1987). See also my "Feminist Contractarianism."

[43] I have been greatly benefited by a number of people in the course of writing this chapter. The impetus to write it came from a discussion of a related paper of mine at Yale Law School's Legal Theory Workshop. I also wish to thank Neera Badhwar, Jules Coleman, David Schmidtz, Elizabeth Willott, the other contributors to this volume [Social Philosophy and Policy 10], and its editors, for all their comments, criticisms, and ideas. (I trust their help was authentically offered!)

3

Mens Rea

The greatest incitement to guilt is the hope of sinning with impunity.
Cicero

Accusing, condemning, and avenging are part of our daily life. However, a review of many years of literature attempting to analyze our blaming practices suggests that we do not understand very well what we are doing when we judge people culpable for a wrong they have committed. Of course, everyone agrees that, for example, someone deserves censure and punishment when she is guilty of a wrong, and the law has traditionally looked for a *mens rea*, or "guilty mind," in order to convict someone of a criminal wrongdoing. But philosophers and legal theorists have found it interestingly difficult to say what *mens rea* is. For example, noting the way in which we intuitively think people aren't culpable for a crime if they disobey the law by mistake, or under duress, or while insane, theorists such as H. L. A. Hart[1] have tried to define *mens rea* negatively, as that which an agent has if he is not in what we consider to be an excusing state. But such an approach only circumscribes and does not unravel the central mystery; it also fails to explain why the law recognizes any excusing states as mitigating or absolving one of guilt, much less why all and only the excusing states that are recognized by the law are the right ones. Moreover, the Model Penal Code, which gives a very detailed

---

[1] See Hart's *Punishment and Responsibility*, ch. 2, "Legal Responsibility and Excuses," (Oxford: Clarenden Press, 1968), pp. 28–53.

account of the kinds of mental states which justify criminal conviction,[2] does not tell us (nor was it designed to tell us) why these states of mind (e.g., knowledge, purposiveness, intention, assumption of risk of harm, negligence) are relevant to an assessment of legal guilt.

In this chapter I want to try to develop a positive account of *mens rea*, or legal culpability, which explains why the mental states detailed in the Model Penal Code are relevant to recognizing it. Because negligence introduces difficulties into the discussion that I cannot properly pursue here, my focus will be on non-negligent culpable acts, although I will have something to say about criminal negligence in the final section of the chapter.

The procedure I will follow for analyzing the legally guilty mind is to clarify, first, what non-negligent culpability is more generally. People can be judged to be "at fault" in three different circumstances: when they act illegally, when they act immorally, and when they act irrationally.[3] I want to argue, however, that there is one distinctive kind of "mental act" that underlies all three kinds of culpability, and which is definitive of the (non-negligent) guilty mind. Hence, I will start by giving an analysis of rational and moral culpability, and then use these analyses as models for the explication of legal culpability.

Let me also make clear that I will merely be analyzing the concept of culpability and not justifying it. Proponents of deterrence theory and consequentialist approaches to legal blame should see this chapter as robbing them of only one of their arguments against their opponents, namely that the concept of *mens rea* is not intelligible. Even if I succeed in making the notion intelligible in the context of non-negligent culpable acts, there is still plenty of room for attacks against it as the wrong notion for our legal system to rely upon in its conceptualization of the point of criminal sanctions. Nonetheless, I am interested in formulating an intelligible conception of culpability because I am committed to it, and

---

[2] The Model Penal Code has been drafted, with commentary, by the American Law Institute and has had considerable influence upon legal reform in the United States during the past 30 years. For a presentation and discussion of the Code's minimum requirements for culpability, see *Criminal Law and Its Processes*, ed. Sanford Kadish and Monrad Paulsen, 3rd ed. (Boston: Little, Brown, 1975), p. 95.

[3] This chapter builds on my initial attempts to understand moral culpability in "The Nature of Immorality," in *The Foundations of Moral and Political Philosophy*, ed. Ellen Frankel Paul et al. (Oxford: Basil Blackwell, 1990); also published in *Social Philosophy and Policy* 7, issue I (Autumn 1989).

so wish to see a deeper understanding of an idea that is (and should be) central to our legal system, and our moral practices generally.

It was common in ancient times to think that there was something about the way human beings are by nature that explains why they are invariably culpable for violations of the norms of morality, reason, and law. This chapter, one might say, tries to cash out that ancient view by arguing that it is because human beings are prone to a particular mental act definitive of being "at fault" in any of these three ways that they have a "fallen" nature. Nonetheless, I will contend that this natural basis for human culpability does not afford us an excuse for our wrongdoings. The following explication of *mens rea* aims to establish why we are appropriately blamed, punished, and (one hopes) finally forgiven for our culpable acts.

I. Defiance of Reason

An analysis of culpability should start not with a discussion of legal culpability, and not even with a discussion of moral culpability, but with an analysis of what I will call "rational culpability," which is a way of being rationally "at fault."

To be rationally culpable is to be irrational, but not every kind of irrationality counts as culpable irrationality, and not every mistake people make when they reason constitutes being irrational. Consider that a person who makes a mistake about how to achieve his goals fails to act rationally, but he is not for that reason alone criticized as 'irrational.' When Henry Hudson headed up the large river that emptied into the Atlantic by the island of Manhattan thinking that it was the Northwest Passage, he wasn't irrational: he was mistaken. Unlike Henry, those we consider culpably irrational are not in some sense "innocent" in their performance of the mistaken action. We think either that they knew that their action was imprudent but did it anyway or that they ought to have known that it was imprudent. Of the former, we might say they demonstrated "willful irrationality"; of the latter, we might say they demonstrated "negligent irrationality." Leaving aside negligence here, I will attempt an analysis of willful irrationality in this section. I will argue that the notion of "fault" implicit in the judgment of someone as irrational in this sense involves the attribution of a mental state to this person which is importantly similar to the mental state attributed to those who are judged morally or legally "at fault."

Being willfully irrational is also not the same as another species of irrationality, which I will distinguish with the term 'non-rational.' There are certain mistakes in reasoning that human beings commonly make and which psychologists study – mistakes in the way they process information, in the way they reason logically, and in the way they think about the world.[4] When we make such errors, we are not thinking or behaving rationally, but there is nothing intentional about our mistakes. We are "afflicted" with the disposition to make them (for reasons worthy of psychological study), and they cannot be considered "our fault" unless others consider us negligent in failing to remedy our tendency to make them. In this chapter I also will not discuss these non-culpable failures of reason, and henceforth when I use the word 'irrational' I will be doing so to refer to those non-negligent failures of rationality which we believe the individual engaged in willfully in order to advance some objective, and not innocent "cognitive slips."

It is not hard to recognize this species of irrationality. "Johnny knows he won't get through college if he doesn't study," says his father, "but, for him, every night is party night. How can he be so irrational?" Johnny's persistence in behavior that we believe he knows will preclude the achievement of a preeminent goal he has is central to our perception of him as "at fault"; it is this knowledge which makes him deserving of our criticism of his behavior. It may be tempting for Johnny's father, who realizes that Johnny is aware that his behavior doesn't make sense given his goals, to explain Johnny's behavior in a way proposed by the American comedian Bill Cosby. Cosby, in order to account for his children's penchant for knowing the better but doing the worse, explains it in two words: brain damage.

The joke highlights the fact that it is difficult to make this kind of behavior intelligible. In order to try to make sense of this difficulty, let me develop and analyze an actual (and I think interesting) example of genuine irrationality. I once knew an 18-year-old who decided he wanted to live the "natural life," raising his own food, living in a house built with his own hands, in a rural area along the coast of Maine. After getting permission to use a piece of his grandmother's land, he attempted to

---

[4] For examples of discussions of such failures of reasoning, see A. Tversky and D. Kanneman, "The Framing of Decisions and the Psychology of Choice," *Science* 211 (1981): 453–58; and David Pears, *Motivated Irrationality* (Oxford: Clarendon Press, 1984), esp. pp. 45f.

build his house – a kind of log cabin affair – despite the fact that he knew little about building houses. His father, on the other hand, knew a great deal about house-building techniques. Nonetheless, this young man refused to take any advice from his father about how to build the house, and refused all offers of help from him because he wanted to live independently of his parents. The result, predictably enough, was disastrous: what was built was poor and did not stand up to the winter storms. In the end, the teenager had to seek refuge with his grandmother, and eventually had to go to his father and accept the help he had insisted on refusing before.

We would not, of course, consider this person immoral for what he had done, but we would not be kind in our assessment of him: 'pig-headed,' 'stupid,' 'imprudent' are the sorts of descriptions we would use – words which indicate a kind of culpability in our minds, but a non-moral one.

We would make this assessment of him because we would believe of him that he "knew better." But what did he really know? If we believe that the boy wasn't insensible and thus paid attention both to the facts of the world around him and all the things that parents, teachers, and friends were telling him, then we have to believe that he knew that he didn't really have enough technical ability to build a log house himself. In particular, we think he knew, first, that he didn't have the technical ability to build a house by himself; second, that the chances of him learning to do this by winter's arrival were very bad; and third, that his father did indeed know how to build one. In virtue of these three beliefs, we can attribute to him at least the following item of knowledge

a) attempting to build the house alone is not the most effective way, and probably not even a possible way, to achieve his goal, so that his actions are irrational.

His abysmal ignorance must have been obvious even, we think, to himself. We would say of any remarks he might make to the contrary that "he's fooling himself."

So why did he try to build the house if he knew the action was impru-dent? Was he simply ignoring the counsels of prudence? To say that he was simply ignoring them would be to say that he was pursuing something else besides the prudent course of action, and that this prudent course of action therefore "lost" fair and square in his calculations about what to do. For example, we might see the son as having to choose between two incommensurable goods, being prudent and something else – say, being independent, and finally deciding to choose the latter because he concluded somehow that he had a better reason to be independent than to be prudent.

But this isn't an accurate picture of what was going on. In this situation there was not some neat clash of incommensurable goods, with the teenager feeling he had better reason to choose the imprudent option. Granted, the goal that the teenager had was independence; nonetheless, that goal could be achieved only if he accepted his father's help to build the house. So to live an independent life, the boy had to depend upon his father in the short term. And given that the boy was not in any way intellectually deficient, we impute to him the knowledge, supplied by reason, that to achieve independence he had to accept his father's help. Reason's directive to this effect, we think, must have had real force for him. He must have appreciated that going to his father and asking for help was what he *ought* to do, given what was necessary to achieve his ultimate goal. To put it in a different way: given his goal, this person knew that he ought to be rational and do that which would allow him to successfully achieve his goal. So reason had authority for the teenager in this situation. We conclude, then, that the teenager had the following knowledge:

b) The fact that the action he contemplates is irrational gives him not just a reason but the best reason in the circumstances not to do the action; reason's directives are "authoritative" in the situation.

But if he knew not just that his action was irrational but that he had the best possible reason in the circumstances to act rationally, why did he persist in irrational behavior? This is the standard sort of question that trips up those who try to recognize and explain akratic action. If we believe, with Aristotle, that every act we take aims at what we believe to be good, then knowing the better but doing the worse seems to be impossible.

So how do we make the teenager's action intelligible? We take seriously the natural characterization we make of him as rebellious and we make sense of his action as a rebellion. Consider that the boy knew both that building the house without his father's help was irrational, and that he hated the idea of having his father help him. Indeed, the prospects of accepting the help were sufficiently repulsive to him that he could not bear to let it happen. Hence he was faced with a choice: he could conform his actions and desires to the dictates of reason, which would mean temporarily giving up his goal of being independent of his father and accepting his help, *or* he could defy reason's authority and substitute in its place the authority of his desire to build the house by himself. He chose defiance. And, as I shall now argue, anyone whom we consider to be willfully irrational is someone whom we believe to be defiant of reason.

Those who defy reason do not merely rebel against its directives, but attempt to install another authority in its place which will endorse the action they wish to perform. To put it in an Aristotelian way, they are able to do what is worse, despite always taking action to achieve the good, by challenging the authority of that which judges the action worse, and choosing instead to respect as authoritative that which makes the action good. Of course every act we take aims at the good, but when we want to see the worse action as the better one, we can depose our reason which judges it worse and install a new authority that makes it an act that aims at the good.

What is the new authority? Normally, it will be whatever desire motivates the interest in performing the action. However, one might also want to install in the place of reason what one thought was a less authoritative norm – for example, a moral or legal norm – to which one had allegiance and which directed one to perform an action one's reason told one not to perform. However, many theorists, particularly Kantians, argue that moral norms have more (rather than less) authority than practical reason; in any conflict between them, the right choice would be the choice to obey morality. In view of this, Kantians would believe any rebellion against the directives of reason in the name of morality would be commendable rather than wrong, and thus improperly classified as defiance (you don't defy a legitimate ruler when you support her and not a rival faction after her throne). Indeed, Kantians would expect to see defiance of morality by those who preferred the directives of reason, rather than the reverse. It also seems strange to think that one would have more allegiance to legal norms than to the directives of practical reason, hence making it unlikely that a person would defy the latter in order to install the former.

What is not strange at all, however, is the defiance of the authority of law in order to install the authority of reason, when it directs one to behave in ways that are illegal. (We will discuss this form of defiance in our discussion of legal culpability.) So the normal and natural explanation for why we would behave irrationally and defy the directives of practical reason is that those directives conflict with the satisfaction of a desire which ought not to have sway in this situation, but which we insist should be authoritative. To use an English locution, when we are defiant of reason we "would have it that" we are right to do what our desires dictate, and not what reason dictates.

There are two ways in which such defiance of practical reason can work. One can either defy the normative power of practical reason directly, or one can defy it indirectly by defying the information provided by theoretical reason on which the disliked directives of practical reason are based.

The form of reasoning constitutive of the direct defiance of practical reason is "I want to do x but I know that doing x will not allow me to achieve y and achieving y is my preeminent goal; nonetheless, I will do x." Here the reasoner is defying the norm that tells him that he ought to do what will allow him to achieve his preeminent goal. He refuses to bow to the authority of this norm, and, as the American expression goes, "he tries to have his cake and eat it too." Children are wonderfully good at this kind of reasoning. A weary babysitter once told me that his little charge had wanted a hamburger but refused to go with him to the only place where she could get the hamburger, telling him that she wanted to "have the hamburger without getting it." She threw a kind of tantrum in the face of an unacceptable directive of practical reason.

Such childish defiance may persist into adulthood, but it is more common for an adult to try another kind of defiance of reason. Adults normally do not defy the directives issued by practical reason because, I suspect, they have learned that it doesn't work – one simply cannot have one's cake and eat it too. But a different and more sophisticated style of defiance can seem more promising: in this case, one defies any pronouncements about the world made by theoretical reason which indicate that one's desired course of action is an ineffective way to achieve one's goal. Thus one reasons, "I will perform the most effective action that I can to achieve my goal y, but I want to perform action x, and so I 'would have it that' x will allow me to achieve that goal." But (one might say) this kind of reasoning is crazy! The mountain won't come to Mohammed, and reality can't be altered to suit your convenience. How could anyone believe that it could?

But we all do. We all find ourselves not only wanting but demanding that the world go our way, and even expecting that it will because we have demanded it to do so. So if our teenage house-builder chose this method of defiance, he defied the pronouncement of his theoretical reason that attempting to build the house was too unlikely to succeed to be worth the risk. "I don't like to believe that this is true," he said to himself, "therefore it isn't going to be that way. I 'would have it that' I have enough expertise to build the house." This method of defiance involves an indirect way of getting around the authority of practical reason. He is accepting that he ought to do what will allow him to best achieve his preeminent goal. But he is defying the information supplied to him by his theoretical reason about what the best thing to do actually is.

There are various ways we can challenge the pronouncements of our theoretical reason about the world so as to allow us to believe that what we want to do is also what will best achieve our goals. And these various ways are reflected in the different kinds of *rationalizations* we offer to justify our irrational acts. For example, a person can postulate a kind of magical control over the world, so that doing what he wishes will also seem consistent with the commands of practical reason. This strategy amounts to saying: "My reason tells me that the world is *x*, but I don't like its being *x*, because that means I can't perform the action I want and achieve my goal. Therefore, because I want it to change, it *will* change." This characterizes the reasoning of a graduate student who once told me that even when he knows his credit card limit has been reached, he still pulls out the credit card at his favorite record store. "Because," he says, "I want the albums."

Or people can decide to believe that they are permitted to try a forbidden activity because they are exempted from the sorts of problems that normally plague those who engage in it. For example, drug users often insist that other people get addicted to heroin, but not them. And the teenage house builder might have insisted that although other people require instruction in the art of house building, he was talented enough not to need it.

People can even decide to revise the rules of logic to achieve their goals. Consider the logic student who must prove a theorem on a problem set, but finds it difficult to do so if she is limited to the standard rules of inference: it is not unusual for a student in this situation to "change" these rules and "prove" the theorem using her new ones, only to wince when the problem set comes back with a bad grade. And when asked by her logic professor why she came up with this proof when she *knew* the correct rules of inference, such a student generally has nothing to say – except, perhaps, "I was hoping it would work." And, in general, we hate to answer such questions because the answer is so embarrassing: we *did* hope that we could fix the pronouncements of reason to suit our interests, and when we're caught, our hubris is brought painfully to our own attention.

So what we call the rationalizations which frequently attend our irrational actions are, in fact, expressions of our defiance of the dictates of theoretical rationality that seem to make it impossible for us to do what we want and still follow the dictates of practical reason. Those rationalizations can either be articulations of the way we defiantly see the world in conformity with our desires, or they can be ways of *bolstering* that defiance in situations where we have some doubt that we can pull it off. "Not everyone is as good with his hands as I am," our teenage house builder might say (following a moment of doubt), "so I'm special enough to be able to do something other people can't do."

No matter which of these reason-defying strategies our teenager chose, and no matter how he rationalized what he was doing, the fact of his choosing one of them means we must attribute to him one further (false) belief:

c) the authoritative directives of reason that tell him to do what he prefers not to do can be successfully defied, and the desire dictating the irrational action can be installed as the authority in this situation, so that this desire, and not reason, will rightly direct him as to how he should act.

His irrationality is therefore the result of his choice to respect an authority other than reason.

It is intriguing to me that in all of the discussions of akrasia and self-deception purporting to make sense of knowing the better and doing the worse, this way of rendering the phenomenon intelligible has never been proposed. (Perhaps it has been missed because those who have worked in this area have not spent a great deal of time with small children, and have therefore missed the opportunity to see the faults of humanity undisguised by the veneer of civilization. Or so it seemed to me one day as I marveled at my three-year-old son determinedly setting out to ride his tricycle to San Francisco.) Yet it is clearly a possible explanatory hypothesis: if somebody knows the better and does the worse, doesn't this suggest that *she does so because she believes she can insist that the worse is better?* Thus the smoker aware of the Surgeon General's report can quit smoking, or she can insist that this report has nothing to do with her because she simply isn't going to get cancer. (Once, in presenting this account to a philosopher who smoked, I gave him this example, and he told me in dead earnest that he really wasn't going to get cancer.) And the Malibu home owner whose home is threatened every year by the winter tides – and who explains why he doesn't move from his home on the beach by saying "Every year it gets worse, but I just bury my head in the surf"[5] – believes he has a choice between accepting the pronouncements of theoretical

5 CBS News, March 1983.

reason and performing the prudent action given those pronouncements, or ignoring those pronouncements so as to enjoy himself. Quite clearly he prefers the second option. "But," we say, "this is nuts! People can't make the world behave the way they want it to behave." That's true; that's why these people are irrational. But they, and we, try anyway.

But why aren't these people (i.e., us) genuinely crazy? The reason is that, on this analysis, they are genuinely ignorant of something; they are ignorant of what they can realistically accomplish in the world. But the nature of their ignorance is not the sort of thing that we normally take to be a sign of mental illness. The person who defies reason has a certain conception of who he is and what he needs which makes him treat a stupid strategy as a plausible one. His parents and friends, when they see him act irrationally, might complain "Who does he think he is?" The answer is that he thinks that he is someone special enough to have his desires prevail. The smoker who knows the statistics about cancer and smoking says, "The disease won't get *me*." And the Malibu coast-dweller who knows the danger of flooding insists that the world dishes out disaster to other people, not to him. So, to use an old-fashioned word, although none of these people behaves immorally, all of them are guilty of the "sin of pride." This pridefulness is not craziness because their defiance of the pronouncements of reason occurs in situations where there is some probability that their wishes can come true. Akratic people don't jump off cliffs wishing they could fly; they do, however, smoke in situations where they know there is a chance that they won't get cancer, and they go to graduate school in philosophy when they know there is a chance (albeit small) that they will be able to get a job, and they attempt to build houses even when they don't know how to do so because there is a chance that they'll be able to build something good enough before winter comes.

So when the teenager in my example realized that his makeshift house was inadequate for the winter, he learned something. He not only learned what he could plausibly accomplish and what he could not, but he also learned something about himself: his place in the world turned out not to be as high as he thought, and he realized he was a lot more like other people in power and importance than he thought.

And now we see why the defiance account can render deliberate irrationality intelligible: it explains the irrational action as that which is precipitated by a defiant act in which one installed as authoritative something other than reason which endorsed the irrational action, and it also explains that defiance as a function of the agent's ignorance about something fundamental. The agent who defies the authority of practical reason, insisting that the worse is better in a situation where he wants to perform the action his reason calls worse, does so because he does not understand that he simply cannot supplant reason's authority with something more congenial. The logic student, the drug addict, the Malibu homeowner, and the teenage house builder all mistakenly attribute to themselves a control over reality that they simply do not and cannot have. Such ignorance is striking in the very young, and it is part of the reason we call young people 'immature.' But such immaturity persists into adulthood, albeit in a less obviously false form. Perhaps human self-love is such that we are invariably inclined to see ourselves as more powerful, more special, and more significant than we in fact are. (Perhaps we are, to borrow a phrase from Hobbes, naturally and irredeemably vainglorious.) As we grow we learn, sometimes painfully, just how much and how little we can accomplish, and thus how significant our wishes will be in determining the future course of the world.

A reader might accept that this style of explanation fits some non-negligent forms of irrationality, but not all of them. Such a critic might argue that to say that the irrational person is "defiant" appears to attribute to him a fist-shaking rebelliousness that not every irrational individual has. For example, even if the defiance account explains the proud but self-deceived smoker, does it really explain the smoker who hates the fact that he smokes, does so regretfully, and longs to quit? It does: the word 'defiance' doesn't describe the emotional attitudes of the irrational agent, but rather the kind of mental act that explains how he can know the better and do the worse. The reluctant smoker, no matter how much he claims to hate smoking and to prefer to refrain from it for the rest of his life, picks up the cigarette on this occasion because, right now, smoking this cigarette is what he badly desires and he "would have it that" doing what he desires at this moment is not the worse but the better course of action. "This cigarette won't matter that much to my health, so I might as well enjoy myself," he might say in order to bolster his defiance of the dictates of reason. Or he might say to himself, "I can't live without these things, so I might as well have one now." This way of representing things makes the better course of action impossible at this moment, so that the worse course of action is now permitted, in defiance of the information given him by his theoretical and practical reason. Even the term 'weakness of will' is itself a defiant misrepresentation of the phenomenon of incontinent action: a person who describes his actions in this way is suggesting that he was "too weak" to avoid the action that he claims to acknowledge as worse, thereby representing his action as somehow inevitable when it was not. On the view I am presenting, what he is actually doing is choosing the action he calls worse, even while understanding that it is worse from the standpoint of reason – a standpoint he knows is supposed to be authoritative – because he believes he can defy that authority and substitute in its place the authority of his desires, which direct him to perform the desired action.

There is one other very important way in which defiance can operate to make someone culpably irrational (a way that some might contend constitutes negligence, or at least what has been called "advertent negligence").[6] Suppose I perform action x in ignorance of the fact that it will prevent me from achieving my goal. Prima facie, such ignorance excuses me; but if that ignorance was something I knew that, at some earlier time, I ought to remedy, then the ignorance does not excuse me because it is itself effected by a culpable act. So if I know that I ought to have my cholesterol level checked, but fail to do so and continue to eat large quantities of beef, cheese, and ice cream, then when I have my first heart attack I cannot say that my ignorance of my high cholesterol level excuses me from charges of irrationality. I knew that I should not remain ignorant, because an extremely important desire of mine, self-preservation, could be effectively pursued only if I obtained certain information. In this example, what could explain the fact that I did not get that information? It is not hard to give a perfectly good explanation; I knew, if I got it, that I might have to give up eating the foods I loved, so therefore I did not do so. In this situation I declared that I "would have it that" these foods posed no risk to my future survival, making it unnecessary for me to procure information that might suggest otherwise. There are many ways in which I could rationalize my defiance, as we discussed previously. The point is, however, that my ignorance in this situation would be culpable precisely because it could be traced to a defiant action: I defied reason (in its theoretical or practical guise) in order to choose to remain ignorant, and for this reason my failure to procure my goals by virtue of that ignorance makes it appropriate to call me 'irrational' rather than merely 'mistaken.'

---

[6] The distinction is from Glanville Williams, *Criminal Law: The General Part* (London: Stevens and Sons, 1953), pp. 49–59. For a nice overview of the controversies surrounding the topic of negligence, see the readings on negligence, recklessness, and strict liability in *Freedom and Responsibility*, ed. H. Morris (Stanford: Stanford University Press, 1961).

II. Moral Culpability

Whether one thinks that moral culpability even exists depends upon what one's moral theory says about the authority of moral imperatives. In particular, if one believes that moral imperatives are hypothetical rather than categorical, then one must consider irrational those people who know that these imperatives offer them the best way to satisfy their desires but who fail to follow them anyway. The term 'immoral' could, at most, designate those irrational agents who violate a species of rationally dictated imperative – for example, the imperatives that direct people as to how to achieve peace, or cooperation, or impartial behavior. Philosophers such as David Gauthier and Philippa Foot, who have proposed that moral imperatives may be just a species of rational hypothetical imperatives, are committed to assimilating immorality to irrationality in this way.[7] And the preceding section on the defiance of reason would be, for such philosophers, all that would be necessary to capture the sense in which those who fail to follow these imperatives are culpable.

If the reader agrees with this view, the analysis to follow postulating defiance of a distinctively moral kind of authority will be at best psychologically interesting – an account of what people who postulate this nonexistent authority think they are doing when they behave immorally.

However, philosophers who are committed to the idea that morality has a distinctive authority and who describe moral imperatives as categorical want an explanation of immorality that makes it something other than irrationality. If these theorists are right that moral imperatives bind with an authority that often (and maybe always)[8] supersedes even the authority of reason,[9] then someone who understands that authority should also understand that she should always act from these moral imperatives – even in situations where moral behavior prevents her from satisfying

---

[7] See David Gauthier's *Morals by Agreement* (Oxford: Oxford University Press, 1986), and Philippa Foot's "Morality as a System of Hypothetical Imperatives," in *Virtues and Vices* (Berkeley: University of California Press, 1988).

[8] Kant appears to insist on the total supremacy of morality in his writings, but this idea has been challenged recently. For example, see Susan Wolf, "Moral Saints," *Journal of Philosophy* 79, no. 8 (August 1982): 419–39.

[9] Note here that the word 'reason' is used in a very narrow sense to refer to a norm of action directed at the individual intent on satisfying his desires. This is the economist's notion of reason, roughly equivalent to prudential calculation. Philosophers such as Kant use the word 'reason' more broadly to cover both prudential and moral calculation. Despite my sympathies with Kant's use of the word, I will retain the narrow use of 'reason' in this chapter to mark the distinction between two quite different forms of normative reasoning.

her desires, and is to that extent irrational. So why would she fail to do so?

Despite enormous interest in the authority of morality, moral theorists as a whole have been not only unsuccessful at but also markedly uninterested in explaining immoral action.[10] The founder of our discipline, Socrates, was one of the few who took on the issue explicitly, but his explanation is one of the most unsuccessful. Immoral people, says Socrates, are ignorant of the good, and hence deserving of pity rather than anger, education rather than pain.[11] Yet unlike genuinely ignorant people, the immoral among us do not seem to welcome instruction! Are they really just ignorant? Moreover, it is striking that despite advocating this account of immorality, Socrates was prepared to support punishment of immoral people; clearly, punishment is an unusual educational technique! The fact that punishment rather than college courses seems to be the appropriate kind of response to those who act immorally suggests that their immoral action is a function of a certain kind of resistance inside them, which the Socratic punishment is somehow supposed to break. Understanding immoral agents simply as ignorant fails to capture or explain this resistance.

Perhaps the most serious problem with Socrates' account, however, is that it does not seem hard to find morally culpable people who not only know but even take delight in the fact that what they are doing is wrong. In fact, isn't this knowledge just what makes us want to blame them? After all, outside of legal contexts, ignorance normally excuses.[12] Consider the foreigner who does not know that his behavior in this culture is rude, or the child who does not realize that her words to a friend are wounding, or the doctor who administers a fatal dose of medication negligently prepared by another doctor who had always been trustworthy before: such people bring about injury through their ignorance, but in view of that ignorance – an ignorance we find reasonable under the circumstances – we do not judge them culpable. If immoral people are assimilated with these kinds of folk, it is no wonder that Socrates thought pity rather than anger was the appropriate emotional response toward

---

[10] The following historical remarks are taken from a much longer and more detailed account of various theories of culpability in my "The Nature of Immorality." See note 3.

[11] See *Meno*, 77b–78b (in the translation of W. R. M. Lamb, Harvard University Press, 1924, p. 289), and *Protagoras*, 357d–e (in the Lamb translation, p. 243).

[12] As the saying goes, "*Ignoratia legis non excusat.*" We will be discussing later why ignorance is not a good excuse in legal contexts.

them. Socrates' explanation seems to destroy the moral culpability it was meant to explain.

If ignorance excuses, then knowledge must convict. But once we attribute knowledge to the culpable agent, it is difficult to know how to explain his immoral action in a way that makes it both intelligible and a genuine instance of *culpable* action. Suppose we say, for example, that the person who acts immorally is genuinely indifferent to the authority of moral imperatives. If she is not making any mistake by ignoring them, then that must mean the imperatives, however wonderful we think them, do not in fact apply to this person. She is outside their scope, and hence does nothing wrong when she does not follow them. Such a person is properly called 'amoral' rather than 'immoral,' since we cannot say about her that "she should have done otherwise." We might hate her from a moral point of view, and wish her to be removed from our world, but this way of viewing her makes her into a kind of monster that, although worthy of our hatred and opposition, is no more a justifiable subject of moral *blame* than any other dangerous creature outside the reach of moral imperatives. So, once again, we see that what was supposed to be an explanation of culpable action actually destroys the phenomenon it was supposed to explain.

There is one more popular style of explanation, which I call the Manichean account of immorality. On this view, immoral behavior is a function of a certain "part" of us (Plato would call it the appetite or the spirited part, Freud would call it the id, St. Paul would call it "sin that has its lodging in us")[13] which fights against (and wins against) the part within us (reason, or the superego, or knowledge of God's commands) that is directing the moral action.[14] But how can this view explain a person's culpability for a bad deed when that deed was precipitated by a force about which he could do nothing? On this view, immoral action is not something chosen but something effected by an event – the event of the good part being overpowered by that of the bad part. This loss is presumably something that the good part could do nothing to prevent. But if the good part of you is too weak to win some or all battles with the bad part, then the bad action precipitated by the victory of the bad part is not chosen by the good part. And since the good part is supposed to

---

[13] Romans 7:14–20.

[14] This style of explanation is also popular with those who want to understand akratic behavior. See the articles discussing this style of approach in *The Multiple Self*, ed. Jon Elster (Cambridge: Cambridge University Press, 1986).

be who you really are, this means the bad action is not chosen by you, and thus it is not something for which you are responsible. If "the devil made you do it" – where the "devil" is understood variously as your id, or your appetites, or your hormones, and "you" are associated with that within you which wanted to do good but couldn't – then "you" are not to blame. You are its victim, and hence not the appropriate recipient of our condemnation. However intelligible this style of explanation for immoral behavior is, it once again destroys the phenomenon to be explained.

After considering the way that these accounts failed to capture our conception of (non-negligent) culpability, I found myself looking for one particular kind of inner event that would be the secret of it. Clearly, there are many kinds of people who do immoral deeds, with all sorts of characters from good to bad to awful. If one undertook the project of "explaining" immorality, one would have to come to grips with the variety of motivations, character traits, and desires that are all part of the reason human beings prefer to act badly rather than morally. But despite this diversity, all people who act immorally, no matter whether they are normally saintly or devilish, have something in common which grounds the judgment that they are "at fault," and thus culpable for a wrongdoing. If it isn't ignorance, or indifference, or weakness in the face of a force for evil, then what could be present in all of them – even in the actions of people whom we think have, by and large, a good character – that makes them the appropriate subjects of blame for the particular immoral action they perform?

To understand what it is, consider the following description of what is supposed to be the first morally culpable act committed by a human being:

The serpent was more crafty than any wild creature that the Lord God had made. He said to the woman, "Is it true that God has forbidden you to eat from any tree in the garden?" The woman answered the serpent, "We may eat the fruit of any tree in the garden, except for the tree in the middle of the garden: God has forbidden us either to eat or to touch the fruit of that: if we do, we shall die." The serpent said, "Of course you will not die. God knows that as soon as you eat it, your eyes will be opened and you will be like gods knowing both good and evil." When the woman saw that the fruit of the tree was good to eat, and that it was pleasing to the eye and tempting to contemplate, she took some and ate it. She also gave her husband some and he ate it. Then the eyes of both of them were opened and they discovered they were naked; so they stitched fig-leaves together and made themselves loin-cloths.[15]

[15] Genesis 3:1–7.

As we all know, when God found out what the two of them had done, he was furious; he punished not only the two human beings but also the serpent for their disobedience.

And that is the point of the tale: human immorality is a function of human disobedience of an authoritative command. Human beings are culpable for the commission of wrongs not because they are ignorant that what they are doing is wrong, but because they *know* they are doing wrong. Indeed, if they were ignorant of the wrongfulness of their act, this would excuse them from culpability. Eve and Adam knew that they were not supposed to eat of the fruit of the tree of knowledge; if they had been ignorant of the command, God would have been filled with sorrow rather than fury at their deed (assuming that the ignorance itself wasn't something for which they were culpable). So their knowledge is central to their culpability.

However, not only knowledge of the command, but also knowledge of the command's *authority* is central to our finding them at fault. Adam and Eve are not culpable out of indifference to an imperative which they happen not to find in their interest to follow. They know they are *supposed* to follow the command – that is, that it is authoritative over them, that it is supposed to rule them. While the tale represents them as having no knowledge of good and evil, and thus no knowledge of moral commands generally until they eat the fruit, it does establish that they had knowledge of God's authority, and hence of the authoritativeness of his commands. (Is knowledge of God's authority moral knowledge? Part of the point of the tale may be that knowledge of this authority is not moral knowledge, so that God's authority is prior to and higher than the authority of morality.) If they had been ignorant of his authority, their ignorance would once again undercut their culpability for the act they took. If I don't know that an imperative issued by someone gives me a better reason to act than my wishes give me, then (even though I act incorrectly) I am the appropriate subject of further education rather than blame (assuming, again, that my ignorance is something for which I am not culpable).

Finally, Adam and Eve's culpability is a function of the fact that the wrongdoing was *chosen* rather than caused. Eve was not pushed, compelled, or under duress when she ate the fruit. The snake, of course, encouraged her to do so, but, in the words of Dante, Eve herself "let Desire pull Reason from her throne."[16] In other words, she chose the action,

---

[16] *Inferno*, Canto V, quoted by Donald Davidson in "How Is Weakness of the Will Possible?," in *Essays in Actions and Events* (Oxford: Clarendon Press, 1980), p. 35.

aware that it was forbidden by an authoritative command applicable to her.

The Genesis story therefore presents the following four elements as necessary conditions of the culpable mind.

1. Making the decision to choose the action.
2. Choosing it in the knowledge that the action is forbidden by a command.
3. Choosing it in the knowledge that the action is forbidden by a command that is applicable to oneself and authoritative in this situation (i.e., it gives one the best possible reason to act in the situation).

These three elements presuppose the fourth:

4. Having both the capacity to make choices and the capacity to have knowledge of authoritative commands.

These last two capacities are necessary conditions for judging someone a moral agent.[17] A person who is either unable to choose how to act despite knowing the authoritativeness of the commands (e.g., a kleptomaniac) or unable to understand the way in which these commands are authoritative (e.g., a sociopath) cannot be considered a moral agent, and hence cannot be appropriately blamed for behavior that is not in accord with those commands. We may very well want to do something about such people – lock them up, execute them, put them into therapy – but they are not people whom we should blame or punish.[18]

---

[17] I am indebted to Peter Arenella for pressing me to make this idea explicit in my analysis.

[18] In "The Legal and Moral Responsibility of Organizations" (in *Criminal Justice: Nomos XXVII*, ed. J. Roland Pennock and John W. Chapman (New York: New York University Press, 1985), pp. 267–86), Susan Wolf suggests that sociopaths, although incapable of understanding or being responsive to moral authority, are capable of the kind of responsibility (call it 'practical') which is the foundation of tort law. "We use," she says, "the practical sense when our claim that an agent is responsible for an action is intended to announce that the agent assumes the risks associated with the action. In other words, the agent is considered the appropriate bearer of damages, should they result from the action, as well as the appropriate reaper of the action's possible benefits" (p. 276). One can, according to Wolf, be capable of being practically responsible but not morally responsible; sociopaths may be one example of such an agent, organizations may be another. If she is right, there is a difference between being a moral agent and being (to coin a name) a "practical agent." One might also say, as we shall discuss in the next section, that the criminal law takes seriously the question of whether or not the lawbreaker is a moral agent, whereas the tort law requires practical agency.

But, readers might protest, if this analysis makes immorality a function of such an informed choice, doesn't it portray wrongdoing as a case of knowing the better but choosing the worse, and haven't innumerable discussions of incontinence shown that such a characterization of human action is highly problematic at best, and perhaps incoherent?

This account does indeed portray culpable wrongdoing as a case of knowing the better and doing the worse, but the preceding section on the defiance of reason aimed to establish that such a portrayal need not be understood as an incoherent account of human action. The view that I will henceforth call the "defiance" account of moral culpability incorporates these four features in a coherent and (I will argue) plausible way. In a nutshell, the view is that a culpable agent is one who chooses to defy what she knows to be an authoritative moral command in the name of the satisfaction of one or more of her wishes, whose satisfaction the command forbids. She is disobedient in the face of knowledge that obedience is expected, and a rebel in the sense that she is attempting to establish something more to her liking as authoritative over her decision making, rather than these moral commands. Just like irrational people, immoral people know the better but do the worse because they believe they can install a new reason-giving authority over their actions that transforms the worse into the better.

I want to argue that such defiance is a distinctively human phenomenon, which normally occurs whenever following a command – which one knows is authoritative in the circumstances – interferes with the perception of what is required to achieve or do something else that one wants. In this situation, a human being has the capacity to "overthrow" the authority in her own mind, and to install a new authority which sanctions the action she wishes to take. Indeed, the previous discussion of irrationality was meant to suggest that defiance of norms generally – including rational as well as moral norms – is a distinctively human capacity, which marks out human beings from other animals and which traditional religious thinkers would consider to be the central element in their fallen natures.

How is it distinctive of human beings? Don't dogs, horses, and monkeys display the ability to break rules, sometimes even exhibiting something approximating shame when they do so? However, the defiant mental act that I claim is distinctive in human beings is not just the act of disobeying a command; it is the choice which leads to the disobedience. Specifically, *it is the choice to supplant what one knows to be an authoritative rule with a different authority that sanctions the act one wishes to take.* Or, to put it another way, it is a rebellion against that which is taken to have final evaluative authority in the situation, in order to install a new evaluative authority which evaluates the action one wishes to take as better and not worse.

Contrast this with the disobedience of a horse. When a horse disobeys his rider's command to canter, the horse is simply doing what he prefers until the rider can use punishments and rewards to induce him to prefer the behavior preferred by the rider. So what the horse does is always determined by his desires. Unless we human beings are badly wrong in our understanding of equine mental life, there is no perception of an 'ought to obey' in the horse's head which can act as a reason-giving authority that competes with his desires. But it is the ability to understand and act from the idea that "I ought to obey" – an ability which involves the appreciation of a moral command as authoritative – that distinguishes a human being from an animal. And it is our ability to challenge that authority and install a reason-giving authority that is more amenable to our interests which makes human beings' disobedience of commands distinctive.

My point is that to be morally culpable, one must be able to recognize the authority of morality even while trying to overthrow it. So wrongdoers are rebels, but rebels always understand the authority of that which they seek to depose. This is why they are, and see themselves as, rebels – people who must depose, bring down, vanquish an authority that they oppose and wish to replace.

In the name of what do they rebel? Normally, one opposes morality for the sake of self-interest, which may or may not be rationally tutored. This is why the question "Why are we immoral?" is so naturally answered by saying, "Because we're selfish." A legal norm might also come to oppose the moral authority, and the agent might be tempted to serve that norm, rather than the more important moral norm. Whatever the source of temptation, the agent gives in to it when she installs that source over morality as her reason-giving authority.

As in the case of the discussion of irrationality, the combative language used to state this view may already have some readers worried that it fits only the very worst immoral people. How can the mental state of the reluctant moral offender, or the offender guilty of only a minor moral offense, be understood as some kind of defiant act?

But such a worry misunderstands the account. The defiance view is not a portrait of human character but an analysis of the "culpable act" inside the head of the agent which occurs whenever a person is guilty of a blameworthy but non-negligent action. The view does not attribute to those who are guilty of a wrongdoing the wholesale rejection of the authority of morality on every occasion. Nor does it attribute to them certain emotional attitudes characteristic of political rebels, such as anger, hatred, hostility, or resentment toward the authority they defy, although it is consistent with the view that the culpable agent have any of these emotional attitudes. All that the view says about the morally culpable agent is that inside her there was an act of "insubordination" resulting in the performance of the prohibited action, and it is that insubordination which constitutes her culpability. Specifically, what makes her the appropriate subject of blame is the choice to install as authoritative something that condones what she wishes to do, rather than to allow the relevant authoritative moral command to prevail. That act of insubordination can be done regretfully, sorrowfully, or even happily – the point is that it is *this* act which constitutes being at fault. It can be a rare occurrence in a person's life or a common one; it can occur when the directives of the moral authority are not terribly serious, or when they are very serious indeed; and it can be accompanied by a variety of emotional states. But it is this defiant act that is the basis of all morally culpable action.

So the person who is a decent member of our community but who nonetheless decides, while in a great hurry to get her shopping done at the mall, to sneak into a parking space someone else has been patiently waiting for – that person is, at that moment, defying the claims of morality and obeying the commands of her own wishes. And Peter, who betrayed his friend Jesus three times before the cock crowed and who wept with guilt after his betrayals, nonetheless believed (regretfully, sorrowfully, tearfully) when he denied he knew Jesus that it was more important for him to satisfy his desire to stay alive than it was to be loyal to his friend and the religious views to which he had previously committed himself.

So, like those who defy reason, people who are culpable for moral wrongs obey what they take to be the authority of their own wishes in defiance of the authority of the moral imperatives proscribing the actions that the satisfaction of their wishes require. Take our parking-space thief. She believes that

a') taking the space herself rather than letting the other person have it (where this other person was there first) was immoral (albeit mildly so; it was at least rude).

b') that, given the authority which the dictates of morality have, she is supposed to have better reason to refrain from this immoral behavior than to engage in it so as to satisfy her desires.

    c′) that the authority of morality can be defied in this case, because her own wishes are too important to "lose" to it.

Unless one is insensible, everyone knows (a′). Knowing (b′) might, however, not be possible for some people, who are thereby precluded from being moral agents. Someone who cannot understand the authority of morality cannot be expected to conform her actions in accord with it when the moral dictates oppose her desires. This seems to be exactly the right thing to say about sociopaths. "Although sociopaths can achieve an intellectual understanding that cheating, stealing, murdering, etc., are *considered* to be immoral, they cannot understand why they ought not to act in these ways."[19] We might say that attributing to someone the knowledge of morality's authority is the same as attributing to him a conscience; sociopaths, therefore, lack consciences.[20] Although we lack, as moral philosophers, a good theory of what moral authority is (to the point where some doubt that it exists at all), still, if such a theory were at hand, it would tell us how one who qualifies as a moral agent has access, cognitively or emotionally, to the authority of moral commands.

    In popular parlance, (c′) constitutes the parking-space thief's belief that she can and should "get away with it" if she decides on the immoral action. It is interesting to note that, in *Paradise Lost*, Milton portrays Eve as someone who believes (c′), and who is thereby emboldened to eat the forbidden fruit. In Milton's poem, before she picks the fruit she reasons

> Here grows the cure of all, this fruit divine,
> Fair to the eye, inviting to the taste,
> Of virtue to make wise: what hinders then
> To reach, and feed at once both Body and Mind?[21]

Eve believes there is nothing hindering her from successfully challenging God's authority, and so she eats the fruit. And all her human progeny, who are prone to immoral deeds, are represented as being inclined to reach the same conclusion about their chances of successfully defying the authority that is giving them the commands they dislike. What distinguishes moral skeptics from moral objectivists is that skeptics seriously entertain the idea that the authority of morality can be successfully challenged, whereas objectivists (perhaps out of faith alone) insist that it cannot.

---

[19] Wolf, "The Moral and Legal Responsibility of Organizations," p. 278.
[20] Wolf says the same; ibid.
[21] John Milton, *Paradise Lost*, Book IX (New York: Doubleday, 1969), p. 212.

The defiance account describes one kind of choice which all immoral agents share that marks them out as morally culpable. But can it help us to grade the extent to which any agent is immoral?

In answering this question, it is important to note that the defiance view denies that any offender is "devilish" in the way Kant described – and the way he refused to believe any of us were.[22] That is, immoral people are not portrayed as people who defy the authority of morality out of some kind of unmotivated hatred of that authority. Instead, they are portrayed as rebels against the authority of morality who aim to substitute as authoritative something they prefer to it. As they fight against the moral authority, they may come to despise it insofar as it persists in interfering with their abilities to follow the imperatives of their preferred authority, but they have no fundamental unmotivated antipathy to cooperative, other-regarding behavior. In fact, even the devil himself turns out not to be devilishly defiant on Kant's way of construing the term! The devil, remember, rebels against God not because he finds God intrinsically hateful, but because he prefers himself as ruler of the world (although, as he continues to fight and lose the battle for supremacy with God, he is generally represented as coming to despise his rival).[23]

Hence, the defiance view is not as negative as it might be in its portrayal of human immorality. Still, I believe it leaves room for distinguishing

[22] See Kant's *Religion within the Limits of Reason Alone*, trans. Theodore M. Greene and Hoyt H. Hudson, ed. John Silber (New York: Harper and Brothers, 1960), pp. 52–53.

[23] Because Kant wished to avoid characterizing people as devilish in this sense, he shied away from using the word 'rebel' to describe evil people. For example, he says in the *Religion within the Limits of Reason Alone* that "Man (even the most wicked) does not, under any maxim whatsoever, repudiate the Moral Law in the manner of a rebel (renouncing obedience to it)" (p. 31). Instead, he maintains that "Man (even the best) is evil only in that he reverses the moral order of the incentives when he adopts them into his maxims" (p. 31), but this kind of "insubordination" (which is different from flat-out renunciation) is characterized as rebellion later on in the *Religion*, when Kant notes that were we to remove the incentive of inclination from human nature, then "though it is true that this rebellion is often stilled, the rebel himself is still not conquered, and exterminated" (p. 51n). The critical debate about whether or not Kant is right to reject the idea that we are devilish in his sense fails to take account of the way in which he does acknowledge a genuinely devilish rebellion in the hearts of all (sinful) human beings. See the Silber edition, pp. cxxivff and cxxixff; Allen Wood, *Kant's Moral Religion* (Ithaca: Cornell University Press, 1970), p. 212n; and Philip Quinn, *Divine Commands and Moral Requirements* (Oxford: Clarendon Press, 1978), p. 9 and n. 3.

　　Those who are familiar with Kant's analysis of immoral behavior in the *Religion* will see strong similarities between his treatment of it as an act of insubordination in one's ranking of motives for action and my account of it as the defiant choice of something other than morality as the authority governing one's choice of action in the situation.

grades of immorality, which are, in essence, represented as degrees of rebellion. The point of the defiance account is that all immoral people (i.e., all people who are morally culpable) are rebels; but there is a difference between rebels who are sorry about having to rebel and rebels who have no qualms about their rebellion, and there is a difference between petty rebellion and major insubordination. We look both to the severity of the offense and to the emotional and intellectual attitudes attending its performance to form a judgment of just how immoral a person has shown herself to be by performing the immoral action. In forming that judgment, I suspect that determining the severity of the offense usually takes precedence, and judgments about emotional attitudes are used to mark out distinctions among those who have challenged the same authoritative command. For example, we would say that two people who, in similar circumstances, betray their friends in order to advance their careers have both engaged in an offense of the same seriousness, but the person who feels no sorrow as he betrays his friend is worse, in our eyes, than the betrayer who is plagued by a bad conscience.

Why isn't the former betrayer better characterized as indifferent, rather than defiant? Some readers may worry that my account of culpability seems to leave out a perfectly good category of wrongdoer: that is, the kind who violate moral commands without in any way flinching, who appear to have no loyalty to those commands and even express contempt for them. These people seem indifferent to the demands of morality, not defiant of them. But what does it mean to call them 'indifferent'? Does it mean that they are outside the scope of moral imperatives? That is, do those imperatives issue directives that give them *no reason to act* in the way directed? If this is so, such people made no mistake in their action, although they acted in ways we dislike. If we called them 'immoral,' the description could only be a reflection of our dislike; it could not convey, as it does in the defiance account, our judgment that the wrongdoer's action has been a mistake not only from our point of view but also from his. Accordingly, if they made no mistake acting as they did, they are best described as 'amoral,' where this label designates those who do not act morally and who are not the sort of creature to whom the moral imperatives apply. We may want to do something about these people – they can be greatly disruptive of societal harmony. But our response to them could not be condemnatory, retributive, or desert-based.

Suppose, however, that someone said of such people: "Well, of course they believe they are outside the scope of morality, and so act in ways that we see as indifferent to the authority that commands them, but we don't believe that this is true. We do see these commands as applying to them: they are assuming that they are independent of morality's rule when in fact they are not. Hence, we can correctly say of them that they should have done otherwise, and hence that they are immoral, without finding in them an explicitly defiant act."

But this way of conceiving of these agents does render them defiant in a sense: they are acting as if they are independent of morality's rule when they are not. Now do they understand that they are at least supposed to be ruled by morality, or do they not? If they *do* know about the claim these directives make to rule them (e.g., if they are aware of and can understand the force of the kinds of admonishments of immoral behavior made by parents, Sunday School teachers, judges, and so forth), then there is, in their heads, a defiant act after all. Although they take no interest in the commands, they are aware of their authority, and they are defying it. On the other hand, if they do not know about their authority, then either they are themselves responsible for putting themselves in this state or else some other, external cause is responsible for their being in this state. If they put themselves in it – if they were authors of their own moral insensitivity – we have some grounds for holding them culpable for the actions committed because of that insensitivity. But if something else was the author of it (e.g., a severely impoverished childhood, a mental illness), then they are *ignorant*, why should we blame them for actions which reflect an ignorance that was not their doing? As we have discussed, ignorance excuses an agent from culpability. So, oddly enough, an account of an "immoral" agent as purely indifferent actually destroys what is necessary for that agent to be immoral.

Interestingly, one can find this very account of our blaming practices (in the context of legal norms) given by the Supreme Court of West Germany:

As a free and moral agent and as a participant in the legal community, the individual is bound at all times to conform his behavior to law and to avoid doing the wrong thing. He does not fulfill his duty merely by avoiding that which seems to him clearly to be the wrong thing; rather he must attempt to determine whether that which he plans to do is compatible with the legal imperatives of the system. He must resolve his doubts by reflection or investigation. This requires that he apply his moral sensibility. . . . If despite the moral sensitivity that can fairly be demanded of him, the individual does not perceive the wrongfulness of the contemplated action, then his mistake is to be viewed as ineluctable; the act would be, for him, unavoidable. In a case of this sort, the individual cannot be blamed for his conduct.[24]

---

[24] 2BGH 194 (March 18, 1952). Translation by George Fletcher, *Comparative Criminal Theory* 72 (2nd ed., 1971, mimeo, UCLA); in Kadish and Paulsen, *Criminal Law*, p. 124–25.

Of course, some kind of response to the harmful acts of those "morally insensitive" people who believe themselves to be part of a different moral realm is highly appropriate, but not a blaming response coupled with retribution. We can either work to remedy their ignorance about moral authority, or, if a remedy seems impossible, we can work to neutralize the threat they pose to others (e.g., through incarceration or execution). But it is not fair to respond to them as individuals who could have acted morally, because in an important sense, they were not able to do so.

However, as the discussion above indicated, there is one kind of morally insensitive agent whose insensitivity is a function of his ignorance; on the defiance view, it does make sense to blame this agent. This is that agent who, although now incapable of conforming his actions to the demands of morality, chose to perform actions and to develop in ways that made such insensitivity likely, and was *fully aware of the risk he was taking*. Such a person now acts immorally out of ignorance, but he is himself responsible for that ignorance in the sense that he chose it knowing he should not. We would call him culpably ignorant.[25] Aristotle insists, for example, that people who appear unaware that what they are doing is wrong are actually people who are

responsible for becoming men of that kind, and . . . make themselves responsible for being unjust or self-indulgent, in the one case by cheating and in the other by spending their time in drunken bouts and the like, for it is activities exercised on particular objects that make the corresponding character. . . . Now *not to know* that it is from the exercise of activities on particular objects that states of character are produced is the mark of a thoroughly senseless person.[26]

So of course they do know what they are doing, in which case they have chosen to make themselves into people who are morally insensitive; in virtue of that choice, they are culpable for being morally insensitive later.

Indeed, perhaps we are sometimes inclined to judge morally monstrous people – that is, people who are incapable of understanding moral norms – as culpable despite their inability to act from these norms, because we believe that earlier in their lives they chose to engage in activities that they knew would likely turn them into moral monsters, and that they did so anyway, in defiance of that knowledge, in order to

---

[25] See Holly Smith, "Culpable Ignorance," *Philosophical Review* 92, no. 4 (October 1983): 543–71. Aquinas considers the culpably ignorant to include every non-negligent performer of immoral actions. See *Summa theologica*, First Part of the Second Part, Question 6, Article 8, "Does Ignorance Render an Act Involuntary?"

[26] *Nicomachean Ethics*, 1114a 3-11; my emphasis; translation is that of W. D. Ross in *The Basic Works of Aristotle*, ed. Richard McKeon (Chicago: Random House, 1941).

satisfy their desires. If they become incapable of being ruled by moral considerations thereafter, they are ignorant, but nonetheless culpably so – by virtue of this prior defiant act. Note that it is because we can trace their immoral actions to a defiant act that it becomes possible for us to call them culpable. Indeed, insofar as it seems appropriate to call such people indifferent to morality, the defiance account will allow that there is some truth to that description. But this kind of indifference is a function of a prior defiant act, and is not itself the source of their culpability.

Other wrongdoers appear indifferent to morality in a different way, but still in a way that the defiance account illuminates. Consider that there is a difference between understanding morality's authority but consistently opposing it and accepting that authority most of the time but fighting it off on occasion – say, when its commands oppose certain important wishes. Occasional disobedience of an authority one normally believes deserves obedience is different from full-scale disobedience of directives whose claim to be authoritative one *knows about* but never accepts. The second sort of rebel, one might say, is attempting to declare himself amoral in a society that (he knows) insists on seeing him as persistently disobedient of his proper ruler. He is attempting to make himself indifferent to the claims of morality. Because such a person continually fights to gain his independence from the authority that in his view makes a false claim to rule him, he is unlike and, from a moral point of view, worse than rebels who only occasionally fight against a realm that, on other occasions, they have admitted is entitled to govern them. We judge the former to be worse, from a moral point of view, than the latter, because the latter has significantly more allegiance to the moral authority than the former.

The cagey reader may now be aware that she can make an interesting attack on the defiance account of immorality in light of these last remarks. Why do immoral people defy the moral authority? Presumably they do so because they think they can "get away with it" – their rebellion, they think, will be successful in the sense that any costs they pay because of their defiant action will be outweighed by the benefits from it. Let me be vague about what "costs" and "benefits" refer to here, because different moral philosophers committed to the objective authority of morality will have different ways of cashing out what they are (for example, Aristotle would talk of human flourishing, Kant would talk of the persistent indictment of reason one would feel following the defiance). For present purposes, choose your favorite way of cashing out these terms. Now are moral rebels right to think they can get away with their rebellion and escape without paying any significant costs? Presumably any moral theorist committed to the authority of morality would argue that they cannot do so in any situation over which the moral authority is sovereign.

Now it may well be correct to conclude that the authority of morality has limits – that there are jurisdictions in life over which it does not rule.[27] One might also think that, either because of one's disposition or early training, one may be inclined to exaggerate the scope of morality's authority. In a situation where morality was not the ultimate authority, one's refusal to act morally would be a good thing, because it would show that one was trying to get out from under a ruler whose rule in this situation was inappropriate. Properly speaking, one is not being defiant of morality in such a case because one cannot rebel against something that has no final right of command (although it might *feel* rebellious to the agent who is struggling to overcome what she suspects is her own false sense of morality's authority).

But in situations in which morality is sovereign, moral theorists (e.g., Kantians) committed to the objective authority of morality would insist that the agent's belief that she could successfully defy its rule is false. And it is the falsity of this belief that the agent doesn't know: in this case, the defiance analysis of immorality represents such a person as ignorant of the fact that a rebellion against the authority of morality cannot succeed. Why doesn't this ignorance excuse this person from culpability?

To answer this question, consider that, on the defiance view, *the defiance itself is what makes the person culpable*, whereas the defier's ignorance of the impossibility of succeeding is the explanation of her defiance, and thus, of her culpability (and that which renders it intelligible). That is, it explains why the defiance occurred, but it does not explain away the defiance – and ignorance only excuses when it explains away the defiance. Or, to put it in another way, when ignorance excuses, it is because the fact of the ignorance shows the agent was not defiant after all. When we say "Mary was reasonably ignorant that the man she shot was a human being and not a deer, so we can't find her guilty of murder," or "Joan had no idea that her words to the visitor brought back painful memories, so we can't blame her," we're attributing to the agent an ignorance of something relevant to her assessment of what the authoritative commands told her to perform; because she was so ignorant, she is not acting out of defiance

---

[27] For an argument to this effect, see Susan Wolf, "Moral Saints."

of those commands. In contrast, the ignorance attributed to the culpable agent on the defiance view is an explanation of her defiance – it explains why she thought it made sense to engage in it; this explanation, however, in no way forces us to redescribe her choice to act contrary to the moral rules as not defiant after all. Indeed, it assumes and must assume that defiance in order to explain it. And it is the defiance which makes her culpable.

But why is our assessment of immorality entirely a function of the culpable agent's decision to defy the moral rules? This is, I find, a deep and difficult question. What are we trying to do or say when we label someone immoral? On the defiance view, it seems that we are making a negative evaluation of culpable people because of their decision to give allegiance to something other than the authority that deserves it. And this evaluation shows our own allegiance to the moral authority they flouted. But if it is their allegiance which we are attacking, then our attack is not fended off by any claim that the immoral agent thought she could succeed in evading the rule of morality. That ignorance explains why she thought she could succeed in switching her allegiance, and so explains why she acted immorally. But it does not touch or explain away the (in our eyes) awful fact that she no longer wanted to be committed to the right ruler. And it is that failure of commitment that we are denouncing.

If this way of understanding our moral assessments of people is correct, then there are still mysteries that need to be unraveled. Suppose a person persists in acting morally, not because she respects the moral authority, but only because she is in some way afraid of it. If she could persuade herself that she could get *away* with defying it, she would defy it. Is such a "closet defier" already in an important sense immoral, since she lacks the allegiance to moral authority which marks out the good from the bad?

And what about the claim made by a long line of defenders of morality's authority that defiance of it is bound to fail: is such a claim really true? The defiance account of immorality assumes what moral philosophers have struggled unsuccessfully to justify for many years: the inescapable authority of moral commands. Perhaps one reason why this has been a favorite and persistent topic in moral philosophy for hundreds of years is that it is the central element upon which our blaming practices rest, and so it must be justified if those blaming practices are to be judged legitimate.

III. Defiance of Law

It is relatively straightforward to apply this account to legal culpability. Take the tax cheat: he knows

a″) that the legal system commands him not to commit the action, that is, that it is illegal.

b″) given the authority which legal commands have, he is supposed to have better reason to refrain from illegal behavior than to engage in it in order to do something else he wishes.

Nonetheless, he also believes

c″) the authority of the law can be defied, and something else that condones what he wishes can be enthroned in its place, thereby allowing him to act so as to satisfy them.

Given his belief in (c″), our law-breaker believes he can "get away with it." It is (c″) which is the defiance that constitutes legal *mens rea*, and which the legal system is looking for when it tries in court those who have committed illegal acts.

Thus, I am proposing that an important component of the criminal law is the defiance conception of culpability. The Model Penal Code gives us criteria for culpability that are, in essence, signs of a defiant mind: for example, knowledge, purposiveness, and recklessness (where the last assumes a defiant choice of the action knowing the risks). And the excuses and justifications recognized by the law make sense as mental states in which no defiance has occurred.

In particular, those who are excused from legal culpability will be found not to have believed (c″). For example, the man who, misled by incompetent IRS consultants and government pamphlets, fails to pay enough tax doesn't believe (c″). His action is explained by his ignorance of the tax law – an ignorance that cannot be traced to any defiance of the law's authority on his part. And the driver who takes proper and sufficient care in her operation of a motor vehicle and who hits and kills a drunken pedestrian who has inexplicably hurled himself in front of her car in no way kills the person because of her defiance of the law's authority in order to satisfy her wishes.

Normally, however, ignorance of the law is not an excuse, because a legal system expects people to do their best to understand the legal rules of that system, and communicates that expectation to the citizenry. Hence, if someone complains that he did not know the rule, the legal system is unimpressed because it believes this person knew he should have learned of the rule but nonetheless failed to do so. In the words of one judge, "everyone is conclusively presumed to know the law."[28] He is culpably ignorant, and his culpable failure to remedy his ignorance makes him defiant of the authority of the legal system, and hence legally culpable. (So the taxpayer who did his best to comply with the law but who failed to do so because the tax code was either ambiguous or inadequately promulgated by the state such that he could not find out what the relevant tax rules were would be unfairly penalized for his failure to comply with those rules.)

As I have already mentioned, not only illegal acts of commission but also acts of recklessness are analyzed neatly by this approach. A reckless offender is another example of one who is culpable in the manner of those who are culpably ignorant. Even if he doesn't mean, for example, to drive the power boat into the dock full of people, and even if he points out, correctly in our view, that his boat was going too fast for him to control, nonetheless we believe that he had to know, as he chose to go at that high speed, that he was taking the risk that he would be unable to control the boat and possibly endanger others' lives. The fact that he did so anyway is a sign of his defiance of legal (and, in this case, also moral) pronouncements against taking that kind of risk. He is therefore culpable for running the boat into the dock not because he wanted to perform it in defiance of legal and moral imperatives (he wanted no such thing) but because he wanted to do that which entailed *risking* the kind of harm ruled out by legal and moral imperatives, so that he undertook the risk in defiance of these imperatives.

But what, the reader may wish to know, is legal authority? This famous question is one that some theorists have had trouble answering.[29] To the extent that one denies there is any authority attaching to law *qua* law, one would say either that the lawbreaker is defiant of the authority of morality upon which one supposes legal commands rely, insofar as they have any force upon us – which is the view of any classic natural law theorist – or that she is defiant of reason, in the sense that she performs the illegal action knowing she may suffer a penalty that she finds unacceptable.

---

[28] Judge Buttles, *State v. Woods*, Supreme Court of Vermont, 1935, 107 Vt. 354,179 A 1, in Kadish and Paulsen, *Criminal Law*, p. 110.

[29] See Elizabeth Anscombe, *On the Source of the Authority of the State*, in her *Collected Works*, vol. 3: *Ethics, Religion and Politics* (Minneapolis: University of Minnesota Press, 1981), pp. 1311–55; Joseph Raz, *The Authority of Law: Essays in Law and Morality* (Oxford: Clarendon Press, 1979); and Leslie Green, *The Authority of the State* (Oxford: Clarendon Press, 1988).

On this latter view, the authority of the law (and particularly the criminal law) derives from reason, because laws are imperatives backed by negative sanctions designed to secure a certain deterrent goal. The lawbreaker, on this view, is not defying any special authority that legal rules have, but he is being irrational (assuming that an expected utility calculation, properly performed and of which he is capable, would tell him not to violate the legal rule).

Those who insist, however, that the law does and should have a special authority will want to see the legal offender as defiant not only of reason but also of that special "positivist" authority. Why would someone want to defy the law? She might do so because she was motivated by self-interested considerations that the law opposed, or because she was motivated by what she took to be her moral duty, which conflicted with the legal requirements. Those who insist that the law has its own special authority must defend the strength and scope of that authority, in order to explain when refusal to obey the law for moral or self-interested reasons is legitimate, and when it is condemnable defiance of the proper authority. The question of which authority ought to take precedence when the legal and moral authorities are in conflict is a particularly thorny one. The conscientious objector insists that citizens must serve morality first and the law second; Hobbes is one philosopher who thought that this way of rating the two authorities was a recipe for civil strife, and who therefore insisted that legal authority come first. ("How many throats has this false position cut, that a prince for some causes may be deposed!"[30]) We have located an important point at which philosophizing about the nature and extent of the state's authority is necessary.

Nonetheless, as the quote from the West German Supreme Court shows, a legal system normally does not want to diverge too far from morality; its architects even expect that people understand and assume the authority of morality in the system's own pronouncements and expectations of their appropriate behavior. It may even be that legal systems require that people understand and respect the authority of morality if its punitive response to them explicitly aims at making a moral point, for example, if the punishment is intended as moral retribution, moral education, or both.

However, the state may actually want to avoid constructing its legal code in strict conformity to morality for certain important reasons. For

---

[30] Hobbes, *De cive: The English Works of Thomas Hobbes*, vol. ii, ed. W. Molesworth (London: Bohn, 1839), preface, pp. xi–xii.

example, even quite vicious behavior, such as libel or slander, can be merely a tort and not a criminal offense in situations where the state is concerned to pursue other values, such as the protection of free speech.[31]

Although the defiance view of legal culpability fits the facts well, it does not fit them perfectly. There are decisions (e.g., *Regina v. Prince*[32]) concerning mistake in law that suggest that the law is much more inclined toward "strict liability" than the defiance account would allow. In *Regina v. Prince*, a man married a woman who was under age without knowing it, and with the reasonable belief that she was not. It seems improper to claim that such a person is defiant of the law. Finding him guilty anyway might be justified on grounds of pursuing a deterrent goal, and, in general, the state's interest in deterring harm may lead it to convict even nonculpable (in the sense of non-defiant) offenders in the interest of making them an example for those who are contemplating the same action.

Are those people convicted of criminal negligence convicted on deterrent grounds alone? They are not if they are judged "advertently negligent," because such people really do fit the *mens rea* test of guilt. This form of negligence is essentially the same as recklessness; one who is guilty of it knew that she was risking an unacceptable level of harm when she undertook her action, but flouted that knowledge and did so anyway. She therefore displayed a defiant act prior to her crime. But an "inadvertently negligent" agent is someone who did not know that she should have done otherwise, and yet (we think) could and should have known better. There appears to be no defiant act inside the agent, but only an ignorance that we find culpable. Is that finding based entirely on the thought that conviction would have desirable deterrent consequences for this individual (or for others in the community)?

Perhaps not entirely. If we take an Aristotelian attitude toward this inadvertently negligent person, we believe that, although she did not know that what she was doing was wrong, that ignorance was a function of her faulty character – a character for which she bears primary responsibility

[31] It may also be that the stringent conditions needed to convict people of certain crimes (e.g., treason) in some legal systems – conditions that require finding not only the defiance which I call *mens rea* but also a certain kind of reason for that defiance – reflect the society's concern to control the power of the state in situations where it might be inclined to overreact and use its power excessively or arbitrarily. I am indebted to discussions with David Dolinko on this point.

[32] *Regina v. Prince*, L. R. 2 Crim. Cas. REs. 54 (1876). The defendant was convicted of marrying a girl under the age of sixteen, in violation of Victorian English Law, despite the fact that he was judged to have the "reasonable belief" that she was eighteen.

and which she knew better than to develop in this way. So we locate the defiance not at the time of the act, but earlier, during the process of character formation. Thus a man who is convicted of gross criminal negligence after killing a pedestrian at a crosswalk while driving 30 miles over the speed limit in a rainstorm may be legitimately culpable not because we *now* find in him any defiance of a legal rule whose authority he understood in this situation, but because earlier in his life he had developed the character of an irresponsible driver in defiance of what he knew to be the authoritative legal and moral norms mandating safe and responsible motoring.

The inclination to try to see cases of inadvertent negligence as cases of advertent negligence or recklessness derives, I believe, from the desire to find the subjective element of defiance of the relevant norm in any person convicted of a legal offense. To convict someone who is genuinely and reasonably unaware of the criminal nature of his actions in order to secure greater deterrence of social harm violates the conditions of fairness in judgment and response implicit in the defiance account. Indeed, it seems to be a (mild) instance of resorting to terror to gain social control. Now perhaps the state is sometimes justified in pursuing convictions on these grounds (although that is controversial) because it must not only exact retribution but also secure a high degree of protection for its citizens through the deterrence of certain forms of behavior. Nonetheless, these convictions offend our sense of justice – which is created, I would argue, by our acceptance of the idea that genuine culpability requires a defiant mind.

Conclusion

Although defiance is critical to behavior that we standardly criticize, condemn, and take action to stop, I wonder whether or not it is also critical to our success as individuals and as groups. A readiness to "take on the world" may well be what is necessary to invent new machines, concoct ambitious dreams such as going to the moon, or fight off self-doubt occasioned by racist, or sexist, or class-based perspectives on one's abilities. It *may* even be (as I have suggested elsewhere) that defiance is a necessary part of certain emotions such as resentment and hatred.[33] To appreciate how our capacity to defy authoritative norms may have helped us survive – as

---

[33] See *Forgiveness and Mercy* (written with Jeffrie Murphy) (Cambridge: Cambridge University Press, 1988), ch. 2.

individuals, as a people, as a species – might enable us to become reconciled to something that exponents of various sorts of norms would argue that we ought bitterly to regret. And perhaps it is because we do see this capacity as important to our survival that it becomes hard to shake the thought that the first two human beings were impressive in the way they took on God.

4

Righting Wrongs

The Goal of Retribution

There has been a steady rise in the popularity of retributivism over the last decade, which is surprising given its near death in the 1950s and 1960s. Yet critics of this approach to punishment are, in my view, right to charge that its supporters appeal to little more than intuition when they defend the idea that all and only wrongdoers "deserve" to suffer. In this chapter, I will develop what I call the "expressive" theory of retribution in order to explain and defend the idea of retributive desert. I have presented this theory in other places;[1] here I want to restate the theory, taking into account critical reactions to the view that have appeared since I first began to develop it. Next, I shall argue, on the basis of this theory, that retribution is a fundamental and necessary component of any morally respectable system of punishment carried out by the state, but not the *only* component.[2] Finally, I will argue that not all retributive

---

[1] See, e.g., Hampton, "A New Theory of Retribution," in *Liability and Responsibility: Essays in Law and Morals,* ed. R. Frey and C. Morris (Cambridge: Cambridge University Press, 1991), which is a modified version of J. Murphy and J. Hampton, *Forgiveness and Mercy* (Cambridge: Cambridge University Press, 1988), pp. 35–87, 111–61, in which I first developed this theory of punishment. See also Hampton, "An Expressive Theory of Retribution," in *Retributivism and Its Critics,* ed. W. Cragg (Stuttgart: F. Steiner Verlag, 1992).

[2] I would also argue that moral education and deterrence should be goals of any well-designed system of punishment. Thus, I am a convert to the pluralist approach to justification of punishment, an approach I thought was wrong when I espoused the moral education theory some years ago. See Jean Hampton, "The Moral Education Theory of Punishment," *Philosophy and Public Affairs* 13, no. 3 (Summer, 1984): 208–38, reprinted in J. Feinberg and H. Gross, eds., *Philosophy of Law,* 4th ed. (Belmont, Calif.: Wadsworth Publishing, 1991). Nothing I say in this chapter should be understood to be critical of the moral education theory espoused in that paper, but I no longer believe (as I did then) that moral education can be the sole aim of punishment.

responses are punitive responses, and I will give examples of non-punitive retribution.

I. The Point of Retribution

To understand retribution, we must link the point of the retributive response to the wrongfulness of the action. The failure of a well-known theory of retribution developed by Herbert Morris as an adequate account of the retributive response effectively makes this point. Morris sees wrongdoers as deserving of punishment insofar as they are free riders: when they commit a wrong, they fail to observe certain moral constraints that others in their society accept; and they are thereby able to enjoy the benefits that come from others' acceptance of these constraints without paying the cost of accepting the constraints themselves. He therefore argues that retributive punishment is a way to even up the score: the legal system takes away the benefits enjoyed by these free riders by inflicting pain upon them equal to those benefits.[3]

Morris's theory of retribution essentially makes retributive justice a species of distributive justice, and it presupposes that it is possible not only to measure benefits that come from crime, but also to compare and measure pain so that we can know how much pain equals these (measurable) benefits. Clearly, this presupposition is problematic.[4] However, a more basic difficulty with this theory is its assumption that the fundamental reason why we censure and punish *all* wrongdoers is because they are free riders. This assumption makes sense only if we believe that constraining ourselves so that we do not rape or murder or steal imposes a *cost* upon us. Yet that idea makes sense only if raping, murdering, and stealing are viewed by us as desirable and attractive (either intrinsically or in view of the ends such actions achieve), and therefore individually rational but collectively irrational actions (for example, because such behavior destabilizes the community or damages the economy). However, surely this is exactly what most of us *do not* think about crime. Very few of us understand our refusal to murder or assault our fellows as imposing a cost upon ourselves, and very few of us resent murderers, muggers, or rapists because they have unfairly enjoyed benefits coveted by the rest

---

[3] Herbert Morris, "Persons and Punishment," *The Monist* 54 (1968): 475ff., reprinted in J. Murphy, ed., *Punishment and Rehabilitation*, 2nd ed. (Belmont, Calif.: Wadsworth Publishing, 1985).

[4] I discussed this problem in J. Murphy and J. Hampton, *Forgiveness and Mercy*, at 114–17.

of us. To make retributive justice a species of distributive justice is to claim that the wrongfulness of criminals' behavior consists in the fact that they have behaved *unfairly*. Although there are a few wrongs that we might be prepared to analyze in this way (for example, when people park for free in "no parking zones," while the rest of us pay a fortune to park in the local garage), it seems absurd to say that this is what is wrong with wrongdoers who murder, assault, or abuse others. (Indeed, it seems particularly indecent to analyze child abuse or rape along these lines.)

So, Morris's theory goes wrong because it links retributive punishment with a particular view of what makes an action wrong, and that view is clearly incorrect. However, the failure of Morris's theory is instructive: Morris instinctively tried to make sense of retribution by linking retributive punishment to *that which makes the wrongful action wrong*. Even if we reject his theory of the wrongfulness of punishable conduct, his strategy for understanding the nature of retribution is promising. What we need to make this strategy successful is a good theory of the wrongfulness of punishable conduct.

II. Harms, Losses, and Wrongs

What is a wrong? People usually conceive of wrongs as involving some kind of loss or harm to a person. However, actual harm is not necessary for a wrong to exist; for example, an attempt at murder that fails and does no harm to the intended victim is still a (highly) wrongful act. Moreover, when thinking about wrongs, we can be misled by the harm, and mistake *it* for the wrong. In this section, I want to distinguish harm from that which is "in" a wrongful action that makes it wrong.

Because harms are the concern of tort law, it makes sense to distinguish wrongs from harms by looking at the difference between crimes and torts. Tort law is a complicated legal practice that, in the eyes of many, cannot be unified by a single, over-arching moral or conceptual goal. However, legal theorists such as Jules Coleman have argued that a central concern of most tort cases is the desire to administer what they call "corrective justice."

Coleman understands corrective justice as imposing on wrongdoers the duty to repair the wrongful losses their conduct causes.[5] Coleman

---

[5] J. Coleman, *Risks and Wrongs* (Cambridge: Cambridge University Press, 1992), ch. 16.

insists that it is with the *losses* that corrective justice is concerned, not with the wrongful actions themselves:

Annuling [*sic*] moral wrongs is a matter of justice: retributive, not corrective justice. There is a legal institution that, in some accounts anyway, is designed to do retributive justice: namely, punishment. The bulk of cases in which claims in corrective justice are valid do not involve wrongs in this sense. If we abandon the view that corrective justice requires annuling [*sic*] wrongs as such, we are left with the claim that corrective justice imposes the duty on wrongdoers to annul the wrongful losses their conduct occasions.[6]

This way of dividing up the concerns of tort and criminal law seems plausible. However, whether it is right depends upon what Coleman understands as a wrongful loss.

According to Coleman, a wrongful loss is a loss that results from wrongful conduct. Although he never offers an explicit definition of 'loss,' he seems to mean by that term roughly what many would understand as harm. Henceforth, to clarify matters I will use 'loss' and 'harm' interchangeably, and I will define them as follows:

A harm or loss is a disruption of or interference in a person's well-being, including damage to that person's body, psychological state, capacities to function, life plans, or resources over which we take this person to have an entitlement.

Harms or losses therefore extend over everything we are prepared to consider to "belong" to a person.[7] Henceforth, when I speak of "correcting" or "rectifying a loss," I will mean the same thing as "repairing a harm."

Not all harms or losses are wrongful. "Innocent" sources of harm, such as natural disasters or animals, can cause harms but not wrongful harms. A new business competitor can harm one's business (and damage one's life plans), but again, we do not think of this kind of harm as wrongful. A wrongful harm or loss only comes from wrongful conduct by an agent thought to be culpable. Like Coleman, I would argue that a significant part of tort law (but not all of tort law)[8] is concerned not with

---

[6] Ibid. Thus Coleman rejects (rightly, in my view) the view of Ernest Weinrib that tort law is concerned with answering the *wrong* rather than the harm. See Weinrib, "Understanding Tort Law," *Valparaiso University Law Review* 23 (1989): 485, 512–15.

[7] Whether children can be said to "belong" to their parents is a highly problematic question in tort law. If they do, a harm to the child is also a harm to the parent. In general, I want to avoid issues having to do with defining the concept of ownership for tort purposes.

[8] Even if economic analysis of tort law is unpersuasive to account for the general operation of civil courts, it is certainly persuasive for some kinds of torts. Calabresi's idea that under tort law, people are allowed to perform certain actions on condition that they compensate

the wrongs or the wrongful conduct that causes these losses but with the losses themselves (insofar as they are caused by such wrongful actions). However, it is concerned with them in a particular way: it insists not only that such losses must be repaired, but also that they must be repaired *by the one who caused them.* We do not ask a wealthy Rockefeller to repair the loss that I have caused by my wrongful conduct, even if that Rockefeller is vastly richer than I. Instead, I must cover it, to the extent that I am able, insofar as I am the one who caused it:

> [Corrective justice] provides wrongdoers with reasons for action that are peculiar to them – agent relative reasons in that sense – to annul losses they are responsible for.... [W]rongdoing changes the nature of the relationship between the parties; it creates duties where none had previously existed. It gives agents reasons for acting that they did not previously have.[9]

Hence, corrective justice is that branch of justice that requires those who cause losses by acting in wrongful ways to repair, correct, or annul such losses. *Therefore, corrective justice is not a branch of justice that is concerned with the wrongdoing itself.*[10] In contrast, while corrective justice is concerned with wrongful harms, retributive justice is concerned with wrongful *actions* from which such harms result. Although a punishment may sometimes involve the wrongdoer compensating her victim in some way, the purpose of punishment is not to compensate the person for the harm suffered, but "to right the wrong."

those they may harm after the fact, if right, would show that some tort remedies are not responses to wrongful actions. They are, at most, a kind of "fine," the cost of doing business in a certain way. See G. Calabresi, *The Costs of Accidents: A Legal and Economic Analysis* (New Haven: Yale University Press, 1970). Moreover, Coleman argues that strict liability rules in tort law are actually a part of contract law, specifying the kind of liability certain firms must undertake in their contractual dealings, and not rules that define, or are responsive to harms caused by genuinely wrongful (and, in particular, culpable) action by those firms. See Coleman, *Risks and Wrongs*, ch. 18. This chapter is concerned with only those torts that are the result of wrongful action, and hence are the subject of corrective justice.

9 Coleman, *Risks and Wrongs.* However, Coleman is prepared to entertain the idea of institutional mechanisms for implementing corrective justice that do not require the injurer to repair the loss entirely by himself. See ibid., ch. 20, for a discussion of the way in which corrective justice can be implemented successfully.

10 Thus, like Coleman, I am opposed to Weinrib's view of corrective justice, which sees tort law as concerned with the wrongful action rather than the loss. However, as I shall explain later, I think that correcting a loss can sometimes play a role in annulling the wrongdoing, and therefore can be a partial response to the wrongdoing.

What does "righting a wrong" involve? To answer this question, we need to appreciate that only a certain kind of wrong needs righting.[11] There are two categories of wrongful action:

1. A wrongful action (potentially resulting in a wrongful loss) that requires a retributive response, and the losses of which require compensation.
2. A wrongful action (potentially resulting in a wrongful loss) that does not require a retributive response, but the losses of which (still) require compensation.

Wrongful losses (or harms) that arise from actions falling into either of the two categories require correction according to corrective justice. Indeed, one might say that the categories are species of the same genus because losses that result from a crime can be the subject of a civil suit distinct from the punishment meted out to the criminal for her act. Not all torts are the result of wrongful action (so that not all torts are the subject of corrective justice). However, of those that are, not all are the result of wrongful actions falling into the first category. The second category of wrongful action recognizes the possibility that there can be a wrongful action which is not the appropriate subject of retribution, but which is wrongful nonetheless and which can cause harms that corrective justice requires the wrongdoer to repair. If we can understand the nature of this second category, then we will be in a position to isolate the element in the first category of wrongful conduct that makes a retributive response to such actions appropriate.

Let me give two examples of tortious action that fall into the second category. The first is the well-known case of *Vincent v. Lake Erie Transp. Co.*:[12] in this case, a shipowner tied his ship to a dock to avoid the virtual certainty of shipwreck by an approaching storm, despite the fact that the dockowner refused permission for him to do so. During the storm, the ship caused considerable damage to the dock.[13] The dockowner sued, and the court decided that the shipowner was liable for the damages, but was in no way legally punishable for having tied his ship to the dock

---

[11] Wrongs are also the product of what might be called a "moral agent." I do not have space here to develop a conception of moral agency, which would involve a complicated discussion of autonomous action. Instead, I will focus on the nature of, and conditions for, culpability by a moral agent.

[12] 109 Minn. 456, 124 N.W. 221 (1910).

[13] Ibid. at 457–58, 124 N.W. at 221.

given the circumstances. Like the court, our overall moral assessment of the shipowner's conduct is positive, but like the court, we agree that there is still a component of his action – tying up his ship at another person's dock without permission – that was wrong in the sense that it violated a right.[14] Because our overall assessment of the shipowner's conduct is positive, we do not think that he should be the subject of retributive punishment. Indeed, any attempt by the dockowner to have him convicted of a criminal offense would have been (rightly) rejected by the court. Nonetheless, something wrongful persists within his action, namely, making use of the dockowner's property without his permission, and because the loss suffered by the dockowner was the causal result of this wrongful conduct, it counts as a wrongful loss, and therefore one which the shipowner must rectify.[15]

This case fits within the second category because the overall assessment of the injurer's action is morally positive, even though there is a component of wrongfulness within it. However, there are also cases in which the overall assessment of the injurer's action is morally negative but that nonetheless also fit within the second category. Consider, as an example, losses that result from non-criminal negligence: these are losses that result from wrongful conduct, but nonetheless, such conduct does not merit a retributive response. Suppose Mary is taking her two children to school in her Honda on a wet day; and after rounding a turn, is unable to avoid hitting Susan's car, which is stopped in preparation to make a left turn after the oncoming traffic clears. Moreover, to make this a clear instance of a wrongful act in the second category, let us suppose that while not perfect, her driving was not grossly negligent; for example, suppose she was going no faster than the speed limit but rainwater on the road made the surface slick in a way that she should have (but did not) notice. Mary has done something wrong; she has driven negligently in a way that has resulted in a loss to Susan (and perhaps to her own kids in the back seat). So to say that she has done something wrong is to say that she has failed to conform to the norms appropriate for good driving in those weather conditions, norms which we believe she does (and should) know. Still, it seems deeply inappropriate to haul her in front of a judge in a criminal courtroom and demand that she be punished for what she has done. The wrongfulness of her conduct is not the *right kind* of wrongfulness to merit such a response. Instead, it is the sort of wrongfulness to

[14] Ibid. at 460, 124 N.W. 222.
[15] Ibid.

which we think a court has completely and adequately responded when it requires her to repair the losses she caused.

We also think it deeply inappropriate to inflict a retributive response on someone who has wronged himself: most liberals – myself included – reject the criminalization of this sort of wrong, and even those who do not are usually reluctant to insist on serious criminal penalties for the crime of, say, attempting to commit suicide. In contrast, if someone has defrauded you of your life savings, we do not think that a court has completely and adequately responded to this wrongful action simply by requiring that this person return your money to you. So what is the difference between the wrongfulness of the defrauder's action and the wrongfulness of the actions of the negligent driver, or the shipowner, or the suicide attempter? Once we understand that difference, we will understand the nature of the wrongfulness to which retribution is a response.

III. Wrongfulness and Intrinsic Value

All wrongful actions are actions that violate a moral standard applicable in the circumstances. However, I will say that some moral actions violate those standards in a particular way insofar as they are also *an affront to the victim's value or dignity*. I call such an affront a *moral injury*. I shall argue that only when moral actions cause moral injuries, and only when those injuries are to a person other than oneself, are those who perform them appropriate candidates for receiving the retributive response. In this and the next section, I want to clarify the nature of a moral injury, and explain how a retributive response is a way of "repairing" this kind of injury.

A moral injury is not the same as a wrongful loss or harm. The latter concept, as I have defined it above, involves material or psychological damage to that over which a person has a right (for example, her possessions, her body, her psychological well-being), and comes about because of a wrongful action. In contrast, a moral injury is an injury to what I will call the victim's "realization of her value." Hence, the idea assumes, first, a certain conception of value, and, second, a certain understanding of how actions can affect that value. Let me develop each of these ideas in turn.

To say that someone has value is to invoke a certain conception of human worth.[16] To hold a conception of human worth is to hold beliefs

---

[16] I am concentrating here only on "human" worth to make my explanatory project more tractable. However, I believe strongly that a certain kind of worth is possessed by animals, whose denial can also warrant retributive punishment.

about how human beings are to be valued, and how to appraise each individual's value. There are many possible theories of human worth, and philosophers have varied in how they have understood the nature of human value. For example, Hobbes regarded human value as no different from the value of any commodity: "The Value . . . of a man," he insisted, "is . . . his Price."[17] Therefore, on his view our value is entirely instrumental: we are worth only what someone would give to make use of our skills, labor, or other characteristics. Naturally, his position accords people different values, depending upon the marketability of their various traits.

There are also noninstrumental conceptions of human worth, which grant people "inherent" or "intrinsic" worth on the basis of one or more characteristics. Many of these conceptions are inegalitarian, granting human beings unequal value depending upon their sex, race, or caste, or alternatively, on the basis of how intelligent, accomplished, or morally worthy they are. Other noninstrumental conceptions are egalitarian, insisting that people are equal in worth insofar as they share certain critical, worth-defining characteristics. One popular egalitarian theory is that of Kant, which grants each of us equal worth insofar as we are rational and autonomous.

These theories of worth are normative, not meta-ethical, theories. I take no stand on the question of whether any of these theories attributes to people what seem to be non-natural properties, making them implausible or nonscientific. Nor will I discuss whether they allow the possibility of genuine (moral) knowledge. To what extent rational people should be committed to any of them is an issue I leave for another day. My only claim in this chapter is that such conceptions are a normal part of a culture's normative practices, animating its ethics and its punitive system.[18]

Because Kant's theory is very significant in what follows, I want to take some time to explicate it. Kant had *two* theories of worth, only one of which is crucial for my present purpose. First, Kant granted us worth insofar as we are "morally worthy," and when we evaluate one another's moral worth, Kant held that – in this sense – we will likely be unequal in value. After all, some of us are vastly better from a moral point of view than others. Second, Kant said we have worth simply insofar as we are

---

[17] Thomas Hobbes, *Leviathan*, ed. C. Macpherson (Hammondsworth: Penguin, 1985), ch. 10, para. 16, p. 151.

[18] The reader may have recognized that a moral theory so conceived is not well described either as consequentialist or deontological. I will discuss the advantages of conceiving moral theory apart from these philosophical categories in another place.

human beings, and calls each of us an "end-in-himself." In this second sense we are equal in value. Only this second conception of value is relevant to defining the kind of moral respect a person deserves. On this view (which has its roots in Judeo-Christian religious teaching),[19] our moral obligations to people do not increase with, say, their moral virtue; instead we are obliged to respect our fellow human beings *equally*, no matter what the state of their moral character, insofar as each human being is an autonomous, rational being (although Kant would certainly maintain that how this respect should be demonstrated can vary depending upon the state of a person's moral character).[20] Thus, Kant's second way of defining human worth is egalitarian, and critical to the concept of moral respect. All of us must be valued as equals insofar as we all have the same value as "ends in ourselves." This "democratic" conception of value has been popular, albeit not universally accepted, in the modern world.

This second sense of value is fundamental to my view of moral respect and retribution. Curiously, one critic of my view took it that by speaking of the "value of the victim" I meant moral worth in Kant's first sense.[21] However, neither I nor Kant (nor anyone I know) would maintain that we should respect people only to the extent that they are moral people. The Kantian view explicitly denies that moral respect is based on a hierarchy of moral merit. Instead, this view maintains that moral respect is based on our intrinsic value as ends, which all of us have equally, and which is not easily capable of aggregation in the way that some utilitarian doctrines characterize it. On this view, morality demands of each of us that we respect the dignity of others and of ourselves, and thus reject the way that,

[19] Jeffrie Murphy, "Afterword: Constitutionalism, Moral Skepticism, and Religious Belief," in A. Rosenbaum, ed., *Constitutionalism: The Philosophical Dimension* (New York: Greenwood Press, 1988), pp. 239, 243–46.

I was struck recently by how many people in American culture accept this view of worth when I read a letter written by parents of children in a Tucson-area elementary school, calling upon the school to foster the idea that "all people are equal." In attempting to explain this equality, the authors of the letter noted that although each of us is different, our differences do not affect our equality: Just as 3+3+1 is different from, but equal to, 3+4, they explained, so too are we different from, but equal to, one another.

[20] For example, Kant maintains that those who are morally bad can deserve punishment, but he is also well known for insisting that punishment is a way of respecting a person's autonomy, and represents neither a violation, nor a suspension, of that autonomy.

[21] David Dolinko, "Some Thoughts about Retributivism," *Ethics* 101 (1991): 537, 554. His confusion is betrayed by his use of the phrase "moral value." According to Kant, we have value even when we are immoral, insofar as we are ends. Our moral worth is not the same as the value we have intrinsically, upon which moral respect is based.

for example, a white supremacist would insist on his own superiority over other racial groups, or the way in which a male might relish the idea that he is the intrinsic superior of all women. Interestingly, it also demands that we reject the idea that any of us "good" people is the superior of any wrongdoer – a thought which, as I will explain below, is important to understanding how to define appropriate retributive punishment.

The Kantian conception of value, insofar as it is connected to the two most prominent religious traditions of the West, has been enormously influential in modern Western societies, and has therefore played a role in setting the normative standards for acceptable treatment of people in our society. To see how (and the extent to which) it has done so, we must appreciate the way in which *human behavior is expressive*, and that what behavior expresses is partly a matter of cultural convention. Judith Martin, the expert on etiquette, has defended this idea in the context of arguing for the importance of manners as modes of behavior that constitute a language for conveying respect:

> The idea that people can behave naturally, without resorting to an artificial code tacitly agreed upon by their society, is as silly as the idea that they can communicate by a spoken language without commonly accepted semantic and grammatical rules. Like language, a code of manners can be used with more or less skill, for laudable or for evil purposes, to express a variety of ideas and emotions. In itself, it carries no moral value, but ignorance in use of this tool is not a sign of virtue. Inarticulateness should not be mistaken for guilelessness.
>
> Like language, manners pertain to a particular society at a particular time. If they were "just common sense" as is often claimed by critics of the field, why should Japanese behavior be any different from American, or medieval from modern? Like language, manners continually undergo slow changes and adaptations, but these changes have to be global, and not atomic. For if everyone improvises his own manners, no one will understand the meaning of anyone else's behavior, and the result will be social chaos and the end of civilization.[22]

So Martin sees manners as defined by convention (in the way that word meaning is conventional). However, she neglects to note that conventions about manners differ not only because societies use different behaviors to convey respect, but also because they have different conceptions of the kind of respect human beings are owed. Inegalitarian hierarchical conceptions of value have been commonplace throughout human history, while egalitarian conceptions have gained popularity only in modern times. Moreover, the "official" or most popular theory of worth in a society may not always be embraced by all sectors of the society: for

---

[22] Judith Martin, *Common Courtesy* (New York: Scribner, 1985), pp. 14–15.

example, the Kantian, egalitarian theory of worth implicit in American political values has always been rejected by white racists, and has been subtly dismissed by sexists (who are egalitarian only when evaluating the worth of males). In any pluralist society, just as there are a variety of spoken languages, or varieties of one dominant spoken language, there are also varieties of value-expressive behavioral language that are "spoken" by different sectors of the society.

As we grow up in a certain sector of society, we do not merely learn the language expressing the "right" ways to behave, we also figure out the wrong ways. Moreover, we learn not only certain conventional behavioral formulae (for example, shaking hands as a sign of respect, eating in ways that are deemed socially inoffensive), but also the behavioral ingredients for expressing messages about value in convention-flouting ways. When we behave "wrongfully," we fail to conform to what our society would recognize as acceptable behavior, either by doing things that are conventionally understood to be wrong or by inventing from conventional behavioral material novel ways of expressing our defiance of what society understands as respectful behavior.

Such defiance is not always understood by us to be *morally* wrong; when Rosa Parks refused to sit at the back of the bus, she defied the manners of 1950s Alabama society in a way that we think was morally right. Yet note that her defiance of those manners was a defiance of a conception of the unequal worth of human beings based on race, a conception that we, along with Parks, reject as wrong. In contrast, those whose behavior defies what we take to be the right theory of worth are people whom we regard as, to some degree, morally criticizable.

It is because behavior can carry meaning with regard to human value that it can be wrongful. The analogies between the meaningfulness of language and the meaningfulness of behavior are striking enough that one can use the Gricean theory of linguistic meaning to distinguish different ways in which human conduct can be meaningful; and in what follows, I will employ Gricean categories in the course of explaining how wrongful conduct is meaningful (although I cannot give any kind of complete Gricean analysis here).[23] I will then explain how that meaning is related to the moral injuries that wrongdoing effects. In brief, I shall argue that a person is morally injured when she is the target of behavior whose meaning, appropriately understood by members of the cultural community in

---

[23] See H. P. Grice, "Meaning" and "Logic and Conversation," in *Studies in the Way of Words* (Cambridge, Mass.: Harvard University Press, 1989).

which the behavior occurs, represents her value as less than the value she should be accorded. However, the insulting meaning of this behavior does not, by itself, constitute the moral injury. As I shall explain, the insulting meaning inflicts the injury in one of two possible ways.

IV. Behavioral Meaning and Moral Injury

It isn't always true that when we fail to conform to the standards of acceptable behavior we are thereby engaging in behavior that should be interpreted as defying or taking exception to the theory of worth motivating these standards. There are other explanations of our failure. For example, when Mary ran into Susan's car, she may have been appalled at what she did, and explain her conduct by saying that she had been distracted, or inexperienced, or over-confident in her ability to control the car. So while she might heartily agree that she ought not to have driven the way she did, she might also insist that her careless driving conveyed no message of disrespect for anyone on the road. Given our reluctance to see her as a suitable target of punishment, we tend to agree with this account of her behavior's "meaning."

The preceding example shows that we cannot maintain that an agent inflicts a moral injury whenever her conduct (for which we hold her responsible) fails to conform to certain moral standards. Moreover, because, as I noted above, a moral injury can be inflicted by an action even when there is no actual harm done to the agent, a moral injury cannot be identified with the harm inflicted by the wrongful action. Indeed, a moral injury cannot even be identified with the psychological experience of pain following the wrong, since such pain is neither a necessary nor a sufficient condition for the existence of a moral injury. First, it is not necessary because there can be victims who for one reason or another fail to experience such pain but are nonetheless wrongfully treated: for example, an elderly man in failing health who, unbeknownst to him, is having his life savings slowly filched by his financial advisor, or a rape victim whose sense of self-worth is so low that she is unable to recognize the rape as wrong, mistaking it for an action permissible for someone as "low" as her. The first victim fails to recognize the wrong because he fails to recognize the action; the second victim recognizes the action, but fails to understand it was wrong. Nonetheless, both are victims of wrongful action. Second, psychological pain is not a sufficient condition for the existence of moral injury because there are people who experience such pain who are not wrongfully treated. White supremacists "brought low" by the actions of people such as Rosa Parks are, we believe, right to be lowered, because they claimed a position for themselves, relative to others, that we believe is too high; hence we do not take seriously the psychological pain they experience as a result of such actions.

Often, perhaps even usually, our sense of being wronged tracks genuine wrongful treatment, but this is not always so, as these examples demonstrate. Hence these examples show that a moral injury is an "objective" and not a subjective injury. By this I merely mean that the existence of the moral injury does not depend on whether or not the agent *believes* she has received dishonoring treatment.

If moral injury is not harm, and if it is not the psychological pain one might feel after the wrongful treatment, then what is it? In particular, what is it an injury *to*? As I shall explain, it is a particular kind of injury to the person's value. In this section I will argue that wrongful actions that merit retributive punishment carry meanings that effect injuries to a person's value in one of two ways: either they can damage what I will call that person's "realization of his value," or they can damage "the acknowledgement of his value." In my previous presentations of this theory, I have been insufficiently clear about the genuine damage to value that results from a wrongdoing.[24] In what follows, I want to explain more precisely the nature of the two forms of damage to value effected by wrongful actions, distinguishing between the value-denigrating meaning of a wrongful action and the injury that the action inflicts by virtue of its denigrating meaning.

Exactly how one conceives of a wrongdoing as injuring value depends upon the theory of value that one accepts. A Kantian theory of value insists that human beings *never* lose value as ends-in-themselves, no matter what kind of treatment they receive. Hence, it is initially hard to see how this theory of value could generate *any* conception of a wrongful action as an injury to the victim's value. Nonetheless, it can, as I shall now explain.

As I will understand the phrase "Kantian theory of value," it is a generic term, subsuming a number of different species of theories of value. What all of them have in common is the belief that human value is intrinsic, equal, and "permanent" in the sense that our value cannot be degraded

---

[24] In particular, I am responding to Dolinko's worry that I have been too focused on the message of the crime, and not sufficiently interested in the crime itself. See Dolinko, "Some Thoughts about Retributivism," p. 552. It is not merely what the act says, but also what it accomplishes, which I want to explain here and which I see as the target of retribution.

or lowered by any kind of action. However, they differ in regard to what it is about human beings that explains why they are valuable, and they differ in regard to why human value is permanent in this sense. For example, one instance of such a theory (and the likely source of Kant's own views) is the Christian conception of human beings as intrinsically, equally, and permanently valuable insofar as each of us is the child of God, made in His image. Degradation is impossible on this view because nothing that any human being could do to another can remove this value. Indeed, not even killing a human being could do so: death is not understood to end the victim's existence, because the dead are thought to persist in an afterlife. Hence this view posits what I will call "strong permanence," that is, the idea that human value can be neither degraded nor destroyed.

A different Kantian view understands human beings as valuable by virtue of their capacities for rationality and autonomy – but note that to remain Kantian, this view must consider value to be present equally in all of us after a certain threshold of these capacities is reached, and thus not to vary with the extent to which our capacities for rationality and autonomy are fully and differentially realized. This view recognizes that the characteristics that give us value can be damaged or extinguished by an immoral action (e.g., by murdering us or destroying our brains). However, it would hold that if this is done, our status as persons is also destroyed; so although immoral actions could destroy our personhood and thus our value, these actions could not *lower* or degrade our value as long as we remained persons. This view therefore posits "weak permanence," that is, the idea that human value can be destroyed but never degraded by immoral actions: the most these actions can do is to extinguish our personhood, in which case *we* are not lowered by such actions, because we cease to exist. To put it another way, even if we are murdered, that action cannot lower us in value (as if we remained behind in the corpse), but only extinguish that which *was* valuable. So whereas the first Kantian view holds that both degradation and extinction are impossible, the second grants the possibility of the latter but not the former.

In different ways, both sorts of views reject the idea that our human value can be literally degraded for as long as we remain persons. However, both theories allow that there can be the appearance of degradation, which I will call *diminishment*. I will argue that diminishment is the normal result of an immoral action and that which constitutes the moral injury inflicted by a wrongdoing. It is therefore the damage or "loss of value" that wrongdoing inflicts.

To understand what I mean, consider what we might say about the marring of some valuable artistic object.[25] Let us suppose that someone spraypainted over the pages of the Book of Kells. We would be furious and deeply angry about the damage this person had done, and that is because we take the book's value to preclude many kinds of treatment with respect to this object, including anything that would mar the artwork. So our view of the value of this object implies that only certain kinds of treatment are appropriate for it. Let us say therefore that its *value generates certain entitlements*. For as long as the Book of Kells has that value, it has these entitlements, which include being preserved, treated with care, and so forth. (One might also want to call these entitlements "rights," but I shall not pursue here the question of whether this term is appropriate.)

Therefore, someone who intentionally does not give the valuable object that to which it is entitled can be said to flout its value. By flouting it, this person is in effect denying that the object really has that value, because he is denying the entitlements which that value generates. So the person's action has meaning; by marring the object he "says" that the value is not what is being represented. (Suppose an art expert slit the canvas of a painting with his pen knife – those watching would be horrified unless he explained that the painting was a worthless fake.) In this way, the person's actions diminish the value of the object.

Marring valuable objects can do more than merely diminish them; marring can actually decrease their value. However, as I discussed above, Kantian theories of human worth deny that crimes can ever lower human value (although as I noted, one kind of Kantian will admit that such actions can certainly destroy a human being and, thereby, her value). These views therefore insist that only diminishment, and never degradation, can be the result of wrongdoings. They are actions that say, and attempt to represent, the person as having some value less than that which the Kantian theory of value would attribute to them.

Diminishment is an "objective" phenomenon, by which I merely mean (as I noted above) that it is not something that can be identified with any psychological experience of victimization. Instead, it is something that we "read off of" the effects of immoral behavior. As I will now explain, diminishment is effected by the meaning of the immoral behavior, and perhaps also by how others respond to the harm that the behavior may

[25] I will leave aside here the issue of the source of the value of such objects; perhaps they have value only because human beings value them, or perhaps human beings value them because they have intrinsic value.

inflict. And as I will go on to explain, it is diminishment that causes moral injury, in one of two ways.

To see further how diminishment works, let me give a heinous example of it. The example comes from a story told by the modern dancer Bill T. Jones, originally related to him by his mother.[26] In her youth, Jones's mother knew a white farmer who employed a black farmhand and his four sons. When one day the farmhand did something that enraged the farmer, the farmer apprehended him and his four sons, put them in large burlap bags, hung the bags holding the men from a tree, and began burning them. Before he was burned, one of the men asked for a cigar. The farmer answered him by using a knife to slit the bag holding him, cutting off the man's penis, and then sticking it in his mouth, saying "Here, smoke that." The message conveyed by the farmer's behavior in this incident is one that not only denies *all* of the humanity these men possess, *all* of their manhood, and *all* of their rights as sentient creatures, but also any part or feature of them that could be thought to make them worthy of any degree of respect. Even mere objects can be taken by us to have worth; this farmer denied that these men had anything that one should respect. By constructing an event that represented the people he killed as degraded and worthless, burning them to death seemed no more significant than burning a pile of trash. Note how many details of the entire event accomplish this diminishment: not only the killing but also the containment in bags; not only the castration, but the mocking reference to the penis as a cigar. From the Kantian point of view, the difference between the value these people actually had, and the (almost nonexistent) value the farmer represented them as having, is what makes his actions so horrendous.

We can use a Gricean analysis of the meaningfulness of the farmer's various acts to show the variety of ways in which the farmer diminished the farmhands' value. Grice has distinguished four different ways in which conduct can be meaningful.[27] First, there is "natural" meaning, as when we say, "Smoke means fire." Note that this use of 'means' is not really a linguistic one, for what we are really saying is "Smoke is evidence of fire." With respect to behavior, if we said, "The fact that the art expert slit the canvas of that painting means that it is worthless," we would really be saying, "His action is evidence of its worthlessness." Nonetheless, a person

[26] The story was told by Jones on "Great Performances – Dance in America: Bill T. Jones/Arnie Zane & Co." (PBS television broadcast, Feb. 12, 1992).
[27] Grice, "Meaning."

can say or do something as a way of intending a person to draw a certain evidentiary conclusion. In which case, even if the natural meaning is not itself linguistic, it is the object of a linguistic expression. Thus the farmer intended anyone present at the killing of the farmhands to infer from the fact that he was killing them that they were, indeed, worthless. He intended his deed to act as evidence of their lack of value (and *not* merely as symptomatic of his mere belief in their lack of value).

The second Gricean category of meaning is "word" meaning: in any language, there are linguistic conventions defining the meanings of words, and these conventional meanings, in certain contexts, will prevail regardless of what one might intend to say when one uses them. Similarly, certain behaviors have fixed conventional meanings, so that, for example, blowing a raspberry will be taken to convey disrespect in this society, even if one intended it as a compliment.[28] The farmer's treatment of his farmhands used conventionally defined behaviors to convey deep disrespect, not only when he burned them alive, but also when he castrated them.

Yet the farmer used more than just the behavioral conventions at hand in order to diminish the farmhands. Consider that the third Gricean category of "speaker" meaning (or non-natural meaning) refers to occasions when a speaker accomplishes something meaningful not through the use of convention, but by making clear in other ways what it is he intends to convey. To be momentarily at a loss for words in trying to describe what one wants to eat and then pointing to a chocolate bar is to convey meaning through one's intentions; similarly, to attempt to blow a raspberry to convey one's disrespect, but fail in a way that, nonetheless, makes one's intentions clear, is also to convey meaning through one's intentions. The story of the farmer gives examples of this form of meaning in his behavior, insofar as it shows that he made novel uses of conventional behavioral material in order to diminish the farmhands more thoroughly than if he had relied solely on the behavioral conventions themselves. For example, he did not merely kill the men, but burned them alive in bags (as if they were, quite literally, bags of trash); and he did not merely castrate them, but did so in a way that denied that their penises could have had anything to do with their manhood. One might even say that the farmer made metaphoric use of the behavioral conventions of his culture in order to convey his intentions regarding these men's worth.

---

[28] I am indebted to Gary Gleb for the example.

Grice's final category is that of "conversational implicature."[29] To respond to a rude store clerk by acidly thanking him for his help is to convey meaning outside of the conventions attached to one's words. The farmer's cutting off the men's penises and treating them as cigars in response to their requests to smoke was a reaction to them that, while in the form of a civil answer to a request, is about as denigrating to human worth as one could imagine.

However, the meaning of a wrong involves not only the victim's worth, but also the worth of the wrongdoer himself. Consider once again the farmer's murder: we do not merely "read off" from his actions an expression of the farmhands' worthlessness, but also an expression of the farmer's vast superiority relative to them. He represented himself as, quite literally, the master of the men he murdered: he conveyed to them through his actions that he had the power as well as the authority to recognize their worthlessness and to decide their fates to the point of destroying them. His treatment is intended to "mean" (i.e., to be evidence of) his superiority. They are his to own and destroy, and thus no different from any other relatively worthless possession. Our fury at his murderous actions is connected with our disgust at the representation of his own value relative to them. Hence the moral injury inflicted by wrongdoers such as the farmer involves more than the misrepresentation of the victim's value, but also the misrepresentation of their own value.

Thus, a wrongful action that produces moral injury and which merits retributive punishment is an action that has a certain kind of meaning, which I will define as follows:

A person behaves wrongfully in a way that effects a moral injury to another when she treats that person in a way that is precluded by that person's value, and/or by representing him as worth far less that his actual value; or, in other words, when the meaning of her action is such that she *diminishes* him, and by doing so, represents herself as elevated with respect him, thereby according herself a value that she does not have.

The example of the farmer shows that there are two potential "carriers" of diminishment in a wrongdoing: the act itself and the harm (if any) which the act effects. Either (or both) can be the object of our moral anger, by virtue of the way each of them presents the victim and the wrongdoer. Consider first the harm: we will be upset about a harm effected by a natural disaster. However, what makes the harm effected by a wrongdoing

---

[29] Grice, "Logic and Conversation."

"worse" for us, and hence the target of a special kind of anger in us, is the way it constitutes a treatment of the victim that violates the entitlements which that person's value requires other human beings to respect. When a wrongdoing effects a state of affairs in which the victim is unable to secure that to which his value entitles him – where that can include his autonomy, his bodily integrity, the possession of property, and even his life – then insofar as we care about this person's value, we object, perhaps violently, to actions that violate those entitlements (and hence that value).

Simply stated, harms anger us not merely because they cause suffering we have to see in others, but also because we see their inflictions as *violative of the victim's entitlements given her value.* Hence one way in which diminishment accomplished by an immoral action morally injures the victim is that it *damages the realization of her value.* That is, the false message about value carried in the action explains why the victim's entitlements are not respected. Indeed, that false message can be taken to license quite ghastly treatments, as the farmer understood when he killed his farmhands in the most humiliating way possible.

Second, even when a wrong action does not inflict a harm, it angers us simply by virtue of what the action says about the person. We care about what people say by their actions because we care about whether our own value, and the value of others, will continue to be respected in our society. The misrepresentation of value implicit in moral injuries not only violates the entitlements generated by their value, but also threatens to reinforce belief in the wrong theory of value by the community. Our views about human value are more or less secure, and we are more or less committed to them. Fear that we are worth less than we wish (or perhaps less than others think we are worth) is a common human phenomenon, particularly in societies in which non-Kantian inegalitarian theories of worth have gained currency. A value-denying act can therefore be frightening to the victim and others like him insofar as it plays into those fears. Perhaps more importantly, it can encourage the action of similar injuries by people who find appealing the apparent diminishment of the victim and the relative elevation effected by wrongdoing. For many, the longing to be better is a lure to behave in ways that diminish another and elevate oneself. I call this *damage to the acknowledgement of the victim's value.*

So I will define a *moral injury* as *damage to the realization of a victim's value, or damage to the acknowledgement of the victim's value, accomplished through behavior whose meaning is such that the victim is diminished in value.*

The more a wrongdoing inflicts damage to value in either way, the more we object to it. If there is minimal damage, we generally find the act minimally immoral; indeed, we might not even bother to respond to it at all. Merely publishing a book proclaiming that, say, men are better than women, or whites are better than blacks,[30] is to deny value and thereby do something morally offensive, but unless other people respond to the book in some way, that damage is negligible and society does not bother to respond. If people take them seriously, and come to believe these assertions of superiority, the books become much more dangerous, because such beliefs can prompt people to interfere with the entitlements of these "inferiors" (to the point of inciting violent acts against them), and to propagate the view that they are not valuable enough to be accorded these entitlements. In a way, such books morally injure not one individual, but a whole class of individuals, leaving them sitting ducks for treatment lower (perhaps much lower) than that which they deserve. When such literature leads to damage to the realization and/or acknowledgment of some human beings' value, societal action against those who write it may be justified. Think of the damage caused by anti-Semitic Nazi literature in the 1920s and 30s, or consider the prohibition by cities such as Los Angeles of racist or sexist video arcade games in public places, or the argument by feminists such as Catherine MacKinnon for prohibiting pornography not only because of its alleged connection with sexual assault, but also because of the role it plays in encouraging a demeaning view of women.[31] So on this view, not only the actions caused by such books and visual material, but also their own *content*, is morally injurious. Such materials denigrate people not only indirectly, by influencing others to inflict harm on them, but also directly, by representing them as inferior. Let me stress that this morally injurious character might not be sufficient to justify their prohibition, since freedom of speech might be thought to be threatened were such censorship permitted. I will discuss this issue briefly in the last section. My point is that not only acts but also words and pictures can do moral injury to others, and thus be morally wrongful.[32]

---

[30] The examples are from Dolinko, "Some Thoughts about Retributivism."

[31] Catherine Mackinnon, *Toward a Feminist Theory of the State* (Cambridge, Mass.: Harvard University Press, 1989), pp. 195–214; Lewin, "Canada Court Says Pornography Harms Women," *New York Times*, Feb. 28, 1992, B7, col. 3.

[32] Liberals supportive of free speech are reluctant to grant this fact, fearing that to recognize the wrongfulness of certain forms of expression is prima facie cause to license their censorship. This is, however, not true; censorship might be precluded by moral concerns

The reader might object that this account of wrongfulness is successful only for crimes that have as their object the degradation of the victim, such as the farmer's murder, or most examples of rape or sexual harassment. How does it explain the wrongfulness of crimes that do not have degradation as their aim, such as petty theft?

Consider a small, rather mundane act of wrongfulness: sneaking a book out of a university library without checking it out. Someone who commits this act is not doing anything nearly as disrespectful of worth as someone who knifes an innocent passerby to get money. Nonetheless, she has acted in a way that makes it impossible for fellow members of her university to trace the book if they need to take it out, makes her immune from recalls or deadlines, and allows her to "forget" to return it, so that it can become effectively her own book. The message we read from her action is that her needs are so important that, at least in this instance, she regards herself as permitted to inconvenience or harm others in the university community to satisfy her needs; hence, her action means (or is evidence of) the superiority of her needs over those of the rest of the university community. That is, her behavior assumes a conception of her own value that elevates her over others in this situation, and conversely diminishes them relative to herself. However, her action is more than an idle "behavioral remark"; her actions actually *make it the case* that she is able to better satisfy her needs than others, thereby enjoying superior services from the library. She has acted to shape the world so that she gets superior treatment. In this case, it is not only the message, but the actuality of what it expresses, that constitutes the moral injury to others inflicted by her behavior. Thus, those who are injured are rightly angered at both the remark and the actuality; "why should *she* get exclusive enjoyment of the book," they ask, "while the rest of us can't use it at all? Who does she think she is?"

In a way, our objection to her conduct is the same as our objection to the conduct of free riders generally, who elevate themselves over those of us stuck paying the costs for the benefits they take for free. Whereas

more important that the desire to deter the creation of such material, and in any case, an effective retributive response to such material might be consistent with the permissibility of its publication.

Moreover, those who support the prohibition of such material, whether or not they are right, are nonetheless unwise, in my view, to think that the issue of prohibition turns on whether or not such material causes harmful actions: my point here is that even if it does not, such material is already morally injurious because of the fact that it diminishes the value of some human beings.

Herbert Morris thought that we objected to free riders merely because they got something for nothing and we did not,[33] I am arguing that this situation bothers us in a morally significant way because of how it represents them as superior to us – with entitlements to goods and services that we cannot claim. So it is not the fact that they are ahead of us in resources that irks us (after all, many people are, and to object to them simply on those grounds is, at least arguably, a function of our envy rather than our moral sensibility). Rather, we object because we believe they have gotten ahead by means that we "read" as inegalitarian and disrespectful to the rest of us. This suggests, contra Morris, that at least here, distributive fairness is implied by retributive fairness, and not the reverse. I will return to this suggestion later in the chapter.

Some immoral actions are immoral only because of what they express, and not because of any concrete damage they inflict. Think of attempted murder. If the attempt fails but is discovered, the behavior is sufficiently alarming in what it conveys about the intended victim's worth that we seek to answer it with punishment, even though no damage has been done to that person's realization of value in the world (and this is mainly because no harm has been done). As I noted when discussing Grice's second category of meaning, there are some actions, just as there are some words, that are so intrinsically and deeply disrespectful that there is no way anyone could use them intentionally without understanding and intending that deep disrespect. And as I noted when discussing Grice's third category of meaning, there are also many actions – and the harm that results from them – whose meaning is more ambiguous. Here, an investigation of the wrongdoer's intentions and motives is necessary to uncover the existence and nature of disrespect: for example, an air traffic controller's failure to separate aircraft sufficiently to prevent a midair collision might be a function of his inability to handle the demands of his job (in which case, he is merely incompetent); it might be a function of a cavalier and reckless attitude on the job, in which case we are angry at him for failing to appreciate the value of the people whose lives were endangered by his behavior, and thus find him criminally negligent; or it might be a function of a deliberate desire to murder someone on the plane, in which case we condemn him severely for having so little regard not only for the person he wanted to murder, but for those whom he murdered along with his intended victim.

---

[33] See Morris, "Persons and Punishment," and accompanying text.

Although all these wrongful actions are "disrespectful of value," exactly *how* they deny value differ. Yet they all convey – and work to effect – the wrongdoer's superior importance relative to the victim understood as an individual or as a class of individuals.[34] In this sense, the message and the result of the actions of the library thief or the cavalier traffic controller is the same: by virtue of what they have done, they count for more than their fellows. However, *how* they conceive of themselves as "more important," and the nature of the diminished status that their action gives to their victims, can differ radically. The library thief strikes us as departing only mildly from our egalitarian standards: she is only a little more important than others (so she will steal the book, but she would not, say, kill for it). In contrast, the husband who persistently abuses his wife "in order to put her in her place," gives her the sort of treatment standardly given to sentient chattel such as animals, which not only conveys to her that this is all the value she has, but also makes that standing a fact of her everyday life (even if it is also a denial of her true standing as a person). Consider the following description by a former athlete of what he took to be many male athletes' attitudes toward women, which he believed encouraged some of them to engage in rape: "The view is that women are 'its.' ... [T]hat women are objects, that women should be attracted to athletes. There's a male machismo there that they can take what they want and that society will overlook their transgressions."[35] Whereas a wife-beating husband's behavior conveys the idea that his wife is mere chattel, a rapist whose behavior conveys this attitude expresses the idea that women are even lower than chattels – mere "objects" who are there to be used whenever the male feels the need to do so. If he succeeds in raping her, not only is this the message one "reads off of" the rape, more distressingly, the rape is a kind of event which seeks to make that diminished status a reality. She has been used as though she is an object, so she is one, right? Finally, there is the complete diminishment of the victim, of the sort that was accomplished by wrongdoers such as the farmer,

34 Immorality can also go in the other direction; I have argued elsewhere that there are people who respect themselves too little and others too much. Whether a retributive response is appropriate for such people is complicated, and an issue I leave for another day.

35 Rhoden, "Tyson Case May Not Yield Lesson," *New York Times*, Feb. 12, 1992, B13, col. 3 (comment made by Jeffrey Sammons, associate professor of history at New York University and author of *Beyond the Ring: The Role of Boxing in American Society* (Urbana and Chicago: University of Illinois Press, 1990), who tried to explain how Mike Tyson, the former heavyweight boxer, could have come to commit rape).

involving the performance of actions, the infliction of harms, and the overall construction of a severely demeaning "event" that intends to rob a human being of everything that could make him worthy of any sort of respect.

So why do we care about these denials of value? Why should we take moral injuries to be objectionable? These questions have been asked of me by readers of my work, puzzled about why anyone should care so much about the *appearance* of loss of value. Does my Kantian analysis not suggest that we should simply take a Nietzschean approach to wrongdoing, and thus shrug off crimes merely as nuisances with respect to our value, ineffective in what they seek to establish given the permanence and equality of our worth as persons?

This question is actually a bundle of questions. I have defined wrongdoing in an objective way, as behavior that denies the value that a human being has. There is nothing subjective about this definition. So what can the theory tell us about why we subjects do care, or ought to care, about diminishment and the damage to value it effects?

The answer to the "ought" question is straightforward: to be valuable is to be something about which human beings should care, and something *for* which they should care. To witness the value of someone being misrepresented is to witness behavior that ought to violate one's sense of what is appropriate for this person, and prompt a reaction that attempts to stop, and repudiate, that misrepresentation. Of course, that people ought to care about the value of others is no guarantee that they do. The psychological requirements for being able to care in the right way are not something I can pursue here; suffice it to say that if someone is unable to respond to this value at all, we have reason to question their sanity, and perhaps their very humanity. Nor does a Nietzschean attitude on the part of the victim suffice to answer the value denial, because regardless of whether an immoral action shakes a victim's confidence in her worth, if it has damaged the realization or the acknowledgment of her value, it is morally offensive, and the representation of her diminishment becomes unacceptable. I cannot explain that offensiveness by appealing to something else, because it is the foundation of our objection to wrongdoing; it is part of what it means to say that something is valuable that we ought to care about preserving and acknowledging that value. Indeed, a Nietzschean self-confidence is useful not so much as an answer, by itself, to the diminishment accomplished by the wrongdoing, but as a psychological attitude that makes it *easier* for a victim to object to a wrongdoing: consider the way in which many feminists want rape victims to come forward openly to accuse their attackers (and, for example, allow their names to be published), throwing off the mantle of shame and degradation which has traditionally been placed upon rape victims, and thereby becoming more effective in securing the conviction of those who wronged them.

Finally, let me note one other aspect of the way in which the moral injury to victims is objective: the message of the action and the actuality of what it accomplishes is not only something that we understand apart from the victim's reaction to it, but also something that we "read off of" the action regardless of the psychological peculiarities of a wrongdoer's psychology that led him to commit the wrong. For example, a psychologist's explanation of the rapist's behavior might well point to the way in which it arises from a poor sense of self, which the rapist tries to bolster through an action of mastery. However, that explanation is irrelevant to the way in which the action is wrongful; it is the expressive content of the action – in both its commission and in its results – representing the rapist as master and the victim as inferior object, and not the causal story we tell to explain why it was performed, that accounts for its being wrongful. Although there may be times when that causal story is relevant to our determination of the action's expressive content (for example, in the evaluation of the air traffic controller's conduct), nonetheless it is the latter, and not the former, which determines wrongfulness.

As I discuss in the next section, a decision not to punish wrongdoers such as the rapist is also expressive: it communicates to the victim and to the wider society the idea that such treatment, and the status it attributes the victim, are appropriate, and thus, in the case of the rape victim, reinforces the idea that women are objects to be possessed and are "there for the taking." Moreover, if nothing happens to people like the farmer (and indeed, nothing did), we feel a special kind of fury at the thought of what they "got away" with. Indeed, if I asked you, "What ought to be done to such a farmer?" surely you would demand the severest possible infliction of pain that you believe morally justified (and even those who do not favor capital punishment might find themselves wanting to respond, "Kill him").[36] What is it that produces this reaction? Surely it is not elicited

---

[36] In *The Brothers Karamazov*, Dostoyevsky has Ivan Karamazov relate to his brother Alyosha a gruesome story of cruelty and injustice. Although a kind and gentle Christian, Alyosha instinctively responds to the question of what ought to be done to the wrongdoer with the answer "Shoot him!" F. Dostoyevsky, *The Brothers Karamazov*, trans. D. Magarshack (London: Folio Society, 1958), p. 284. Dostoyevsky's aim seems to be to show the reader that the retributive instinct is alive and well in even the most mild-mannered and

in us because we believe that such behavior ought to be deterred: of course we want it deterred, but that goal has nothing to do with our fury at this man that our reaction expresses. Nor does that reaction betray any interest in morally educating or changing him for the better; maybe after some consideration we might agree that these goals are appropriate (so that killing him would be inappropriate), but regardless of whether he can be changed, we want him to pay *severely* for what he did to those men.

What we want, in a word, is retribution. In the next section, I will discuss how retribution is a response to the damage to value implicit in such wrongfulness.

V. Retribution

Traditionally, theorists who have defended retribution have assumed they were defending a theory of punishment. However, I will argue in what follows that retribution includes all sorts of responses to human beings, only some of which are punitive. Moreover, it is a mistake to focus, as philosophers have always done, on the punishment of felons to explain and give examples of retribution because constructing retributive responses for those who commit serious wrongdoings is extremely difficult, and there is good reason to believe that our legal system does not do a very good job of it. Hence, existing punishments in our criminal law may often be poor instances of retribution. I will proceed to explicate retribution by using examples drawn from both inside and outside the criminal law, some of which illustrate nonpunitive retributive responses.

The preceding analysis has isolated the ingredient in wrongful conduct that makes it the sort of conduct for which a retributive response is appropriate: this conduct causes a moral injury, which means that it expresses and does damage to the acknowledgment and realization of the value of the victim. When Mary hit Susan's car, her conduct caused no such injury, nor did the conduct of the shipowner in *Vincent v. Lake Erie Transp. Co.*[37] The same is true of a starving man's theft of food; however much this action may be thought to break legitimate rules arising from the rights of the victim, nonetheless it carries no insult, and therefore should not be punished. In contrast, those who abuse their spouses, murder in

---

generous of us: "So that's the sort of little demon dwelling in your heart," says Ivan to Alyosha. Ibid. Indeed, the cruelty in the story is probably more likely to inflame those who are beneficent to others than those who are selfish.

[37] 109 Minn. 456, 124 N.W. 221 (1910).

rage, or commit acts of theft from greed rather than necessity engage in behavior that we take to be expressive of disrespect for people's worth, and therefore are appropriate candidates for a retributive response.

In short, retribution is a response to a wrong that is intended to vindicate the value of the victim denied by the wrongdoer's action through the construction of an event that not only repudiates the action's message of superiority over the victim but does so in a way that confirms them as equal by virtue of their humanity. What do I mean by "vindicating the value of the victim"? Understanding the nature of the vindication accomplished by a successful retributive response is necessary to understanding what it means to say that a wrongdoer "deserves" punishment. To vindicate the victim, a retributive response must strive first to re-establish the acknowledgment of the victim's worth damaged by the wrongdoing, and second, to repair the damage done to the victim's ability to realize her value.

Re-establishment of the acknowledgment of the victim's worth is normally not accomplished by the mere verbal or written assertion of the equality of worth of wrongdoer and victim. For a judge or jury merely to announce, after reviewing the facts of the farmer's murder of the farmhand and his sons, that he is guilty of murder and that they were his equal in value, is to accomplish virtually nothing. The farmer, by his action, did not just "say" that these men were worthless relative to him, but also sought to *make* them into nothing by fashioning events that purported to establish their extreme degradation. Even if we believe that no such degradation actually took place, to be strung up, castrated, and killed is to suffer severe diminishment. This representation of degradation requires more than just a few idle remarks to deny. When we face actions that not merely express the message that a person is degraded relative to the wrongdoer but also try to establish that degradation, we are morally required to respond by trying to remake the world in a way that denies what the wrongdoer's events have attempted to establish, thereby lowering the wrongdoer, elevating the victim, and annulling the act of diminishment. How does a retributive response do this?

Marc Galanter and David Luban have argued that the theory I have articulated works well as an account of the appropriateness of large punitive damage awards in certain recent tort cases.[38] They note the similarity

---

[38] See M. Galanter and D. Luban, "Poetic Justice: Legal Pluralism and the Jurisprudence of Punitive Damages," *American University Law Review* 42 (1993): 1393–463. Galanter and Luban even speculate than my theory may actually do a better job of justifying punitive damage awards than it does justifying punishment by the criminal justice system.

between the way I describe the aim of retribution and the way a tort historian has described what he takes to be the point of punitive damage awards in tort law over the last several hundred years:

The reported cases from roughly the first quarter of the seventeenth century through the first quarter of the nineteenth century . . . included cases of slander, seduction, assault and battery in humiliating circumstances, criminal conversion, malicious prosecution, illegal intrusion into private dwellings and seizure of private papers, trespass onto private land in an offensive manner, and false imprisonment. *Diverse as they may have been, all of these cases share one common attribute: they involved acts that resulted in affronts to the honor of the victim[s].*[39]

Galanter and Luban note that what was actually said in many of these cases is not only consistent with my theory of retribution but was also said using terms that are quite like my own. For example, in *Grey v. Grant*, the court awarded a punitive award because "the plaintiff [had] been used unlike a gentleman."[40] In *Forde v. Skinner*, the jury was told that if the hair of female paupers was cut off in a poor house against their will "with the malicious intent . . . of 'taking down their pride,' . . . that will be an aggravation, and ought to increase the damages."[41]

Perhaps even more strikingly, Galanter and Luban argue that the punitive damage awards in certain recent American cases, which many have regarded as inexplicably and even grotesquely large, actually make sense as retributive responses to the wrongful behavior of the tort-feasor. Consider, for example, *Grimshaw v. Ford Motor Co.*, in which the family of a boy who had been badly burned in the explosion of a Ford Pinto in which he was riding sued Ford Motor Company.[42] The jury awarded the family $125 million in punitive damages.[43] As Galanter and Luban explain:

The jury arrived at this figure after learning that Ford relied on a study showing that the costs of recalling the Pinto for modification would outweigh the benefits (estimated at $200,000 per burn death avoided and $67,000 per injury avoided) by $100 million; the punitive award consisted of $100 million plus interest.[44]

Galanter and Luban find the jury's action a perfect case of "letting the punishment fit the tort," whereas they regard the judge's reduction of

---

[39] Ibid. (quoting Ellis, "Fairness and Efficiency in the Law of Punitive Damages," *University of Southern California Law Review* 56, no. 1 (1982): 14–15 (emphasis added) (citations omitted)).

[40] Ibid. (citing Grey v. Grant, 95 Etg. Rep. 794, 795 (K.B. 1764)).

[41] Ibid. (citing Forde v. Skitter, 172 Etg. Rep. 6897 (Horsham Assizes 1830)).

[42] 119 Cal. App. 3d 757, 174 Cal. Rptr. 348 (1981).

[43] Ibid. at 771–72, 174 Cal. Rptr. at 358.

[44] Galanter and Luban, "Poetic Justice."

the punitive damage award to $3.5 million as close to unintelligible.[45] They represent the jury's reasoning as follows: Ford's calculations showed contempt for Grimshaw and other human beings who would be affected by the defects of Ford's products; indeed, Ford quite literally understood people to be worth only a price – indeed, a rather low price that was quite easily outweighed by the profits Ford would earn if they did not repair the defect. Without necessarily rejecting cost/benefit analysis altogether, the jury rejected Ford's use of it in this case because of the low valuation Ford's calculations gave to the human beings whose lives or limbs would be saved if the Pinto were recalled.[46] As Galanter and Luban put it,

> Ford had determined Grimshaw's and other customers' prices through the technique of cost/benefit analysis. For this reason, the jury chose to inflict a monetary defeat on Ford that incorporated within it a reference to Ford's own cost/benefit analysis – a defeat that Ford could not help but understand because the jury held up the cost/benefit analysis as a kind of mirror in which we would all recognize the moral truth of the situation. Finally, the jury recognized the particular kind of wickedness displayed in Ford's reluctance to recall the exploding Pintos: it was greed, allowing its decision to be swayed by the sheer magnitude of money. For this reason, taking the amount of money by which Ford was swayed as the measure of heinousness seems especially appropriate.[47]

Using the facts of the case, the jury therefore figured out a way to fashion a defeat for Ford that vindicated the value of the victims of Ford's greed. Ford's sense of the importance of its own profits, as opposed to what it thought to be the rather paltry value of human lives, was denied by the jury's awarding *all* of those profits to one of those victims. The message? People are worth far more than Ford's cost/benefit analysis recognized. Ford's low valuation of the price of a human life surely reflected its belief that its profits were more important than the lives and injuries that would be saved by repairing the vehicle. This behavior therefore conveyed a message of superiority over its potential victims that required countering. That countering was not simply symbolic but quite literal – the jury intended Ford to lose any gain that accrued to it from its offensive attitude and conduct.

[45] Ibid.

[46] Indeed, the *Grimshaw* court acknowledged that in some product liability cases, the defendant *is* allowed a cost/benefit analysis as a defense. See *Grimshaw v. Ford Motor Co.*, 119 Cal. App. 3d 757, 803, 174 Cal. Rptr. 348, 377 (1981) (citing *Barker v. Lull Eng'g Co.*, 20 Cal. 3d 413, 435, 573 P.2d 443, 143 Cal. Rptr. 225 (1978)).

[47] Galanter and Luban, "Poetic Justice."

From a retributive point of view, it is unfortunate that the jury's decision was not allowed to stand. There is an important sense in which Ford "got away" with something, and indeed, by being allowed to keep most of the profits from its decision not to recall the Pinto, effectively established (with the government's help) the superiority of its profits – and, indeed, of itself – over individual consumers of its products. The moral offensiveness of this state of affairs is unchanged by the fact that, in an ideally moral world, Ford's act of elevation, and the profits it was able to enjoy by virtue of it, would not be tolerated.

Retributive responses in the criminal law rarely seem as effective or as well aimed as this jury's decision. Controversies about how to structure criminal punishment are commonplace and often intense, perhaps reflecting how hard it can be for a society to develop retributive responses (rather than hateful reactions) that succeed in vindicating the victim's value without compromising the wrongdoer's value as a person. However, perhaps our society is beginning to do better. For example, I have been told of innovative punishment programs for sex offenders now being used in the United States (for example, Vermont), Canada, and Great Britain,[48] which go some way toward doing both. In such programs, convicted sex offenders undergo a different kind of experience while in prison: in small groups and led by a therapist, they are forced to listen to the words and accusations of rape victims, and they engage in role playing in which they assume the role of the women they raped. Such experiences force them to deal with the feelings of anger, hurt, and frustration that they come to realize their actions have caused others. Experience has shown that many of these men have been victims of sexual assault themselves, usually as children; but whatever part such assault played in their becoming rapists, no sympathy is offered to them, and no respite from the relentless insistence by those who run the small group sessions that they must confront what they did to other human beings, and appreciate how badly their actions affected them. Thus, these programs are intended as an experience in retribution, not rehabilitation. Notwithstanding that fact, these programs seem to have changed many of these men for the better. However, they also have desirable moral results from the victim's standpoint, because the state, in the victim's name, forces the rapist to

[48] For a brief discussion of such a program in Grendon Underwood Prison in England by a feminist lawyer and member of WAR (Women against Rape), see Glasman, "Discussing Rape with Rapists – or Can Men Change?," *University of New South Wales Law Journal* 139 (1989): 969. Such programs can be controversial, and as of this writing, their constitutionality is under attack.

undergo an experience that, even while never denying his own dignity as a person, insists that he experience the rape from the victim's point of view. By doing so, not only does the state confirm the victim's importance, but it also defeats the rapist's claim to mastery by putting him in a position where he must, through his imagination, *become* her, and suffer as if he were her. By making the rapist imaginatively become the victim, the state thereby takes away from him any claim to mastery or superiority over her established by his action.

These programs also illustrate another important feature of my approach to punishment, namely, its denial of the claim that the *lex talionis* (which requires that one inflict as punishment on an offender something like what he did to his victim) is the morally appropriate formula for constructing a retributive punishment. Granted, the theory does insist on proportionality of the punishment with the offense. The more awful the wrong, the larger the purported gulf between wrongdoer and victim, and thus the more substantial and severe the punishment must be in order to defeat the wrongdoer and thereby deny his claim to superiority. If the punishment is too severe, society can wrongfully deny the relative equality of wrongdoer and victim, and thus commit a kind of crime itself. If in the name of the victim, the state is prepared not merely to defeat but also to attempt to degrade the wrongdoer, then its punishment will violate the egalitarian standard of worth that motivates retribution.

This violation is exactly what would frequently occur if the state followed the *lex talionis* in its construction of punishment. Now one can see why people might have thought the *lex talionis* was the right retributive formula: after all, doing to the offender what he did to his victim seems exactly the right way of rendering him the equal of the one he hurt. However, even if there are times when following this formula is appropriate, there are other occasions when the wrongdoer's deed has been so violative of the victim's dignity that doing the same to him would strike us as morally indecent or repulsive. For example, if he tortured or removed body parts of his victim, or threw acid on his victim's face, then doing the same to him would certainly "defeat" him, but in a way that also denied his worth as a human being. The theory I am commending insists that the value of both offender and victim be recognized in a retributive response; to do otherwise is to use the punishment in a hateful attempt to degrade the wrongdoer and represent him as worth less than other human beings. While he may be *morally* worse than others, the Kantian theory of value insists that he is still an end-in-himself, and thus still someone whose value requires respect. I take it to be extremely difficult for a society to fashion retributive punishments for serious felons that simultaneously respect the wrongdoer and defeat him in a way that destroys his claim to mastery. When reflecting on the kind of murderous crime committed by the farmer, it is not obvious to me that capital punishment does not succeed in meeting both criteria, but I shall leave that issue aside for now. What the controversy over capital punishment illustrates is the way in which acceptable forms of retribution are not obvious responses to wrongdoing that we can simply take off some shelf and inflict on wrongdoers. The construction of a retributive response is difficult and may at times require creativity and flexibility on the part of those charged with determining the punishment insofar as it is often difficult to determine how to annul the wrongdoing in the appropriate way (and that difficulty increases if there are some in society who want revenge rather than retribution).[49]

From a retributive point of view, punishments that are too lenient are as bad as (and sometimes worse than) punishments that are too severe. When a serious wrongdoer gets a mere slap on the wrist after performing an act that diminished her victim, the punisher ratifies the view that the victim is indeed the sort of being who is low relative to the wrongdoer. When the American courts, until recently, responded to spousal abusers with light punishment or no punishment at all, they were expressing the view that women were indeed the chattel of their husbands. When the present-day Canadian courts use a sentencing policy that gives certain types of sexual offenders lighter sentences, on average, than those given to people who have been convicted of burglary, they are accepting a view of women that grants them standing similar to – but slightly lower than – mere objects.[50] Moreover, the widespread tolerance in the American South in the past for the sort of treatment meted out by the farmer to his black farmhands demonstrates societal support for the message about relative value which that farmer's act conveyed. Behavior is expressive, and the state's behavior in the face of an act of attempted degradation against a victim is itself something that will either annul or contribute further to the diminishment of the victim.

Who must formulate and inflict the punishment, in order that it work as an effective vindication of the victim's value, and what kinds of denials must the state, through the criminal law, attempt to vindicate? One critic has claimed that under my theory, the state could never carry out

---

49 Like most partisans of retribution, I distinguish it sharply from revenge, which I take to be a response of hate rather than moral vindication. I discuss revenge in Murphy and Hampton, *Forgiveness and Mercy*, pp. 137–38.

50 See generally Lewin, "Canada Court." Many Canadian women have attacked this sentencing policy. Ibid.

punishment because, to establish equality, the victim must carry out the defeat herself, and not rely on someone more powerful than herself to act on her behalf.[51] But this criticism misunderstands both my theory of retribution and the state's role as an agent of retribution. There have always been societies in which people believe that human worth is a function of strength and power, and there are sectors of our own society in which this tenet is held. In such communities, a victim defeated by a stronger opponent would have to fight her own battles to re-establish her worth, since her worth is something that is a feature of the strength she *in fact* manifests. However, on the Kantian view, which undergirds my retributive theory, it is not strength, power, intelligence, or skill that creates worth; it is our bare humanity, something possessed equally by the weakest and the strongest among us. To restore this value, the wrongdoer must be defeated in a way that makes the relative value of victim and wrongdoer apparent. Yet ironically, the victim is often ill suited to deliver the defeat, not only because it will often be the case that he is unable to deliver it (for example, he may be an infant or in some way infirm), but also because he may be unable to deliver it in a way that focuses on what is morally relevant in assessing worth – namely, their common humanity. The attractiveness of the state as the agent for accomplishing retribution (for example, through a jury, judge, or legislative sanction) is that the state is – or at least purports to be – an impartial agent of morality, with greater capacity to recognize the moral facts than any involved individual citizen.

Of course, there are occasions when the state's assumption of its moral impartiality and competence strikes us as ridiculous, even offensive,[52] so that we resist the idea that it should be the agent of retribution. Certainly

---

[51] Dolinko, "Some Thoughts about Retribution," at 553.

[52] Fans of Rex Stout's Nero Wolfe detective series will recall that Wolfe's own acid evaluation of the morality of his state prompts him to encourage the murderers he uncovers to commit suicide in response to what they did – which Wolfe seems to regard as a kind of self-imposed punishment that is morally cleaner than the state's capital punishment. Here the defeat is self-inflicted, but it is no less a defeat for all that, and no less an action that repudiates the wrongdoer's elevation with respect to the victim. Hence, it is an interesting instance of the offender inflicting a retributive response upon himself. Perhaps Wolfe is right that there are often times in which agents other than the state are best suited to inflict the retributive response – perhaps even including the offender himself.

Rather than emphasize the role of the state, many Greek literary artists emphasized other retributive agents. Often nature itself punished. Moreover, "the furies" were perceived as efficient agents of retribution who, as the Sophist Critias put it, attempted the enslavement of "hubris" through their punishments. Mary Mackenzie, *Plato on Punishment* (Berkeley: University of California Press, 1981), p. 109. For more on Greek theories of punishment, see ibid., pp. 106–12.

in our private lives we often inflict – and receive – retributive responses
for the commission of private wrongs. Galanter and Luban give some
clear examples of non-legal retributive practices in our society. Consider,
for example, the following account of a retributive response to some
parking offenders in an urban New York neighborhood:

> One winter we did have that problem with father's parking space being taken,
> because we [have] a large apartment building up there and all the young people
> who live there, of course, most of them don't own shovels but they all own cars
> so, of course, if you've . . . shoveled your spot as soon as you've left they were in it.
> But you know it was nothing for someone to just get behind them and give them
> a shove up into the snowbank. . . . People wouldn't think anything about giving
> them a little nudge.[53]

Here the punishment of the crime fits neatly, and the apartment dweller's
"do it yourself" attitude toward infliction of retributive response seems
both appropriate and effective. We would do well to remember that retribution is neither the exclusive, nor perhaps even the primary, responsibility of the state.

Nonetheless, some crimes are so serious that we cannot imagine any
person or institution sufficing as an adequate agent other than the state.
For example, the offense of the farmer who killed the farmhand and
his sons is so awful that only the state, in its capacity as impartial moral
representative of the entire community, is in a position to send the kind
of profoundly humbling message, and the kind of profoundly humbling
experience, that stands any kind of chance of vindicating the value of the
victims. As Hegel appreciated, the modern state is the citizenry's moral
representative – in the face of pluralism and religious controversy, it is the
only institutional voice of the community's shared moral values. Serious
crimes represent serious attacks on those moral views and, in particular,
on the conception of worth animating those views, and thus the state is the
only institution that can speak and act on behalf of the community against
the diminishment accomplished by the crime. *Which* crimes are the state's
business is, I believe, not a question to which a theory of retribution by
itself can answer; liberals who have particular concerns about preserving
individual liberty in a political environment will answer the question one
way, non-liberals another. There are all sorts of denigrating behaviors and

---

[53] Galanter and Luban, "Poetic Justice" (quoting Thomas-Buckle and Buckle, "Doing unto
Others: Disputes and Dispute Processing in an Urban American Neighborhood," in
R. Tomasic and M. Feeley, eds., *Neighborhood Justice: Assessment of an Emerging Idea* (New
York: Longman, 1982), pp. 78 and 84.

statements to which the modern liberal state, for the sake of preserving freedom, will believe it cannot respond. I have already noted the way even denigrating speech can be a candidate for retribution, and yet the state might want to try to avoid punishing such speech for the sake of preserving liberty. An action can be a candidate for retribution, without being an action that the *state* should punish. Just as there are many ways in which we could morally injure people, there are many different persons or institutions that are possible agents of retribution. It is misleading and naive to try to understand the point of retribution by concentrating only on the traditional crimes and punishments to which the criminal law in modern Western societies has responded, especially given the extent to which all these societies have been unjust (a point to which I will return in the last section of the chapter).

Recognizing how each of us as private citizens acts as an agent of retribution enables us to see perhaps the most surprising aspect of the theory of retribution I have developed, namely, that the retributive response need not be in the form of a punishment to count as retribution. There are many occasions in our private lives when we inflict retribution without inflicting punishment. Among other things, punishment involves inflicting upon a wrongdoer an experience which will, in some way, interfere with his ability to satisfy his desires. Consider the seemingly passive and loving response of "turning the other cheek," which certainly cannot count as punishment so defined. Nonetheless, this sort of response, far from being the opposite of retribution, is actually an instance of it in many circumstances. Consider the following remarks by St. Paul: "[I]f your enemy is hungry, feed him; if he is thirsty, give him drink; for by so doing, you will heap burning coals upon his head."[54] Acting benevolently toward one's enemy cannot be said to be a way of inflicting punishment, as it is defined above. Yet Paul argues that it can be the equivalent of "heaping burning coals on someone's head" – hardly a "nice" thing to do. How does a beneficent response toward an enemy accomplish this? The pain Paul describes comes from the emotions of humiliation and shame, which kindness can evoke in us when we are benefited by those whom we have wronged. Such treatment startles us, prompts us to rethink how our own responses to our benefactor have been so much uglier than our victim's behavior toward us, and (assuming we have a decent conscience) makes us ashamed of what we have done. Through that shame we are humbled. The person we have wronged has defeated us, and robbed us

---

[54] Romans 12:20 (Revised Standard Version).

of our pretense of elevation over him. We are chastened, just as surely as if we had been punished.[55]

Appreciating that retribution can include more than punishment is important in another way. A critic of my view of retribution once asked me, "If we want to vindicate the value of the victim after a wrongdoing, why not simply hold a parade for her? Why do anything to the wrongdoer?" I argued in reply that punishment of the wrongdoer was uniquely suited to do the vindicating, insofar as it created a state of affairs (a *real* state, not a hoped-for moral state) in which the victim was elevated with respect to the wrongdoer.[56] Then David Wasserman pointed out to me at there is a story in the Biblical Book of Esther in which a parade for the victim was indeed used as an effective retributive response to a wrongdoing. In the story, the Persian King Ahasuerus marries the Hebrew woman Esther, whose uncle Mordecai had helped the King in the past to defeat two would-be usurpers of his throne. Mordecai offended one of the King's highest counselors, named Haman, by refusing to show obeisance to him. Haman then decided to destroy not only Mordecai, but also all the Jewish people, and was permitted by the King to construct a plan to do so after Haman convinced him that these people were dangerous and disrespectful of his rule. However, the King began to feel guilty about the treatment Mordecai had received, given Mordecai's previous help to him. So the King decided to honor Mordecai in some way, and asked Haman, "What shall be done to the man whom the king delights to honor?"[57] Assuming that he would be the honoree, Haman said,

For the man whom the king delights to honor, let royal robes be brought, which the king has worn, and the horse which the king has ridden, and on whose head a royal crown is set; and ... (find a servant to) conduct the man on horseback through the open square of the city, proclaiming before him; "Thus shall it be done to the man whom the king delights to honor."[58]

The King agreed to Haman's plan, only the man he honored was Mordecai, and the servant he chose to escort him through the city was Haman. Haman's reaction? Following the parade he "hurried to his house, mourning" and was told by his wife and friends that he had begun to "fall" before Mordecai.[59] Note that the King had not "done" anything to Haman, but

---

55 For another discussion of this point, see Hampton, "An Expressive Theory of Retribution."

56 Murphy and Hampton, *Forgiveness and Mercy*, pp. 124–34.

57 Esther 6:6 (Revised Standard Version).

58 Ibid., 6:7–9.

59 Ibid., 6:12–13.

nonetheless Haman had been brought low by a parade, humbled before the man he had tried to destroy. Moreover, the parade worked in the circumstances not merely to "state" Mordecai's value, but also to *realize* it in the social milieu (Mordecai was genuinely honored by the experience and Haman was placed in the position of his servant) in a way that undercut the elevation Haman had sought over Mordecai – something that Haman well understood. Hence, it was a very successful retributive response – which the story implies was engineered by the God of the Jews (and which ultimately resulted in the King's rescinding the order to kill the Jews).[60] Nonetheless, it is quite unlike anything we would normally recognize as punishment.

What is particularly nice about this retributive response is that it repairs the damage done both to the acknowledgment of the victim's value and to his ability to realize that value. The parade re-established Mordecai's ability to live in conditions in which his entitlements (generated by his value) would be respected, and it re-established the acknowledgment of his value. What often makes it difficult to construct a retributive response is that it is hard to conceive of an event which will do both. Repairing acknowledgment can be much easier than repairing loss of entitlement – particularly if the wrongdoing has resulted in harm that has seriously impaired the victim's capacities in some way. Nonetheless, the demand for a wrongdoer to "make amends" to his victim is a retributive idea, arising from the retributive claim that repairing diminishment requires, among other things, repairing the wrongdoer's damage to the victim's entitlements (generated by her value). A punishment can have built into it actions or services that constitute such amends; otherwise, these amends can be conceived as separate from the punishment, for example, understood as restitution or as a civil remedy, in which case the retributive response would have to be understood as including not only the punishment (which would be primarily concerned with repairing damage to

---

[60] In addition to depicting God as the agent of retribution, stories and myths from around the world portray wrongdoers as brought down by nature. The ubiquity of the theme of "poetic justice" most likely reflects human beings' desire to believe that the power of moral norms is sufficient to prevent nature from allowing a wrongdoer to defy human value for long. That this defiance often appears to succeed is surely part of the reason why human beings have had faith in the existence of God and an afterlife, thereby enabling them to believe that what fails to be put right here will finally be righted by God later. Indeed, these ideas are suggested by Kant as the reason for believing in the idea of immortality. Immanuel Kant, *Critique of Practical Reason*, trans. L. W. Beck (New York: Macmillan, 1956), pp. 126–36.

the acknowledgment of the victim's value), but also these remedies.[61] Tort remedies can therefore function as part of a retributive response, although, as I noted in discussing the case of Mary, the poor driver, they need not do so.[62]

The retributive importance of making amends has, I think, one other implication, namely, that the most common and successful retributive response to wrongdoing – at least of the small-scale variety – is the one that all of us, when we commit a wrong, standardly inflict upon ourselves when we come to understand ourselves as guilty of an offense: it involves an apology followed by the attempt to "make it up" to the one we have hurt. An apology is a way of humbling ourselves in front of the one whose value (and entitlements) we have failed to respect. Such humbling is not easy for us prideful wrongdoers, which is why apologies come hard. But by apologizing, we deny the diminishment of the victim, and our relative elevation, expressed by our wrongful action. And by trying to "make it up" to our victim, we attempt to repair the damage we have done by failing to respect their entitlements. If we are successful, our response annuls the appearance of degradation accomplished by our act, and establishes the right moral relationship between us.

What these reflections show is that retribution is actually a form of compensation to the victim. Whereas tort damages are supposed to be awarded to place the victim in the situation she would have been in had the tort-feasor not acted, retribution is supposed to be inflicted to nullify the wrongdoer's message of superiority over the victim, thus placing the victim in the position she would have been in had the wrongdoer not acted. Hence the real contrast between corrective justice and retributive justice is not that the former is compensatory whereas the latter is not,

---

[61] Indeed, one problem with the jury's retributive response to Ford in the Pinto case is that it would have distributed *all* the punitive damage awards to only one victim of the company's policies, over and above the damages that victim was already due to receive. This strikes us as giving this victim too much, and other victims too little, in the way of amends. See *Grimshaw v. Ford Motor Co.*, 119 Cal. App. 3d 757, 174 Cal. Rptr. 348 (1981).

[62] But might not corrective justice be understood as requiring the correction of harms (understood as interference with or loss of entitlements), not only for "retributive wrongs," but also for wrongs committed by poor drivers such as Mary? Even if Mary did not do anything value-denying when she hit Susan's car, if she indeed respects Mary, and thus respects that to which Mary is entitled, then would not she believe she was morally required to repair those things of Mary's that she harmed by not driving ideally? Corrective justice may simply be one aspect of retributive justice – the only aspect that applies to wrongs such as Mary's, but only one aspect of the retributive response which, say, a wrong such as murder deserves. A discussion of whether this conception of corrective justice is sufficient I leave for another place.

but rather that each compensates a different form of damage. Corrective justice compensates victims for harms, whereas retributive justice compensates victims for moral injuries.[63]

VI. Politics and Punishment

Some have worried that my theory of retribution does not adequately explain the appropriateness of punishment for people who commit crimes who are from impoverished backgrounds, and whose crimes are largely explained by those backgrounds. The theory assumes that the wrongdoing has elevated the wrongdoer relative to the victim, but how can it be that, for example, an inner-city teenager who is from one of society's lowest social rungs could ever be thought to elevate himself by his action, such that punishment could be justified to "lower" him? Isn't he already too low as it is? The question is important, illustrating how difficult it is to apply ideal moral theory to a messy, morally compromised world. Ironically, the theory of retribution I have articulated is actually stronger for its inability to justify neatly the punishment of such a teenager, because the theory also implies that the teenager was himself the victim of wrongdoing insofar as society has treated him in a way that has lowered him (rather dramatically) in value relative to others in his society.

Laws are the product of legislators, and these human beings can come under the influence of those with money and power in ways that result in the construction of social and legal institutions that inflict wrongs in and of themselves – and to which there is, of course, no politically sponsored retributive response. A society easily recognizes, and is prepared to punish, a person who commits armed robbery against someone who is wealthy; it is much less ready to recognize how, say, the racism that animates that society results in the wrongful denial of appropriate opportunities for a child, so that he comes to see armed robbery, and even the mere possession of a gun, not only as a means (one of the few available to him) of making money, but also as a way to elevate himself. To permit children to grow up in situations where they are often in danger, where they often do not get enough to eat, where they are unable to get adequate health care, and where their schools are ineffective or worse, is to permit severe value diminishment. That this is permitted by our

---

[63] I am indebted to Gary Gleb for this way of putting my point.

political system demonstrates that it often pays mere lip service to equality of worth, if it admits it at all.

So of course there is a problem in punishing the inner-city teenager given this theory of retribution – but that is a strength of the theory, because punishing such a person *is* problematic. One cannot straightforwardly endorse the punishment of people whose value-denying acts are causally connected to the value-denying behavior of others toward them. This is not to say that, all things considered, such people should not receive a retributive response; their victims, many of whom might be other inner-city residents, have suffered moral injuries that deserve to be repaired. However, the injuries of those who committed these offenses must also be remembered and repaired. How one fashions a legal system that can accomplish both ends is not easy to conceive. It would be far better if the legal system prevented large-scale diminishment of certain classes of people.

Thus, a considerable advantage of my theory of retribution is that it redefines (and enlarges) who counts as someone who has been wronged. One reason (maybe the most important reason) to create a world that is distributively just is to ensure the mutual respect for value that I have argued is always the goal of retribution. Traditionally, as I discussed above, philosophers such as Morris have tried to use distributive justice to understand the point of retributive justice, but it may be that the former is properly understood and defended only when it is founded on the principles of human worth animating the latter.

Although there are times when political considerations can lead to too little concern for inflicting deserved retributive responses, there are also times when a society is right to put other concerns before retribution. As I understand the point of retribution, all actions that are wrongfully committed in a value-diminishing way are actions that we are obliged to answer with a retributive response, but that obligation is certainly not absolute.[64] This obligation may not be the most important moral obligation in the circumstances. Which wrongful actions should be criminalized, so that they receive a retributive response inflicted by the state, must be a political decision that takes into account other moral obligations the

---

[64] Thus, I am puzzled by Dolinko's attempt to decide whether I regard retribution as rationally justified, or only morally permissible. Dolinko, "Some Thoughts about Retribution," at 550–51. Neither description is appropriate; the infliction of retribution is both morally permissible and a moral obligation, but not an absolute one, so that it can be overridden by other moral obligations that are more important in certain circumstances (for example, the obligation to be merciful).

state ought to consider. For example, a liberal state will believe that even though it has an obligation to respond in a retributive fashion to libel and slander and to a wide variety of racist and sexist literature, it also has an obligation not to threaten freedom of speech, which might occur as a result of such punishment. Hence, the state might sometimes find itself responding to this damaging speech by means of punitive damages in tort law, or it might decide that its moral obligations are such that it is morally precluded from inflicting retribution in any way.

Moreover, legal systems are concerned with punishment not only for the purpose of inflicting retribution on wrongdoers. The moral obligations of states include deterring certain kinds of offenses to promote the well-being of the community. I have argued elsewhere that they also include morally educating the criminal – or at least not inflicting punishment in a way that precludes moral education. These obligations can affect, and sometimes override, the obligation to inflict retributive punishment, causing the state to inflict a punitive response other than the one retribution would recommend. Therefore, nothing I have said on behalf of retribution here should be taken as an argument against the idea that punishment can also justifiably be used as a deterrent, or as a means of moral education,[65] because these other concerns might be, on occasion, more important than retribution.

Finally, let me note one other political implication of this view of retribution. If I am right that morality demands that the state inflict retribution for certain serious moral wrongs, then even the most liberal state will have a moral role to play in the society it governs. It is currently fashionable for many liberals (for example, Rawls) to portray the liberal state as "morally neutral" – one that does not take moral sides as it governs a pluralist society.[66] However, were a state to try to be morally neutral, it would be unable to inflict retributive punishment. The demands of

---

[65] Hence, I now take a pluralist approach to the justification of criminal punishment, whereas I argued for a unitary approach when I supported the moral education theory. I still think moral education of the criminal is one important moral obligation that the state has, and which justifies the infliction of certain kinds of pain in response to a wrongdoing. However, it is not the only reason to punish. Nor do I believe now that it is the main reason. I take retribution to be the primary justification of punishment; but the theory of retribution I have elaborated understands punishment in a way that may often be consistent with and supportive of the goal of moral education.

[66] Much of Rawls's recent work centers around this idea, e.g., Rawls, "The Priority of Right and Ideas of the Good," *Philosophy and Public Affairs* 17, no. 4 (Autumn, 1988): 251–76. See also Nagel, "Moral Conflict and Political Legitimacy," *Philosophy and Public Affairs* 16, no. 3 (Summer 1987): 215–40.

retribution require a legal institution not only to take moral sides, but also to strive to implement a moral world in which people are treated with the respect their value requires.

As I see it, no liberal state would be worth supporting if it did not assume this role. A state that would truly be neutral about morality could not be animated by any conception of its citizens' worth as it punished offenders, and whatever its punishment goals, could not be properly responsive to that which matters most deeply to all of us: our value. What liberal would want to live in such a state? How could an acceptable liberal state be morally neutral in the face of the white farmer's treatment of his farmhands? How could an acceptable liberal state punish burglars more than it punishes sex offenders? Just as an individual's behavior has moral meaning, so too does a state's response to the behavior of its citizens. Liberals should wish not for a morally neutral state, but for a morally reputable and conscientious one that accepts that it has a role to play in ensuring that each of us is accorded the value we ought to have. The old liberals, including Locke, Rousseau, and Jefferson, as well as modern liberals such as Joel Feinberg, have had no trouble with this limited moral conception of the state's role. Nor should we: for how can human autonomy be realized in a society without mutual respect for human worth?[67]

[67] I would like to thank David Dolinko for his critical comments on this project, Peter Arenella for his interest in it, and Gary Gleb for his editorial help during the writing of this chapter.

5

The Common Faith of Liberalism

Early in the introduction of his new book *Political Liberalism*,[1] John Rawls states the problem his book will address: "How is it possible that there may exist over time a stable society of free and equal citizens profoundly divided by reasonable though incompatible religious, philosophical and moral doctrines?" (p. xviii). Rawls appreciates, but rejects, the traditional liberal answer to this question:

Sometimes one hears reference made to the so-called Enlightenment project of finding a philosophical secular doctrine, one founded on reason and yet comprehensive. It would then be suitable to the modern world, so it was thought, now that the religious authority and the faith of Christian ages was alleged no longer dominant. (p. xviii)

Henceforth I will call "Enlightenment liberalism" the view that there exists a secular political conception, that we can find and know to be correct via the use of our reason, which can unify a pluralist society and provide a just and stable foundation for its political life. Such a liberalism is an example of what Rawls calls a "comprehensive moral view" insofar as it makes moral commitments in a number of areas – commitments which it takes to be true and which it claims all persons can understand to be true if they reason correctly.[2]

---

[1] John Rawls, *Political Liberalism* (Cambridge, Mass.: Harvard University Press, 1993). Henceforth all references to this book will appear in the body of the text.
[2] Rawls defined a comprehensive moral view as follows: A moral conception is "comprehensive when it includes conceptions of what is of value in human life, and ideals of personal character, as well as ideals of friendship of familial and associational relationships, and much else that is to inform our conduct, and in the limit to our life as a whole. A conception is fully comprehensive if it covers all recognized values and virtues within one rather

Rawls quite clearly rejects the Enlightenment idea that reason can yield a true comprehensive (and secular) conception of justice that can bind a pluralist society. The problem with Enlightenment Liberalism, on his view, is that it is a partisan doctrine, one among many comprehensive views that members of a society might hold, making it unfit to serve as a unifying conception for such a society. As Rawls sees it: "Holding a political conception as true, and for that reason alone the one suitable basis of public reason, is exclusive, even sectarian, and so likely to foster political division" (p. 129).

Now it is worth pointing out immediately that Rawls is wrong to say that any Enlightenment liberal would regard the truth of a political conception as the *sole* justification for its serving as the basis of public reason; as I shall discuss, such liberals insist not only that a political conception be true, but also that it must be accepted (or consented to) by the people who will be governed by it in order for it to be a legitimate ruling conception in that political society. But he is certainly right that liberals have generally made the truth of a political conception a necessary, albeit not a sufficient, condition of its legitimacy. And their advocacy of their own (often conflicting) views has largely been based on the claim that their views (alone) were true. Rawls worries that these conflicting truth claims only serve to make these liberal theories sectarian, and thus unable to serve as a unifying foundation for a pluralist society.

Therefore he attempts to construct a new kind of liberalism, one that avoids making such divisive truth claims. He calls it "political liberalism," and it is not so much different in content from previous liberal theories as different in *methodology*:

> political liberalism takes for granted not simply pluralism but the fact of reasonable pluralism, and beyond this, it supposes that of the main existing reasonable comprehensive doctrines, some are religious.... The problem of political liberalism is to work out a conception of political justice for a constitutional democratic regime that the plurality of reasonable doctrines – always a feature of the culture of a free democratic regime – might endorse. (p. xviii)

His political liberalism is therefore meant to provide a charter for a pluralist society, formulated so as not to be sectarian or divisive, and accordingly, puts forward central tenets of liberal theory without grounding them in

---

precisely articulated system; whereas a conception is only partially comprehensive when it comprises a number of, but by no means all, nonpolitical values and virtues and is rather loosely articulated" (p. 13). On the basis of this definition, Enlightenment liberalism would seem to qualify only as a partially comprehensive moral doctrine.

partisan (and controversial) philosophical or religious justifications that could not be universally agreed to in a pluralist society.

But despite what Rawls says, is his political liberalism really different from Enlightenment liberalism? Has he really succeeded in formulating a kind of liberalism that is "less" than a comprehensive moral view and genuinely non-sectarian, or has he subtly built into it the reason-based moral commitments that have always been the hallmark of Enlightenment liberals from Jefferson to Mill to liberals of our time? I will argue that a thorough explication of his views reveals that his political liberalism is little different from anything that would count as Enlightenment liberalism. Thus I will be extending the argument I have made in two earlier papers,[3] that Rawls's attempt to build a neutral form of liberalism, that is more than a *modus vivendi* for a democratic society but less than a comprehensive moral conception, ultimately fails. If, as seems to be the case in his new book, Rawls rejects a conception of political stability that is based on a politically expedient (and likely temporary) consensus, he must endorse a conception of liberalism little different from the Enlightenment liberalism he claims to reject.

I. Enlightenment Liberalism

What is Enlightenment liberalism? I shall argue in this section that traditional liberal theories are forms of Enlightenment liberalism, insofar as they are informed by the "Enlightenment conception of reason."

So what is a liberal theory? As I understand this question, it asks us to focus on how liberalism has been understood in the philosophical tradition in the modern world, and does not ask about how the term has been used in the political life of various countries over the years. Although Rawls speaks as if there is *one* traditional comprehensive liberal doctrine in the philosophical tradition, in fact there have been many different liberal theories in the modern political world. Clearly, from the definition of the word, liberals believe in liberty, prompting one philosopher to refer to liberals as "philosophers of freedom."[4] The phrase is felicitous, and yet

---

3 See Jean Hampton, "Should Political Philosophy Be Done without Metaphysics?" *Ethics* 99 (1989): 791–814, and Jean Hampton, "The Moral Commitments of Liberalism," in *The Idea of Democracy*, ed. D. Copp, J. Hampton, and J. Roemer (Cambridge: Cambridge University Press, 1992), pp. 292–313.
4 Maurice Cranston in the entry "Liberalism" in the *Encyclopedia of Philosophy*, ed. Paul Edwards (New York and London: Macmillan and Collier, 1967).

those who are held to be in this tradition have had strikingly different conceptions of what freedom is.

We can distinguish two prominent types of liberalism in terms of how they conceive of liberty: the first conceives of it in Lockean terms, the second conceives of it in more Rousseauian terms.[5] The Lockeans focus on the danger to liberty coming from the power of the state, and thus advocate minimal government and certain liberties (or rights) of subjects (such as habeas corpus and the right of bail); such Lockeans include Montesquieu, Constant, Humboldt, and many of the American revolutionaries. Philosophers such as Joel Feinberg also work within this tradition when they insist that a liberal society can admit only laws sanctioned by the "harm principle" and the "offense principle," which require that the state can interfere only with behavior that either harms, or gives offense, to people other than the person interfered with.[6]

Particularly in the nineteenth century, and particularly in England, Lockean liberals tended to endorse the economic doctrine of laissez-faire; today Locke's descendants are invariably committed to markets, and market-based solutions, both because of their economic efficiency and because, these Lockeans say, markets best realize freedom. This style of liberalism has also been developed into the political position called libertarianism, and in countries such as the United States, has inspired certain "right wing" political parties and movements (although some of these have evolved in ways that make some of them better exemplars of Burkean conservatism, rather than Lockean liberalism).

However, the term 'liberal' is slippery, and particularly in America it is often used in political contexts to refer to the "left wing" Rousseauian opponents of the Lockeans. The Rousseauians focus on the danger to liberty that comes from a society that is distributively unjust and unequal. Those oppressed by poverty, on this view, cannot be said to be free, nor can those suffering from a social system that favors and ranks some over others. Nor does it make sense, on this view, to design a political system

---

[5] Cranston has a particularly nice discussion of different movements of liberalism in ibid.

[6] To be precise, Feinberg's harm principle is "state interference with a citizen's behavior tends to be morally justified when it is reasonably necessary (that is, when there are reasonable grounds for taking it to be necessary as well as effective) to prevent harm or the unreasonable risk of harm to parties other than the person interfered with" (*Harm to Others* (Oxford: Oxford University Press, 1984, p. 11)). And the offense principle sanctions state interference with a citizen's behavior when that behavior gives offense to others in the society (see ibid., p. 13). Feinberg then defines liberalism as "the view that the harm and offense principles, duly clarified and qualified, between them exhaust the class of morally relevant reasons for criminal prohibitions" (ibid., pp. 14–15).

that tries to implement freedom by uncritically trying to maximize the satisfaction of preferences, since preferences are affected by social structures, and can be corrupt, distorted, and damaging to the realization of an individual's autonomy, properly understood. The remedy, according to these liberals, is not a limited but an active state, one that reflects and implements the will of the people who own it, that strives to end poverty and secure equal opportunities for all, that attempts to ensure that the people who develop within it have authentic preferences whose satisfaction will realize their autonomy, and that attempts to create not only a democratic party but also a democratic social culture. Such liberals include certain American and French revolutionaries, certain English thinkers such as T. H. Green and Matthew Arnold, and, in contemporary times, "left wing" thinkers in left-of-center political parties. Whereas the Lockeans emphasize ideas such as freedom of conscience and toleration and tend to think in individualistic terms, the Rousseauian liberals tend to emphasize equality – especially economic equality – and are more collectivist in outlook. Despite their collectivist outlook, however, Rousseauians remain committed to the individual as the basic political unit of political justification. Indeed, Rousseau himself was so concerned about the importance of ensuring each individual's voluntary participation in his political society that he argued against any form of representative government.[7]

Some liberals are noted for wanting to unify both strands of liberal thought. For example, in *Utilitarianism* Mill emphasizes the well-being of the community and the role of the state in securing it, whereas in *On Liberty* he emphasizes the liberty of the individual and the need for the state to stay out of private concerns. But philosophers have been persistently troubled about how mutually consistent Mill's two books finally are, reflecting the fact that it is not at all obvious that Lockean and Rousseauian ideas can be consistently fitted together in one position. In *A Theory of Justice* Rawls tries to fit them together by repudiating Millian utilitarianism, and putting forward two principles that together constitute his conception of justice, the first of which requires each individual to enjoy "the most extensive total system of equal basic liberties compatible with a similar system of liberty for all," and the second of which requires that social and economic inequalities be arranged so that they are to the

[7] See Rousseau's *The Social Contract*, trans. G. D. H. Cole (London: Dent, 1968), esp. pp. 73–80 (III, chs. xi–xv). For discussions of voluntarism in modern liberal theory, see P. Riley, *Will and Political Legitimacy* (Cambridge, Mass.: Harvard University Press, 1982).

greatest benefit of the least advantaged, and attached to offices and positions open to all under conditions of fair equality of opportunity.[8] However, the union of these principles has struck some critics as optimistic;[9] Rawls insists that the first principle is prior to the second; but little is said in *A Theory of Justice* about the tensions and conflicts that many are convinced must exist between policies that pursue individual liberty, as the first principle commands, and policies that pursue economic equality in the way that the second principle requires. And a common libertarian reaction to Rawls's conception of justice is that, if the first principle really is prior to the second, the second has no force, because the implementation of the first principle precludes legislation or policies that would be required to implement the second. Rawls clearly has a conception of what the first principle requires that differs from a libertarian conception, such that its implementation does not jeopardize the pursuit of economic equality, a conception that Rawls's followers have subsequently attempted to make precise.

These differences in their conceptions of freedom and equality affect how various liberals conceive of justice; although all of them agree that a political society should be just, and although all of them agree that the notion of justice must be explicated in terms of the freedom and equality of the citizenry, nonetheless because they have disagreed extensively about how the notions of freedom and equality are to be understood, they have put forward very different conceptions of justice. It is also worth pointing out that their commitments to these ideals generally have not stopped them from acquiescing in, and sometimes even arguing for, the subordination of some kinds of persons to others, in particular, the subordination of women to men. Mill is a notable exception in this regard.

Disagreements among liberals over the meaning of freedom and equality are also associated with differences in the kind of philosophical arguments they have used to provide a foundation for their views. Some liberals are utilitarian and some are contractarian. Some are committed to the centrality and priority of the notion of individual rights, and some believe that the idea that there are natural, non-derivative rights is nonsense and seek to find a better foundation for their liberal views. And some liberal positions are formulated so as to avoid involvement in any of these

---

[8] See John Rawls, *A Theory of Justice* (Cambridge, Mass.: Harvard University Press, 1971), p. 302.

[9] See H. L. A. Hart's article in *Reading Rawls,* ed. N. Daniels (Stanford: Stanford University Press, 1989), and Robert Nozick's criticisms of Rawls in Part II of his *Anarchy, State and Utopia* (New York: Basic Books, 1975).

theoretical debates: for example, Joel Feinberg presents his liberal conception of law as (merely) a middle-level theory,[10] one which describes the extent of state interference in the life of the citizenry, but which does not take a stand on deep foundational questions regarding the source of justification in political theory. Liberal thinking also tends to differ along national lines: for example, the American experience of religious pluralism has produced the doctrine of the separation of church and state as one of the hallmarks of American liberalism, and yet no European democracy has accepted the idea that church and state should be completely separated. What institutions are required to realize the creation of a liberal state is controversial, and connected to the very different historical experiences of Western democracies.

So is there one traditional doctrine of liberalism to which Rawls's views can be compared? There is, but only if "traditional liberalism" is defined as a kind of umbrella theory, which can include a variety of particular liberal philosophies. One might distinguish among the various and competing liberal conceptions of our political life and the liberal "movement" in political philosophy. Or alternatively, we might call traditional liberalism a kind of over-arching "secular political faith," consisting of many rival denominations. As Jeremy Waldron puts it: "The terms 'socialism,' 'conservatism,' and 'liberalism' are like surnames and the theories, principles and parties that share one of these names often do not have much more in common with one another than the members of a widely extended family."[11]

So any account of philosophical liberalism must be formulated so as to be able to accommodate the diversity of views denoted by this label. Some liberals have been reluctant to deal with that diversity, arguing that all forms of (so-called) liberalism that are substantially at odds with their view do not count as 'liberal,' properly speaking. I call these *disowning arguments*; my formulation of traditional theory will try, as far as possible, to avoid such arguments, and seek to determine the common characteristics of all theories whose authors welcome the word 'liberal' as a description of them. Moreover, these common characteristics must be stated in a highly general, imprecise form, in order to take account of the variety of ways in which that form has been concretized in theory. To

---

[10] See Hampton, "Liberalism, Retribution and Criminality," in *Essays in Honor of Joel Feinberg*, ed. J. Coleman and A. Buchanan (Cambridge: Cambridge University Press, 1993).

[11] Jeremy Waldron, "Theoretical Foundations of Liberalism," *Philosophical Quarterly* 37, no. 147 (1987): 127–50.

use Rawls's terminology, liberalism must be stated in terms of "concepts" rather than "conceptions": liberals are, I shall argue, largely united on the issue of what concepts a liberal society should affirm, but they have different conceptions of these concepts.

With these caveats, let me propose that all theories which are properly considered 'liberal' share the following five fundamental commitments:

(1) A commitment to the idea that people in a political society must be free.

As I have already noted, the concept of freedom can be understood in a variety of ways, some highly individualistic, others more collectivist.

(2) A commitment to equality of the people in the political society.

Again, the concept of equality can be understood in a variety of ways, ranging from pure procedural equality for all people, to substantive economic equality.

(3) A commitment to the idea that the state's role must be defined such that it enhances the freedom and equality of the people.

Different liberals will disagree quite severely about how the state best enhances freedom and equality – some maintaining that it can do so only by taking a very minimal role in the society, others maintaining that it must take a very extensive role. Despite this disagreement, all liberals tend to agree on the following three general theses about the state's role and structure.

(3a) The state has the best chance of securing the freedom and equality of its citizenry when it is organized as a democracy.

The idea that democracy is central to the construction of a liberal polity has been largely unchallenged in recent times. And although this commitment to democracy tends to go along with a commitment to certain procedures that a liberal state must follow in its legislative and judicial processes, such as habeas corpus, in general liberals in different liberal societies have disagreed about what procedures and practices best implement the democratic ideal.

(3b) The state can only ensure freedom by pursuing policies that implement toleration and freedom of conscience for all citizens.

As we shall see, for theorists such as Rawls, this is a particularly important feature of liberalism, but again, how toleration and freedom of conscience are best implemented is the subject of controversy (e.g., consider the controversy over the best construction of freedom of speech laws).

> (3c) The state must stay out of the individual's construction of his own life plans – his "conception of the good."

The agreement on this last thesis is, however, matched by controversy over its interpretation. Some liberals believe that when they say this, they are committing the state to a minimal role; others insist that the state's neutrality with respect to life plans will require rather extensive state involvement in the life of the community, for example, in assuring the economic equality necessary in order for individuals to have a free and equal chance to pursue their own conceptions of the good.

The fourth tenet of liberalism is that which focuses on the importance of individual consent in the legitimating of a political society:

> (4) Any political society must be justified to the individuals who live within it, if that society is to be legitimate.[12]

Again, controversy surrounds this tenet: how do we understand the individuals to whom the justification is made? Are they real individuals in the society, or should they be appropriately cleansed of bias, irrationality, and bad reasoning in order for the justification to be morally compelling? What form does the justification take? Does it have to be contractarian in nature, or can a utilitarian argument be responsive to individuals in the right way? And does the justification require that individuals respond with their actual consent, or does the hypothetical consent of their fully rational counterparts suffice? Different liberals have given a variety of answers to these questions.

But all of them construct their answers in such a way that they take them to be justified by reason. Rawls's reference to liberalism of the "Enlightenment" points up this "common faith" in reason that all liberals have had:

> (5) Reason is the tool by which the liberal state governs. Whatever the religious, moral, or metaphysical views of the people, they are expected to deal with one another in the political arena through rational argument and reasonable attitudes, and the legitimating arguments directing at individuals in order to procure their consent must be based on reason.

---

[12] Jeremy Waldron has a very nice discussion of the importance of this idea to the liberal tradition in ibid.

Implicit in this commitment is the idea that reason is common to all human beings – indeed, definitive of what it is to be a human being. But liberals differ on the nature of reason: some have a Kantian conception, others a utilitarian conception, others a rational choice conception. And these different conceptions of reason are associated with different conceptions of how morality, and thus liberal values, are "based on" reason, some of which support moral objectivism, and some of which do not. So there is a great variety of positions on moral metaphysics held by liberals. And that means there are a variety of liberal positions on how we should understand the "truth" of normative prescriptions about our political life. But amidst these differences, all liberals have been committed to the Enlightenment idea that human beings have the rational capacity to grasp the nature of the world – not just the physical world, but also the moral and social world whose truths a legitimate society must respect. Although they disagree about what the rational capacity is, and what truth it reveals, the idea *that we can eventually know the truth through reasoning,* and that this knowledge can enable us to construct a legitimate and well-functioning political society, has been a fundamental liberal belief.

It is this commitment to reason that makes all traditional liberal theories descendants of the Enlightenment. But having said this, I want to be careful to distinguish liberals' general commitment to reason's power to reveal politically relevant truth from any particular conception of how reason informs us of political truth. For example, some liberals have been committed to reason as *superior* to religious belief or revelation, and held the view that religion is mere superstition which good reasoning enables us to overcome. This particular view about reason has not been universally held among liberals; Jefferson, for example, specifically rejects it.[13] By "Enlightenment liberalism" I do not mean a theory that would embrace such a particular view, but rather, a theory that holds there is a "normal faculty" of reasoning "common to the typical theist and the typical atheist" that suffices for working out how our political societies ought to be structured.[14] This latter view is compatible with a host of positions on religion and religious revelation, both hostile and friendly. And it is this latter view, and not any particular stand on the relation between reason and religion, which has been the hallmark of all liberal theory.

---

[13] See Richard Rorty, "The Priority of Democracy to Philosophy," in *The Virginia Statute for Religious Freedom,* ed. M. Peterson and Robert Vaughan (New York: Cambridge University Press, 1988), p. 257, for a discussion of this point.

[14] See ibid.

Note that there is a connection between the liberals' commitment to reason, and their commitment to human beings as free and equal. To maintain that public policy is to be pursued via the use of reason is to be committed to the use of rational argument in the setting of public policy. When you argue with an opponent, as opposed to, say, fighting with him, you seek to win him over to your side not by coercing him, but by asking him to *choose* to accept your position, in view of its rational superiority. Thus you are respecting his autonomy, and rejecting the idea that his views make him inferior to you, and thus subject to coercion by you or by those who hold your views. To be committed to persuading by rational argument is therefore to be committed to respecting the individual, not necessarily as a virtuous person, or as a smart person, or as a person satisfying some normative ideal, but as a human being who, like you, can and should choose what he believes in his life.[15]

Traditional Enlightenment liberalism defined in these deliberately general terms does not qualify as what Rawls terms a fully comprehensive moral doctrine, that is, one that "covers all recognized values and virtues within one rather precisely articulated system" (p. 13); it is too limited and too imprecise in its normative commitments. So is it what he calls a partially comprehensive doctrine, that is, one that "comprises a number of, but by no means all, nonpolitical values and virtues and is rather loosely articulated" (p. 13)? Well, yes and no: No – because there is no single, clearly worked out philosophical doctrine that is denoted by this phrase, but only a set of general, vaguely defined commitments which have been articulated in a variety of ways and which have fostered a variety of concrete political positions, some of them bitterly opposed to one another. Yes – because traditional Enlightenment liberalism is at least unified in support of some moral ideals – in particular, freedom and equality – even if liberals have disagreed about how these moral ideas are to be understood. And there is enough commonality in their understanding of these ideas to unite them in some respects. For example, liberals unite in opposing practices such as slavery, racism, sexism, and anti-Semitism insofar as they all agree that such practices deny freedom and equality and prevent individuals from being able to work out the details of their own lives.

So in seeking to understand Rawls's political liberalism we need to ask not whether it differs in the details from other conceptions of liberalism,

---

[15] I discuss this in "Should Political Philosophy Be Done without Metaphysics?," *Ethics* 99 (1989): 791–814.

because all liberal doctrines will disagree about the details, but whether it repudiates one or more of the five general commitments which have been the hallmark of the liberal movement in modern political theory since the Enlightenment.

II. How "Political" Can Liberalism Be?

How exactly is Rawls's "political" liberalism different from the traditional liberal theories that preceded it? I want to answer this question by considering the extent to which he accepts each of the five defining characteristics of traditional liberalism.

Rawls clearly embraces the fourth tenet of liberalism, which requires that a political regime receive the consent of those subject to it in order to be justified, in his advocacy of what he calls the "Liberal Principle of Legitimacy":

> Our exercise of political power is proper and hence justifiable only when it is exercised in accordance with a constitution the essentials of which all citizens may reasonably be expected to endorse in the light of principles and ideals acceptable to them as reasonable and rational. (p. 217)

Of course Rawls's conception of that which is acceptable to "reasonable and rational" people may be controversial enough to make his particular conception of tenet number four controversial. We shall pursue this point below.

Rawls also embraces the third tenet of liberalism (and its associated theses). *Political Liberalism* clearly endorses democracy as the polity by which a liberal regime should operate, and vigorously defends democratic institutions, and the principle of toleration as implementing the ideals of freedom and equality.

Moreover, Rawls accepts that freedom and equality are the two ruling concepts in a liberal political regime, and thus would seem to endorse the first two tenets of liberalism. But does Rawls's theory commit itself to freedom and equality *in the way* that traditional liberal theories have done? Rawls, I believe, would claim that it does not. Whereas Enlightenment liberalism understands freedom and equality not only as political but also as *moral* values, Rawls says he wants to affirm them merely as "political" values, and avoid endorsing them as part of some kind of comprehensive or partially comprehensive moral view. To say these values are 'political' is to say that they apply to basic political and social institutions, that they can be understood and affirmed independent of comprehensive doctrines of any kind (although they may certainly be supported by such doctrines), and that they have been developed from fundamental intuitive ideas viewed as implicit in the public political culture of the society.

Now all liberals understand freedom and equality as "political" in the first sense, insofar as all of them take it that these values apply to the basic political and social institutions whose structure their theory prescribes. But would they all accept that these values are "political" in the second and third ways described above?

Let us consider, first, whether Rawls is departing from tradition in presenting them independently of any supporting doctrines or comprehensive views. He calls the values of freedom and equality "freestanding" and because they do not need, on his view, to be buttressed by foundational views that will invariably be controversial, he takes it that all citizens in a democratic regime are able to affirm them regardless of the kind of foundational view they happen to like. Thus, with respect to freedom he writes:

I stress that full autonomy is achieved by citizens: it is a political and not an ethical value. By that I mean that it is realized in public life by affirming the political principles of justice and enjoying the protections of the basic rights and liberties; it is also realized by participating in society's public affairs and sharing in its collective self-determination over time. This full autonomy of political life must be distinguished from the ethical values of autonomy and individuality, which may apply to the whole of life, both social and individual, as expressed by the comprehensive liberalisms of Kant and Mill. Justice as fairness emphasizes this contrast; it affirms political autonomy for all but leaves the weight of ethical autonomy to be decided by citizens severally in light of their comprehensive doctrines. (pp. 77–78)

Rawls's original position is also supposed to "model" this political conception of freedom: that is, given the way in which the parties are situated relative to one another, and given the limits on information to which they are subject, they are in a position where they will reason, and act from, fair terms of social cooperation that "they would give to themselves when fairly represented as free and equal persons" (p. 77).

But have not other traditional liberals endorsed freedom as a (more or less) free-standing value, and argued for it in ways that have avoided controversial philosophical or religious commitments? As Rawls notes, his theory takes no stand on the "weight" that autonomy has in some over-arching moral theory, but most liberal theories, particularly those developed in this century, are uninterested in the large project of explaining or describing the extent of human autonomy generally. And while some liberals (e.g., the utilitarians) take care to embed their conception of freedom within a larger theory of morality, many liberals do not. The most striking example of someone who does not is Joel Feinberg, who explicitly says that he is interested in developing a liberal theory of law without having to tackle deep and controversial foundational issues in moral philosophy.

Feinberg's theory is perhaps the best example of a liberalism that embraces the idea that freedom and equality can be "free standing." In explaining his method, Feinberg writes:

> It would be folly to speculate whether the moral theory implicitly in this work is utilitarian, Kantian, Rawlsian, or whatever. I appeal at various places quite unself-consciously, to all the kinds of reasons normally produced in practical discourse, from efficiency and utility to fairness, coherence, and human rights. But I make no effort to derive some of these responses from the others, or to rank them in terms of their degree of basicness. My omission is not due to any principled objections to "deep structure" theories (although I must confess to skeptical inclinations). I do not believe that such an approach is precluded, but only that it is unnecessary. Progress on penultimate questions need not wait for solutions to the ultimate ones.[16]

Note the last sentence: Feinberg believes that he can still argue for these values even if he does not embed them in a "deep structure" theory, and that he can still arrive at a conception of them, and their application to political structures, that is true – or at least on the way to being true (we can make "progress" on the questions of freedom and the law, he writes).

Rawls's use of the term 'political' to describe his methodology gives the impression that it is not like Feinberg's method which, even if it eschews foundational theorizing, still proceeds by way of philosophical argumentation and the search for moral truth. So how is it different?

Some might contend that it is different insofar as Rawls appeals to particular conceptions of freedom and equality not as "moral ideas" necessary to developing a particular political conception of justice, but as ideas which, as it happens, are accepted in modern democratic regimes. On this view, these ideals are assumed as conventional elements of the regimes in which we live, and are therefore useful starting points for the development of a stable unifying conception of justice. In previous papers, Rawls has certainly suggested this strategy as a way to explain his "political" methodology, and as a way to distance himself from any

---

[16] Joel Feinberg, *The Moral Limits of the Criminal Law*, vol. 1: *Harm to Others* (Oxford: Oxford University Press, 1984), pp. 17–18.

partially comprehensive moral view.[17] But this strategy is not defended in his book, and there is every indication that Rawls rejects it, for two important reasons.

First, even if it were true that everyone in these regimes just happened to accept the Rawlsian understanding of these ideals, nonetheless assuming them because they happen to be accepted is no way to generate a theory of *justice* for a pluralist society. Such a foundation makes the ideals a mere *modus vivendi*, a politically convenient starting point in our time, but one that may be inappropriate for other political societies, and for our political society in years to come when and if new ideals replace these ones. Rawls speaks as if he wants a permanent and "just" solution to the problem of pluralism he introduces at the start of the book; hence he must reject all *modus vivendi* strategies, which are merely politically expedient, temporary, and contingent.

Second, it is strikingly implausible to claim not merely that freedom and equality are accepted features of our democratic regimes, but also that *the Rawlsian conceptions* of these ideas are commonly accepted in all these regimes. Rawls does not merely embrace the concepts of freedom and equality, he also interprets and develops these concepts into particular conceptions. For example, the original position, on his view, is supposed to model freedom, but that position can model only a certain *conception* of autonomy, that is, one that people realize when they act from principles that they "give to themselves when fairly represented as free and equal persons" (p. 77). There is a puzzle here: what is the notion of "free" that describes the original position of parties, who choose the principles, action from which realizes full autonomy? Rawls says that it is the same notion as full autonomy, and is "modeled by how the original position is set up" (p. 78). Earlier in the book, Rawls attempts to give a sense of what this fundamental notion of "freedom" is, which generates the "reasonable conditions" operating in the original position model:

The basic idea is that in virtue of their two moral powers (a capacity for a sense of justice and for a conception of the good) and the powers of reason (of judgment, thought, and inference connected with these powers), persons are free. (p. 19)

While this is not a detailed or robust notion of freedom, nonetheless because it is a conception that makes reference to "moral powers," it presupposes a certain understanding of human beings, and is at least a

---

[17] See especially Rawls's "Justice as Fairness: Political Not Metaphysical," *Philosophy and Public Affairs* 14 (1985): 223–51.

minimal theory of human agency. Those who take issue with the idea that we have both these moral powers will take issue with Rawls's conception of freedom. For example, Hobbesians will likely reject it, given that it presupposes people have a "capacity for a sense of justice" of the sort that Hobbes explicitly denies that any of us has.

So Rawls's notion of full autonomy is particular – and not universally accepted. That point is perhaps even more clearly made by noting the fact that it is a notion that is used in a certain kind of contractarian model. Recall that full autonomy is realized only by acting from the principles of justice that are justified by this contractarian model, but this means that it is clearly at odds with a variety of political conceptions, including not only utilitarianism but also libertarianism, neither of which can be justified by that model. So, in the eyes of utilitarians and libertarians, Rawls's conception of freedom is not universally assumed in Western political societies (in which these competing liberal conceptions persist), and thus his advocacy of that conception is (of necessity) sectarian. I do not wish to criticize Rawls's conception of political autonomy, because I admit to liking it better than its theoretical rivals. The point, however, is that like all liberals, Rawls not only advocates "freedom," but gives it a particular conceptual development. Indeed, he *must* do so in order to put forward his liberal political theory – the word is vague, overly general, and of little use unless it is filled out at least to some degree. Participation in the liberal movement has always meant developing a particular conception of this fundamental ideal, and liberals have differed about the details of its development. Rawls is clearly siding with liberals such as Feinberg, who believe that for political purposes, a fairly narrow development of freedom is sufficient. But he is just as committed as Feinberg or any other liberal to developing a particular interpretation of it, and to do so he must take issue with those in his society who disagree with that particular conception. Nor can he label illiberal all those who disagree with his interpretation: his various opponents are not incorrectly classed as liberals because they hold views at odds with his views, although Rawls can certainly argue that his views are better articulations of the ideals of liberalism than theirs.

Rawls not only interprets the concept of freedom but also uses certain arguments to develop and defend it. Thus, for example, he explicates autonomy in terms of human beings' moral sense and moral capacity. But this means he takes at least a minimal stand on the nature of human agency in order to develop his conception of freedom. So even if he tries as far as possible to eschew foundational theorizing in his development of his conception of freedom (and his contractarian tendencies suggest that he succeeds less well in this regard than someone such as Feinberg), nonetheless he must still take a stand on some non-political moral and philosophical issues in order to develop that concentration. And in this regard his methodology is no different from that of many other traditional liberals.

The story is the same with respect to equality. Rawls says he is appealing to "the fundamental idea of equality as found in the public political culture of a democratic society" (p. 79), and he fleshes out that idea by saying that "having these powers [i.e., the two moral powers referred to above – having a capacity for a sense of justice and a conception of the good] to the requisite minimum degree to be fully cooperating members of the society makes persons equal" (p. 19). But again, insofar as attributing these powers to people is taking a moral stand with which some philosophers have disagreed, the Rawlsian conception of equality that presupposes them is particular and partisan. And again, the use of this conception within a contractarian argumentative model underlines the fact, for no utilitarian is going to accept that the utilitarian notion of free and equal could receive such a modeling, and hence will reject a conception of free and equal that can. Even certain egalitarians will have problems with Rawls's conception of equality, insofar as Rawls says it "recognizes that some persons have special traits and abilities that qualify them for offices of greater responsibility with their attendant rewards" (p. 80). The implication of this sentence is that the "attendant rewards" are greater for these people, given their greater responsibilities, and there have been many egalitarians who have resisted the "recognition" of the necessity of such greater rewards.

The preceding arguments would seem to show that Rawls's brand of liberalism is little different in its general outlines from any other liberal theory. However, I believe Rawls would reply to these arguments by maintaining that they missed the way in which his reasoning supporting his conceptions of freedom and equality is different from traditional liberal reasoning. And this brings us to the tenet of liberalism that Rawls really does seem to reject, namely the fifth tenet, that is, the commitment to an Enlightenment conception of reason that will (eventually) reveal to us the "truth" about moral matters relevant to our political life. Despite his commitment to the free-standing nature of freedom and equality, Feinberg is clearly committed to this conception of reason, insofar as it is reason, so understood, that helps us to understand and apply (or at least helps us to make progress on understanding and applying) these concepts. In this sense, Feinberg is like any traditional Enlightenment liberal in treating reason as the discloser of universal moral truth, and hence the vehicle through which citizens of a liberal society should seek to get across to the nature of freedom, equality, and justice.[18] Even John Dewey, whose views in political philosophy Rorty compares to those of Rawls,[19] sees reason as that by which we pursue that component of moral reality that is politically relevant, although Dewey regards reason not as something that readily delivers up eternal moral verities but instead as a faculty that works within the context of certain traditions and accepted beliefs within society.[20] Dewey prefers to use the term 'social intelligence' rather than 'reason,'[21] insofar as the former term more than the latter is inherently involved in action and better incorporates emotion: "There is such a thing as passionate intelligence, as ardor in behalf of light shining into the murky places of social existence, and as zeal for its refreshing and purifying effect."[22] He elaborates on the idea of social intelligence as follows:

There is the technical skill with which to initiate a campaign for social health and sanity analogous to that made in behalf of physical public health. Human beings have impulses toward affection, compassion and justice, equality and freedom. It remains to weld all these things together.[23]

Note that Dewey's belief in this "social intelligence" presupposes that there are some moral values, relevant to social and political life, which we pursue via this intelligence, in particular, the nature of justice and equity. Social health is like physical health for Dewey: there are techniques for securing both that we can know and put into effect if we use our intelligence effectively. As it happens, Dewey thinks that belief in the supernatural actually impedes the development and use of this secular social intelligence (so that he is implicitly committed to the idea that there are better and worse ways of using it to attain social health). Of course religious liberals will claim the opposite, insisting that certain kinds of religious beliefs actually encourage and support the development of social intelligence. But all traditional liberals, no matter what their

---

[18] For a discussion of this conception of reason, see Rorty, "The Priority of Democracy to Philosophy," pp. 262 and 268.

[19] See ibid.

[20] John Dewey, *A Common Faith* (New Haven: Yale University Press, 1934).

[21] Ibid., p. 76.

[22] Ibid., p. 79.

[23] Ibid., p. 81.

religious views, will agree with Dewey that this social intelligence exists, and that its use in the society is part of the common faith that binds all factions in a liberal democracy.

How does Rawls's idea of "public reason" differ from the traditional Enlightenment notion of reason as that by which we pursue politically relevant moral truth?

Like all traditional liberals, Rawls makes public reason something that is common to all members of the society, no matter what their philosophical or religious beliefs. We all have "similar powers of thought and judgment," and we all "draw inferences, weigh evidence, and balance competing considerations" (p. 55). Moreover, Rawls says this reasoning is not merely common, but also public, in three ways:

as the reason of citizens as such, it is the reason of the public; its subject is the good of the public and matters of fundamental justice; and its nature and content are public, being given by the ideals and principles expressed by society's conception of political justice, and conducted open to view on that basis. (p. 213)

It is also the reason used in adjudication by courts (particularly in any supreme court: see pp. 231–40), and in legislative arguments (pp. 216–18). More generally, it is the reason of equal citizens (p. 214) committed to respecting each other. So like all traditional liberals, Rawls identifies a reason implicit in liberal society that is used to justify, debate, and decide political issues, no matter what moral or religious views those involved may have.

However, whereas traditional liberals generally treat reason as a form of thinking – a capacity or ability – common to all human beings and that by which we seek out the truth, Rawls treats it as something that is *constructed* out of commonly accepted values. Public reason involves appeal to *reasons,* that have three characteristics: first, these reasons are concerned with the good of the public; second, these reasons are ones all citizens appeal to in the course of political argumentation; and third, the nature and content of these reasons is fully public (see p. 213). The implication of Rawls's discussion is that such reasons are commonly accepted because there is an overlapping consensus on them, whereas traditional liberals assume that the reasons to which people appeal in political argumentation are commonly accepted because reasoning has shown them to be "right." A liberal society, says Rawls, needs "a conception of justice that may be shared by citizens as a basis of reasoned, informed, and willing political agreement" (p. 9). And once constructed, such a conception "expresses their shared and public political reason" (p. 9). But even though it is constructed out of the beliefs of the citizenry, this public reason is vigorously non-partisan:

> to attain such a shared reason, the conception of justice should be, as far as possible, independent of the opposing and conflicting philosophical and religious doctrines that citizens affirm. In formulating such a conception, political liberalism applies the principle of toleration to philosophy itself. (pp. 9–10)

So on Rawls's view, liberals are not supposed to say to one another, "It is a moral fact that x, therefore we must have policy y." Instead, they are supposed to work with one another to develop an overlapping consensus, accepting that reasoning yields plural results, and looking for political values and policies that all of them, despite their different starting points and moral views, can accept. And Rawls notes that the public reason they develop is unlikely to be some simple unitary doctrine, fixed for all time, but fluid and changeable in virtue of the ongoing public debates among the citizenry in such societies (see p. 16).

So how should Enlightenment liberals react to Rawls's notion of public reason? I see no reason why they should not accept it as long as it is added to, and not substituted for, their conception of reason as a mode of access to politically relevant normative truth, since the two notions are thoroughly compatible. Liberals can, and I believe should, accept the idea that citizens in a liberal society must work out a conception of political reasons to which every person appeals in the course of participating in public political life. Even if they believe that human reason is, say, Kantian in nature, liberals need not believe that the access it gives us to normative reality is either immediate or clear. Hence, insofar as moral reality is difficult to discern (just as difficult as, and perhaps more difficult than, the physical reality which scientists strive to understand), liberals can recognize that the citizenry in a liberal society have to work out, via discussion and debate, the ground rules and the normative commonalities that are necessary for the construction of policy and that may, in and of themselves, further progress in understanding and attaining social justice. Arguably, the American Constitution is an attempt to make explicit such ground rules and normative commonalities for American society. The American experience has surely influenced Rawls here.[24]

But traditional Enlightenment liberals will still believe that the citizenry of a liberal society must not be content merely with the construction

[24] This has been noted by Stuart Hampshire, "Liberalism: The New Twist," *New York Review of Books* 40, no. 14 (August 12, 1993).

of some kind of consensus on shared values; they will insist that through their reasoning with one another citizens can make progress toward the normative truth about the structure of our political and social life. Is this what Rawls repudiates?

III. Rawls's Reliance on Reason

Thus far it would appear that the difference between Rawls and the Enlightenment liberals is that Rawls rests content with public reason, whereas Enlightenment liberals insist on the possibility of reasoning toward the truth about normative matters relative to politics. However, in this section I will show that the Enlightenment notion of reason appears in Rawls's theory after all.

Consider his persistent use, throughout *Political Liberalism*, of the word 'reasonable.' Given his conception of public reason, one would think that the term 'reasonable' functions as an adjective to commend or designate those ideas or policies which are consistent with or follow from public reason, understood as an overlapping consensus constructed by the citizenry. And yet this cannot be right, because the overlapping consensus is supposed to be developed out of (only) those comprehensive views that are *reasonable*; hence the notion of the reasonable is conceptually prior to the notion of an overlapping consensus, and thus to the notion of public reason. Moreover, Rawls continually talks as if there is a *fact of the matter* about what is reasonable and what is not. This is most obvious in his presentation of what he calls the "burdens of judgment" argument:

The idea of reasonable disagreement involves an account of the sources, or causes, of disagreement between reasonable persons so defined. These sources I refer to as the burdens of judgment. The account of these burdens must be such that it is fully compatible with, and so does not impugn, the reasonableness of those who disagree. What, then, goes wrong? An explanation of the right kind is that the sources of reasonable disagreement – the burdens of judgment – among reasonable persons are the many hazards involved in the correct (and conscientious) exercise of our powers of reason and judgment in the ordinary course of political life. (pp. 55–56)

Rawls goes on to detail these "hazards" among which he does *not* include such things as prejudice or bias, but only "reasonable" sources of divergent views. For example, he notes that "in a modern society with its numerous offices and positions, its various divisions of labor, its many social groups and their ethnic variety, citizens' total experiences are disparate enough for their judgments to diverge, at least to some degree, on many if not most cases of any significant complexity" (p. 57). He insists, "It is unrealistic – or worse, it arouses mutual suspicion and hostility – to suppose that all our differences are rooted solely in ignorance and perversity, or else in the rivalries of power, status or economic gain" (p. 58). So fully reasonable people will inevitably disagree. *And, he concludes that this fact is itself something that all reasonable persons must recognize.* Those who do not, and who insist that only their point of view is right, are unreasonable. The burdens of judgment is therefore, on Rawls's view, one of the foundations of the democratic ideal of tolerance:

> reasonable persons see that the burdens of judgment set limits on what can be reasonably justified to others, *and so* they endorse some form of liberty to conscience and freedom of thought. It is unreasonable for us to use political power, should we possess it, or share it with others, to repress comprehensive views that are not unreasonable. (p. 61, emphasis added)

These passages raise a myriad of questions, but I want to focus on three here.

First, note the fact that Rawls believes there is an argument, relative to the nature of the social structure in which he believes we should live, that has a conclusion no reasonable person could doubt. This undeniable bit of reasoning goes as follows:

(1) There are (ineliminable) sources of disagreement in moral, philosophical, religious, and political matters among reasonable (and conscientious) people that are not the product of bad reasoning, bias, prejudice, etc. These include differences in weighting of values, and differences in experiences that make certain views or conclusions more plausible to some than to others.

(2) These sources of disagreement can result in fully reasonable people reasoning "correctly" and yet reaching different conclusions.

(3) Therefore, reasonable people who reason correctly can reach more than one conclusion on moral, philosophical, religious, and political matters. (The results of good reasoning in these areas are plural.)

(4) And therefore, a political society must be so constructed that it is tolerant of the differing views of such responsible people.

So the reasonableness of disagreement, and the policy of political toleration, given certain ineliminable features of human life, are, on Rawls's view, conclusions of an argument that must be accepted by reasonable people.

But note this means that although the results of reasoning are often plural, they are not so *here*. Conclusions (3) and (4) are taken by Rawls to be *right* – which is why he says that reasonable people cannot deny them. It is not that people in contemporary societies happen to think they are right, nor that they are conclusions which are somehow the product of some kind of consensus in society; instead they are the conclusions of a bit of reasoning that Rawls believes is undeniable. But this means that, in his burdens of judgment argument, Rawls is relying on reason, in Enlightenment fashion, to yield moral truth, at least in this rather restricted area. So although it seems as if, by using the word 'reasonable,' Rawls is distancing himself from endorsing the idea that any moral truth relevant to political matters is attainable, the preceding passages show that this is not so. What Rawls is really saying is this: we can't pin down or "know" with any certainty the "facts" regarding many, perhaps most normative notions, such as justice. But we *can* know some normative facts about how a political structure ought to work: and we know them *indirectly*, by virtue of knowing something about what is, and is not, 'reasonable.'

This means that the distance between Rawls and traditional liberals is ultimately small: both accept that good liberals should recognize that there is better and worse reasoning, that good reasoners can differ in the conclusions they draw, that this last fact is supportive of policies of toleration, and that good reasoning can lead us to some conclusions which are indisputable. They differ, perhaps, in how often good reasoning can yield such indisputable conclusions, but even Rawls acknowledges the power of reasoning to yield truth in some normative matters relevant to our political life, *truths that all people must recognize no matter what their moral, religious, or philosophical views.*

Second, throughout the discussion of the burdens of reason argument, Rawls assumes there is a difference between good reasoning and bad; for example, he is at pains to resist the idea that all disagreement is a product of, say, self-interest or prejudice, each of which distorts or perverts the reasoning process. So there is a fact of the matter, for Rawls, about what counts as good reasoning and what counts as bad, or distorted, or biased reasoning. And note that in the passage above, Rawls assumes good reasoning is something that we rely on in order to construct an overlapping consensus; it is not itself the product of such a consensus. Were it the latter, then presumably any view held by a significant percentage of the population would have to be included in the construction of that consensus, and hence would have to be involved in the definition of what counts as political reasons in this society. But Rawls wishes, understandably, to avoid including "unreasonable" views in that consensus, in which case, like any traditional liberal, he is committed to thinking that there is such a thing as good reasoning which is sufficiently recognizable to us that it can form a common starting point even for a highly pluralist people.

Third, there are some suppressed steps in the burdens of judgment argument that, once scrutinized, make the argument little different from traditional liberal defenses of political toleration. In that argument, Rawls says that because the conclusions of reason are invariably plural, it is unreasonable for a social system to repress them. But why? Since most of the human beings who have walked this planet in the last few thousand years have believed otherwise, the conclusion is neither inevitable nor obvious. For example, Hobbes certainly accepted whole-heartedly the inevitability of disagreement among rational human beings on a wide variety of topics, but never considered – and would have derisively dismissed – the idea that, as a result, a political society should be tolerant of all reasonable views! So on what basis can Rawls argue that reasonable disagreement mandates toleration?

Consider the following three (mutually consistent) ways of linking the fact of reasonable disagreement with the political practice of toleration:[25]

(1) The fact of reasonable disagreement shows that morality is complicated, and that some moral theories grasp some aspects of it better than others, which means that a political society must allow many views in order that the full extent of morality can be pursued and understood;

(2) The fact of reasonable disagreement shows that we must be epistemically humble, as Mill has argued, and hence refrain from suppressing views we cannot be sure are not right;

(3) The fact of reasonable disagreement is an intrinsically good thing, because it is a sign of a society of individuals reasoning independently and freely via an uncoerced conscience, as Jefferson has argued.

Any of these three views is a way to make the link between reasonable disagreement and toleration, and could be used in an argument to counter the views of opponents such as Hobbes (although the tone of Rawls's discussion is most suggestive of (2)). So if Rawls embraced any or all of

---

[25] These ways of formulating them have been suggested by Timothy Jackson, "To Bedlam and Part Way Back: John Rawls and Christian Justice," *Faith and Philosophy* 8, no. 4 (Oct. 1991): 423–47.

them, he would explain exactly *why* reasonable people who recognize the plural results of good reasoning also support political toleration. But these three views are the stock in trade of traditional liberals. Each of them has been used by liberals to justify (rationally) the political practice of toleration. So if he used any of these three views to flesh out his burdens of judgment argument Rawls will have given us nothing to justify the political practice of toleration that is different from, or more "political" than, any argument traditionally used by a liberal. Nor do I see any "new" distinctively Rawlsian argument in the text of his book that would make the connection between the plural results of reasoning and the policy of toleration.

Suppose Rawls were to reply that his "political" liberalism accepts any of these arguments – indeed, that it refuses to "take sides" by embracing any one of them, and thus allows liberals with different views about the nature of human beings and moral truth to opt for any of these different ways of linking the plural results of good reasoning to the political policy of toleration.[26] But this reply will not work. Consider that Rawls cannot support just *any* way of making this link: insofar as he accepts that there are good and bad ways of reasoning, he must accept that there are good and bad ways of arguing for political toleration from the burdens of judgment argument. So he must be committed only to "good" arguments for this conclusion, and to that extent he is forced to "take sides" and oppose any argument for this policy that does not pass rational muster. The other side of this coin is that he must commit himself to regarding certain arguments for this conclusion as "good" or "reasonable," and presumably that includes any of the three arguments above. However, even this latter commitment is not enough if he is going to be able to mount an argument against a Hobbesian's claim that only the policy of intolerance follows from the plurality of reasonable disagreement. Even if the results of good reasoning are often plural, Rawls must believe that the Hobbesian has made a mistake here. But if that is so, Rawls must produce one or more arguments for the policy of toleration that are undeniable by any reasonable person, and that means explicitly taking a stand on the link between reasonable disagreement and political toleration.

Surely Rawls is not advocating a liberal methodology that is distinctive only insofar as it fails to make explicit crucial components of the arguments for liberal political policies in order to avoid appearing partisan. Such a methodology produces only the most anaemic and

---

[26] This counterargument was suggested to me by Joshua Cohen.

unconvincing liberal theory – if it can be said to generate a theory at all. As we have seen, like any philosopher, liberal or otherwise, Rawls tries to win adherents for his liberal political theory through rational argument. But this means he is as much reliant on good reasoning as the discloser of politically relevant truth as any other heir of the Enlightenment.

IV. What Counts as "Reasonable"?

Rawls's theory may still strike some readers as both different from, and better than, traditional Enlightenment liberalism because his insistence on the recognition of plural results of good reasoning seems to allow more conceptual room for disagreement and discussion in a liberal regime than the traditional liberal's conception of reason. Indeed, Rawls certainly appears to believe that his way of thinking about liberalism is less sectarian, and more truly appreciative of the diversity of views in a liberal society, than that of his Enlightenment predecessors. But in this section I want to argue that this is not so; indeed, I believe there is something that is illiberal in Rawls's use of the term 'reasonable' in certain contexts.

Political unity is purchased in a Rawlsian state committed to political liberalism via an overlapping consensus on substantive matters, where those who participate in this agreement are only those whose views are 'reasonable.' The notion of the reasonable therefore acts as a standard that views must meet in order to be included in the consensus. The burdens of judgment argument would seem to suggest that the 'reasonableness' standard is quite broad, and yet there are places in the book that suggest the standard is actually much narrower, and therefore harder to meet.

Consider an interesting footnote in the book on the issue of abortion policy in a liberal society. I will quote rather extensively from it:

consider the troubled question of abortion. Suppose . . . that we consider the question in terms of these three important political values: the due respect for human life, the ordered reproduction of political society over time, including the family in some form, and finally the equality of women as equal citizens. (There are, of course, other important political values besides these.) Now I believe any reasonable balance of these values will give a woman a duly qualified right to decide whether or not to end her pregnancy during the first trimester. The reason for this is that at this early stage of pregnancy the political value of the equality of women is overriding, and this right is required to give it substance and force. Other political values, if tallied in, would not, I think, affect this conclusion . . . any comprehensive doctrine that leads to a balance of political values excluding that duly qualified right in the first trimester is to that extent unreasonable; and depending on details of its formulation, it may also be cruel and oppressive; for example if it denied the right altogether except in the case of rape and incest. Thus assuming that this question is either a constitutional essential or a matter of basic justice, we would go against the ideal of public reason if we voted from a comprehensive doctrine that denied this right. (pp. 243–44, n. 32)

He goes on to note that just because a comprehensive doctrine leads to an unreasonable conclusion, this does not necessarily mean that it is itself unreasonable, and presumably this is meant to mollify certain readers from traditions, for example, Catholicism, that reach the "unreasonable" conclusion that abortion is not fully justified in the first trimester.

Now let me start the discussion of this passage by saying that I am in complete passionate agreement with Rawls about what abortion policy a liberal society should adopt. But I would have thought that if the burdens of judgment argument works at all, it works here. People who reason about this issue, sincerely and in good faith, have reached, and will continue to reach, different conclusions. Indeed, even those who agree with Rawls about what values are most important in making the choice (i.e., the due respect for human life, the ordered reproduction of political society over time, and the equality of women as equal citizens) can disagree with him about how to *weight* these values, and thus (if they weight the first value heavily) can conclude that first trimester abortions should not be allowed. Such disagreements about weighting are, according to Rawls, commonly why reasonable people reach different conclusions on some matter: "even when we agree fully about the kinds of considerations that are relevant, we may disagree about their weight, and so arrive at different judgments" (p. 56). Hence, the abortion issue would seem to be a paradigm case of an issue on which reasonable people can reach different conclusions, by virtue of the fact that they weight the relevant considerations differently.

Moreover, for Rawls to call those opposed to first trimester abortions "unreasonable" seems to fall foul of what Rawls has called the (moral) "duty of civility" that he believes should prevail in a liberal society. Contrast the Millian liberal with the Rawlsian liberal on this matter. The Millian will say to his opponent on the abortion issue: "You are not unreasonable to have reached this conclusion, but I believe you are wrong, and here's why." In contrast, the Rawlsian who says to his opponent, "This is an unreasonable conclusion," has not only dismissed his opponent's conclusion, but also done so in a way that casts doubt on the opponent's ability to reason about this particular issue. In general, we regard an unreasonable belief as one that cannot be reached by reasoning that meets the standards appropriate for that agent, given his knowledge and capacities, in that time and place.[27] So the implication of calling a belief unreasonable is not only that the belief should be rejected, but also that the person who holds it has violated applicable standards of reasoning. And depending on why he failed to reason effectively (suppose he was overwhelmed by emotion or highly biased), a Rawlsian should perhaps not bother to construct an argument to persuade him to reason differently. Indeed, if he cannot reach reasonable conclusions on this issue, then his ability to participate as an equal in the political discussion of at least *this* issue is under question. The opponent is surely going to treat the Rawlsian response as disrespectful – and thus as an illiberal response to him.

Perhaps, however, we should simply treat this footnote on abortion as a regrettable mistake on Rawls's part – an illiberal moment in the book that can (and should) be excised from the text without affecting the liberal theory put forward there. But I worry that this was no simple mistake. In particular, I worry that there is something about Rawls's theory of liberalism that encourages anyone who embraces it to use the notion of "reasonable" in the illiberal way it is used in this footnote. Consider that the Millian liberal can agree with Rawls that good reasoning can yield plural results (this is, after all, true in all sorts of non-moral realms, including science), even while insisting that some results are just wrong. Rawls, albeit grudgingly, must admit the last point if he is going to commend to us his burdens of judgment argument, but in general he wants to disengage liberals from the project of "looking for the right moral answer" and interest them instead in the project of creating an

---

[27] We can describe these standards generally.

(1) They would not be terribly difficult to meet. For example, normally we do not think that someone who holds a false belief about the probability of some event, after performing some bit of reasoning that yields the right answer 90% of the time but that did not do so here, in a situation where discovering the right answer would involve performing a bit of mathematical reasoning that only 10% of the population is capable of, has a belief that is "unreasonable."

(2) These standards vary with time and place. What it was reasonable for an ancient Aztec to believe is not the same as what is reasonable for a twentieth-century American to believe.

(3) These standards vary with capacities and knowledge. What it is reasonable for an expert to conclude or believe is not the same as what it is reasonable for a non-expert to conclude or believe (so what would make a belief of a cardiologist about her patient's condition reasonable is not the same as what would make a belief about that condition held by a medical layman reasonable).

overlapping consensus among views that, whether or not they are right, are nonetheless "reasonable." However, Rawls needs to be able to rule out a variety of ideas and policies in his liberal society if the overlapping consensus that results is going to instantiate liberal justice. But since he cannot rule them out by calling them wrong, he rules them out using the notion of the reasonable. That notion therefore begins to do a lot of work in his theory.

However, there is no place in Rawls's book where the notion of the reasonable is given clear and precise definition. Such a vaguely defined notion will therefore be filled out by one's intuitions, and, of course, intuitions can vary. When Rawls uses his intuitions to fill out the word, and then classifies some views as unreasonable, he will come into conflict with those whose intuitions on such matters are substantially different (and in a pluralist society we can expect that there will be such people), whether the issue is abortion, or capital punishment, or redistributive justice. And when he goes on to rule out views he considers unreasonable from the overlapping consensus, it is unsurprising that he will encounter opposition from those whose views he opposes. It is this attempt to secure stability by *excluding* views using an intuition-dependent notion that I regard as an illiberal idea.

Modern liberal states do not spend any time developing such intuition-dependent principles of exclusion in order to secure stability. Although some states have excluded some views from the political debate (consider Germany's banning of neo-Nazi political parties), in general in modern liberal states there are all sorts of opposing ideas on every sort of issue among the citizenry, and legislation is frequently designed so that it is a response (albeit often muddled) to lots of them. There are political winners and losers at any given time, but they can easily trade places after the next election or the next legislative session. People call one another's views 'wrong,' but they do not develop arguments calling for some to be placed politically 'out of bounds.' The process is chaotic, full of inconsistencies, and tensions; people do not try for a consensus – they try for a political win, aware that if they win, it is likely only temporary insofar as their competitors will try to supplant them. Virtually nobody is excluded from playing the game or winning, but no one is a political victor for very long. What unifies such a brawling and changeable society? I shall now argue that it is not some kind of substantive consensus on issues (for none is possible – witness the abortion debate), but a substantive consensus on a framework for discussion and decision making, and a set of values that inform and define the operation of that framework.

V. Reason and Liberalism

Although I worry that there are illiberal aspects to Rawls's use of the notion of 'reasonable,' the fact that he uses it, and the way that he uses it, show that he embraces what is arguably the most important component of the Enlightenment tradition of liberalism: namely, that reason has the capacity to effect harmony in a society of conflicting lifestyles and points of view. This commitment may strike some as, to put it mildly, questionable. Waldron calls it a "hunch" (p. 145), and notes that it is far from clear that such a commitment is justified. Stuart Hampshire, who correctly appreciates the fact that Rawls's use of the notion of the reasonable implicitly commits him to the idea that reason is able to provide a common framework of values and rules for political life,[28] attacks the idea outright:

everywhere, both in the soul and in the city, the mark of vitality is conflict, so much so that it seems a law of life that any individual's desires and feelings should be at all times in a state of conflict and properly unstable, and that in public life social classes should at all times be in conflict and society should be properly unstable. The narrative of a person's life shows the constantly shifting predominance of one set of contrary dispositions and ambivalent feelings over another, as she matures and decays, and the historical development of a state or society depends on the competition between different social groups in an unceasing struggle for power. This is the engine of history and we do not expect it to come to a dead stop, although in some moods of despair we may indulge in a fantasy of a final stage, of a Utopia, or we may dream of stability and harmony, as Plato did after the failures of Athenian democracy. Nowhere is there evidence, whether in the individual soul or in society, of a sovereign reason which can secure a consensus, the end of conflict, a uniform order, a harmony of interests, the heavenly city of philosophers.[29]

---

[28] After quoting from the abortion footnote I have just discussed, Hampshire says: "This passage (the abortion footnote) makes it clear that Rawls's new 'political liberalism' still preserves the full creed of traditional liberalism and that this is the effect of a very extended and substantial use of the words 'unreasonable' and 'public reason.' The political liberal leaves space for the plurality of moral views to be found in any society, but only if they can be called reasonable, and this means reasonable as judged by the traditional standards of liberalism itself " (p. 44). However, I disagree with Hampshire somewhat here, because I believe, as I have argued above, that Rawls's use of the term 'reasonable' actually has illiberal overtones, and is not a simple invocation of traditional liberal standards of judgment.

[29] Hampshire, "Liberalism," p. 46. It is interesting that Hampshire would think Rawls is opposed to diversity and conflict, given Rawls's explicit commitment to reasonable diversity in his burdens of judgment argument. Hampshire is, I believe, picking up the way in which Rawls's conception of the "reasonable" can be used to restrict the diversity he claims to respect.

But even if we cannot defend the actual way in which Rawls uses the notion of the reasonable in his theory, I believe that the reliance on reason – by Rawls or any other liberal – can be defended against Hampshire's worries if one correctly appreciates the way liberals believe that reason can effect stability and order.

Most liberals do not believe that either now or in the future, reason will deliver to us all the right answers, and that everyone will know them to be the right answers. The naive confidence of a liberal such as Bentham in the truth of his version of liberal political theory is rare; more common is the attitude taken by theorists such as Mill, that in their time all political and moral theorizing – including their own – is provisional, open to doubt and challenge, capable of being improved through rational discussion. And the participation by such liberals in the process of democratic discussion and decision making shows their appreciation of the fact that good reasoning need not yield *their* conclusions, so that they cannot dogmatically insist on the truth of their views.

So all liberals, and especially Rawls, are appreciative of the ever-present conflicts within the soul and within society, and they do not naively expect that reason will remedy all such conflict any time soon. Indeed, even liberals are in conflict over the meaning of the basic tenets of liberalism, as we have seen. The liberal reliance on reason to produce order is, therefore, based not on the idea that reason can hand us the moral truth any time soon, but on the idea that it can provide us with a *political process* and a *structure* enabling us to work out what each of us believes, and to deal with the inevitable differences in our beliefs civilly, and peacefully.

Hampshire himself implicitly accepts this when he insists that the liberal remedy for conflict is a democratic procedure. But Hampshire assumes that people who agree on a *process* to resolve conflict need not agree on anything else. Indeed, he assumes that order in a liberal regime must be purchased through process because people cannot agree on anything else.

But this cannot be completely right. Let us grant that agreement on process can produce orderly decision making when agreement on substance is not possible; nonetheless *in order* to agree on a process, people must be in substantive agreement about the values underlying the process they select. In particular, if they agree on a certain liberal democratic process as a remedy for conflict, they must be in agreement on values that make this type of procedure preferable to some non-liberal autocratic method. Hampshire forgets that there have been those, such as Hobbes, who have certainly recognized the ever-present conflict in human society, but who have recommended non-liberal solutions for it. (And note that Hobbes maintained his solution was justified by *reasoning*, making him as much an heir of the Enlightenment as any liberal, even though the way he believes reason tells us to produce order out of conflict is not the liberal way.[30]) So a liberal who agrees with Hampshire about the desirability of liberal democratic processes for producing social order is going to have to mount a rational argument for his remedy, either as the most instrumentally effective available, and/or as the morally right remedy. The second and (in my view) preferable way will likely involve arguing that such processes respect the idea that people are free and equal. Both answers involve an appeal to rational argument, and the second appeals to moral ideas that are supposed to be accepted by those who reason correctly about political matters. So both assume that reason will show us the way to achieve order in a pluralist society, not by handing members of the community the right moral answers on a variety of questions, but by showing them a structure of social and political life, supported by certain values, in which conflict can be contained and channeled in useful directions.

So if Hampshire would commend to us democratic processes as the solution to conflict in a society, he is just as committed as Rawls to the power of reason to effect social unity – not because reason can define a substantive consensus on various political issues, but because reason can justify a process that respects certain shared values (especially the values of freedom and equality). This kind of unity permits, and even encourages, (non-violent) conflict and alternative ways of looking at the world because it is not a unity purchased via substantive consensus on issues but by consensus on value-informed procedures. And his own commitment to this reason-based unity explains why Hampshire commends liberals for fighting "for the habit of allowing each side of each case to be heard. That is their passion, a passion for civility within conflict" (p. 43). The rational argumentation which justifies that civility is the foundation of the kind of unity Hampshire – and any other liberal – wants for society: not a unity in belief and lifestyle, but a unity on democratic processes based on a common commitment to certain values instantiated by these processes, that permits radical disagreement on every sort of issue.

---

[30] Hampshire's remark (p. 46) that Hobbes is a philosopher who rejected the Platonic faith in reason is therefore incorrect. Hobbes is perhaps the pre-eminent Enlightenment thinker in early modern political theory, albeit a non-liberal one.

Is a liberalism committed to the idea that reason is the discloser of politically relevant normative truth supportive of political structures and the source of political unity too old-fashioned for people in these "post-modern" times to take seriously? Is there really a universal reason that will enable us to work out processes and structures for living together, and that will enable us to work together to decide policy for our society in the face of our many (permanent) disagreements?

There are many who do not believe such a reason exists. My arguments will be resisted by those who have welcomed Rawls's new views as a kind of post-modern liberalism, or by those who, because they distrust normativity on scientific grounds, see Rawls's version of liberal theory as a kind of "naturalized liberalism."[31] But I have argued that, contrary to appearances, Rawls does not abandon the traditional liberal commitment to the idea that reason is universal enough and powerful enough to allow us to make progress on the *right* kind of social structure in which (free and equal) individuals flourish. Nor do I regard this liberal notion of reason as hostile to a naturalist metaphysics: there are theorists, such as Gibbard, who have put forward a naturalized conception of norms, and who still have a conception of reason that is arguably consonant with this liberal commitment.[32] Indeed, I suppose Rawls's implicit commitment to this notion of reason is as much a function of the fact that Rawls is a *philosopher* as it is a function of the fact that he is a liberal. Philosophizing is an Enlightenment project, commended by people impressed by the teachings of Socrates, Plato, and Aristotle. No philosopher who *argues* for his conception of liberalism can claim to be renouncing a commitment to the Enlightenment notion of reason in his political philosophizing.

Of course, there is no way to say whether this commitment is justified. One might say that philosophical liberals are united by a common *faith* that there is a way to design a social and political structure that is reliant on reason and respectful of all individuals' dignity and autonomy, and that this is the best and the right social and political structure in which any of us could live. That faith has many denominations: liberals have different conceptions of how morality is "based" on reason, and different conception of the ideals of freedom, equality, and democracy that are supposed to form the foundations of the liberal party. Depending

---

[31] This phrase was suggested to me by Jules Coleman.

[32] Allen Gibbard, *Wise Choices, Apt Feelings* (Cambridge, Mass.: Harvard University Press, 1990). And if it can be shown that such a view is not consonant with this commitment, liberals would have to reject such a naturalized conception of reason.

on how a liberal state understands and implements any of these ideals, it will be uncongenial to those who disagree with that understanding or implementation. Thus, liberal states will exercise power in a way that will inevitably make some in the society discontent. Moreover, although liberal theorists defend a theoretically pure and defensible role for the liberal state, in fact existing liberal states operate on an inconsistent jumble of ideas, and are pulled and tugged by their citizenry in many (often inconsistent) directions. So all of us will be discontent with respect to some aspects of the liberal state in which we live. But we cannot hope for a liberal state that does not offend anyone; and if we are offended, we can only continue the debate, defending our point of view until we win, or until better views force us to stand aside and yield to them. It is our reasoning together about political issues within a process that respects us and treats us as equals, that provides an essential part of the "glue" holding a liberal state together. I have argued that Rawls turns out to be as much a believer in the liberal faith in the unifying power of reason as any traditional liberal.[33]

[33] This chapter was read at a conference on Rawls's *Political Liberalism* held at the University of Notre Dame in December 1993. I am grateful to the audience at that conference for their thoughtful discussion of it. Thanks also go to Jon Mandle, Cass Sunstein, and Alan Ryan for their very helpful comments on the chapter.

6

The Contractarian Explanation of the State

How do governments originate? How are they maintained? These are two causal questions about how states originate and persist through time that have always been of interest to anthropologists and historians. To answer them, however, one also needs to know the answer to a conceptual question "What is a state?" This chapter attempts to answer all three questions by using ideas drawn from the social contract tradition. Together the answers constitute what I will call an explanation of the state.

It may seem fantastic to some that the social contract argument could provide plausible answers to the two causal questions. Doesn't the contract argument make the state's creation and maintenance the result of each subject's contractual consent to it? And isn't this a wildly inaccurate explanation of virtually every state's origin and continued existence? As Hume wryly observes:

> [W]ere you to ask the far greatest part of the nation, whether they had ever consented to the authority of their rulers, or promis'd to obey them, they wou'd be inclin'd to think very strangely of you, and wou'd certainly reply, that the affair depended not on their consent but that they were born to such obedience.[1]

In response to such ridicule, supporters of the contractarian methodology have tended to back away from claiming that their contract talk has any explanatory import. The contracts in the argument are generally represented as "hypothetical" occurrences and not historical events: the theorist is, on this view, using the contract talk not to give any dubious

[1] David Hume, *A Treatise of Human Nature*, 2nd ed., ed. L. A. Selby-Bigge, rev. P. H. Nidditch (Oxford: Clarendon Press, 1978), III, ii, viii, p. 548.

history lessons but merely to justify the state in terms of what people *could agree to* in an equal and impartial setting. However, I do not want to give up on the idea that the contract methodology has explanatory power. In this chapter, I will construct an explanatory theory which I will argue is implicit in the traditional social contract argument but which does not make use of the literal notion of contract. I will conclude by considering, first, in what sense this is a *contractarian* model given that it incorporates only an attenuated notion of agreement, and second, whether or not the explanation is true, and thus usable by an historian or anthropologist exploring the origins and histories of particular states, or by a political or legal theorist attempting to understand the nature of the institution itself.

It is important to stress that as I attempt to answer these questions, at no point will I be discussing the justificatory force which contractarians have believed their argument has. Whether or not one can construct a social contract argument justifying the state's authority (and in this chapter I take no position on that issue), I am arguing that this form of argument can at least offer a partial explanation of what kind of institution the state is. I leave for another day a discussion of how much justificational force the social contract might have in political contexts.[2]

I. Solving the Leadership Selection Problem

There are a variety of social contract arguments concerned with the justi-fication of the state: my claim that we can distill from all of them a single explanatory theory of the state means that I believe they share, despite their differences, a common causal account of the state's creation and maintenance, and a common conceptual analysis of the state. It is one of the difficulties of my project that I must isolate these two common threads even while acknowledging the differences that divide members of this tradition.

We can find the end of that common thread by reflecting on the fact that those who present an argument in which people in a state of nature create a government are assuming that political subordination is not a

---

[2] The project of developing a contractarian explanation of the state may, however, help one to understand how social contract talk can have justificatory force. It is hard to understand how an appeal to a nonexistent promissorial agreement to create the state can provide a foundation for the legitimacy of that institution. On the other hand, if we can develop a theory that explains in what sense citizens really do "consent" to the states that rule them, it may be easier to understand how that consent could justify the institution.

natural feature of our social world. In contrast, those who believe that political subordination is natural will insist that one has no more reason to explain the subjugation of a human population to their ruler than one has to explain the subjugation of a group of mares to a stallion. Such subjugation is understood as inevitable, either because the natural masters are born with the power to dominate the natural slaves, or because the natural slaves are, for psychological or intellectual reasons, incapable of assuming the leadership role.

However, someone can believe that there is a hierarchy of talents and abilities which *ought* to be – but frequently is not – respected in the structuring of existing political societies. Or, more radically, he can deny that any such hierarchy exists and insist, as the traditional contractarians did, that human beings are similar enough in talent and abilities to make them equal, such that any of them could be leader. Either view is consistent with the contractarian methodology insofar as each accepts the fundamental tenet of that methodology, namely, that the state is an "artificial" institution (to use Hume's term) created (albeit perhaps not intentionally) by the actions of the human beings who would be rulers or subjects in it. (However, note that the second view would make not only political power but also the *reasons* entitling anyone to hold that power a human creation.) Most members of the contract tradition also believe that the state is not only created but also *maintained* by human action. The model I will present aims to clarify the nature of this maintenance activity.

If states are not only created but also maintained by the people, then this suggests that the people want them. In order to persuade his readers of the desirability of political society, the contractarian paints life without government in a "state of nature" as conflict-ridden, and presents people concluding that the state is a remedy (either the best or the only remedy) for that conflict. In the process of telling that story, the contractarian constructs a psychology which explains both why people tend to engage in conflict in a natural state, and why they would prefer to leave this state of conflict and enter political society. The psychologies of the traditional social contract theorists and the reasons they give for state creation have varied considerably over the years. But if one looks closely, one sees that although their arguments differ on the questions of why the state is desirable and what kind of state people have reason to generate, all of them contain roughly the same account of how the state is created and maintained.

I want to propose that the reason why contractarians share a common explanation of the state is that, despite the use of different psychologies

and ethical theories which justify the institution of different kinds of political regimes, each believes that the generation of the state involves solving
the same game-theoretic problem. In order to make this claim plausible
without going into taxing detail describing every contract argument in
the tradition, I will sketch how it is true for the two most important members of that tradition, Hobbes and Locke. If this common element exists
in their importantly different arguments, then we have at least the basis
for a claim that it is definitive of the contractarian explanatory strategy.

Let us start with Hobbes's theory. People in his state of nature are
largely, but not exclusively, self-interested, and pursue above all else their
self-preservation. Their desire for this latter goal, along with their desire
for glory, generates violent competition for objects that leads to a climate
of distrust precipitating more violence. Hobbes presents the institution
of a sovereign as not only a sufficient but also a necessary condition for
peace. The people in his state of nature believe this, and hence desire
to institute a sovereign. But they still face considerable disagreement on
the question of *who* should be sovereign. What precisely is the nature of
their disagreement?

To specify it exactly, suppose there are three people in Hobbes's state of
nature who are unable to resolve prisoner's dilemma problems and who
are therefore inclined to aggress against one another. Suppose further
that these individuals accept the Hobbesian argument that the warfare
in this state can be remedied only by the institution of a sovereign. To
simplify the problem for the time being, let us also suppose that they
agree with Hobbes that the state will operate best if sovereignty is invested
in one person, so that they aim to create an absolute monarch. Their
preferences over the various possible outcomes in this situation are as
follows. First, each party will rate lowest the situation in which he is not
a member of the state while the other two are, because here he is a lone
individual in a partial state of war facing a unified group of two who can
likely beat him in any conflict. Each of them will rate the partial state
of war in which he is a subject in a two-person state higher than this,
because here he would enjoy the increase in security which association
with another person brings. He would prefer even more being subject in
a state in which all three of them are members because in this situation
peace finally prevails. Hobbes also tells us that individuals would rather
be rulers than subjects in any state;[3] hence, each would prefer being ruler

[3] See Thomas Hobbes, *Leviathan*, ed. C. B. Macpherson (Hammondsworth: Penguin, 1968)
ch. 15, para. 21 (pp. 76–77 in the 1651 pagination).

TABLE 1. *Two-player version of "who shall reign?"*

		B	
		Choose A as ruler	Choose B as ruler
A	Choose A as ruler	3, 2	1, 1
	Choose B as ruler	1, 1	2, 3

of a two-person state rather than a subject in it, and each would prefer even more being ruler in a three-person state. But the importance of avoiding war and imminent death or injury is such that (assuming these people are not badly vainglorious) each individual would prefer being a subject in a three-person state to being the ruler in a partial state of war. So the question to be settled is, "Who shall reign?"

This situation is actually a kind of conflict-ridden coordination game much discussed in the game-theoretic literature called "the Battle of the Sexes" after Luce and Raiffa's unfortunately sexist example of a husband and wife who each prefer different evening activities (he prefers a prize fight, she prefers a ballet) but who would also rather go with the other to his or her preferred evening activity than to go to his or her own favorite alone.[4] A two-player version of this game is given in Table 1.

It is important to note that this type of interaction is a *coordination* rather than a conflict problem because it has coordination equilibria. Coordination equilibria are defined as those situations where the combination of the players' actions is such that no one would be better off if any one player, either himself or another, acted differently.[5] In the matrix in Table 1 there are two coordination equilibria (AA and BB), which come about when A and B choose the same person as ruler. Each prefers either of these outcomes to the outcomes that result when they choose different leaders, because their disagreement prevents them from installing a government. For a population of n people in the state of nature, the matrix representing their deliberations will be n-dimensional, with n coordination equilibria, but that game will be closely analogous to this two-dimensional game.

So the major problem people with these preferences face in their efforts to create a commonwealth is a coordination problem with

[4] See R. Duncan Luce and Howard Raiffa, *Games and Decisions* (New York, 1957), pp. 90–94, and ch. 6.
[5] From David Lewis, *Convention* (Cambridge, Mass., 1969), p. 24.

considerable conflict of interest on the issue: "How shall we be governed?"
I call this the "leadership selection problem." And it really has two components. In the example above, the players agreed that only one of them
would rule – amounting to an agreement to create a state with an absolute monarch. But of course there can be a dispute over whether to invest
sovereignty in one person or a group of persons, which is, in effect, a dispute over what form of government to institute. Resolving this dispute
involves determining how many leaders will rule them, and what power
he/she/they will have, and it, too, would likely have a battle-of-the-sexes
structure.[6]

After resolving these matters, the people must decide (as in the example above) *which* person or persons to choose as leader to fill whatever
offices in the government they have defined. If there is no disagreement
on these questions, the people's dilemma is an easily solvable coordination problem with only one coordination equilibrium. Disagreement
makes the coordination problem conflict-ridden, but unless it is so severe
that people would rather remain in the state of nature than accept someone other than their favorite candidate as ruler (a preference driven by
the desire for glory which Hobbes would condemn as irrational), it will
not destroy the coordination character of the game.[7] As long as irrationality is not widespread, there should be sufficient support for achieving
some resolution to generate an institution powerful enough to coerce
any recalcitrant glory-seekers into submission. Later I will discuss procedures, for example, voting, that help to create a salient solution to
this kind of coordination problem, which could be used to generate the
state.[8]

Does Locke's argument for the state also assume that a conflict-ridden
coordination game describes the problem of creating government? It
does. Consider that unlike Hobbes's people, Locke's people can be motivated not only by self-interest but also by God's "Fundamental Law of
Nature" which directs them to preserve the life, health, and possessions

---

[6] Kavka agrees, noting that people may also agree at this stage on a constitution, explicit
legislation, procedural safeguards to be followed in the regime, and so forth. See his
Hobbesian Moral and Political Theory (Princeton, N.J., 1986), p. 188.

[7] Gregory Kavka cites passages from *Leviathan,* ch. 18, in support of a similar analysis of the
game-theoretic structure underlying the state's creation, but he does not go on to stress
the way in which that structure underlies a convention-based rather than a contract-based
explanation of the state. See *Hobbesian Moral and Political Theory,* 180ff; and see below,
note 18.

[8] See my *Hobbes and the Social Contract Tradition* (Cambridge, 1986), ch. 6.

of others as long as their own preservation will not be compromised by doing so.[9] Were people to act strictly in accordance with God's law, the state of nature would be a state of peace. But warfare is precipitated by irrational members of society, who either harm others for their own gain ("In transgressing the Law of Nature, the Offender declares himself to live by another Rule, than that of Reason and Common Equity"[10]) or fail (because of personal bias) to interpret the Fundamental Law of Nature correctly, especially when they use it to justify the punishment of offenders.[11] In virtue of the violent or uncooperative actions precipitated by this irrationality and self-bias, "nothing but Confusion and Disorder follow."[12] Reason directs men to pursue peace, but like Hobbes, Locke believes they can do so only by instituting a government:

I easily grant, that *Civil Government* is the proper remedy for the inconveniences of the State of Nature, which must certainly be Great, where Men may be Judges in their own Case. . . . the State of Nature is therefore not to be endured.[13]

Hence, for self-interested, religious, and moral reasons, men "are quickly driven to [political] Society."[14]

Locke argues that political society remedies the disorder by providing impartial bodies which can fairly interpret the Fundamental Law of Nature and impartially adjudicate disputes using that law, and also by providing agencies that enforce the law effectively through punishment:

Mankind in general, may restrain, or where necessary, destroy things noxious to them, and so may bring such evil on any one, who hath transgressed that Law, as may make him repent the doing of it, *and thereby deter him,* and by his Example others, from doing the like mischief.[15]

In other words, Locke believes that the use of fear can control the actions of those who refuse to live by the law of reason; on his view only the state can effectively and fairly generate that fear.

---

9 See Locke's *Two Treatises of Government*, ed. P. Laslett (Cambridge, 1960), sec. 6 of the *Second Treatise*, p. 311.

10 Ibid., sec. 8, p. 312.

11 Locke writes, "it is unreasonable for Men to be Judges in their own Cases. . . . Selflove will make Men partial to themselves and to their Friends. . . . Ill Nature, Passion and Revenge will carry them too far in punishing others." Ibid., sec. 13, p. 316.

12 Ibid.

13 Ibid.

14 Ibid., sec. 127, p. 397.

15 Ibid., sec. 8, pp. 312–13; my emphasis, and see ch. 9 of the *Second Treatise*.

Given that this is the solution to their problems, what difficulties do Locke's people face creating that solution? Let us again consider our three-person state of nature, this time described in Lockean terms, and assume once again that they each prefer that only one of them rule. Consider that because Locke's people want the state in order to promote greater respect for a divine law that defines their obligations to one another, they desire political power not only for self-interested but also for moral and religious reasons. For all three reasons, each person would prefer least being a lone individual facing a unified group of two, because outside the state a person does not enjoy the enforcement of his rights according to this law. Locke would represent being a subject in a two-person state as better than this insofar as it would allow a person to enjoy some enforcement of rights and an increase in security (both of which are, at least in part, moral goods). Better still would be membership in a three-person state; here the person would enjoy a cessation of violence (or at least, depending upon the effectiveness of the ruler's enforcement, a lower threshold of violence). What about preferences for being ruler rather than subject in a two- or three-person state? Locke is not as committed as Hobbes is to the idea that each person would rather be ruler than subject, so it is theoretically possible that everyone would have the same favorite candidate, making the selection of a ruler easy. But if there were disagreements, Locke is clear that because it is highly desirable to institute government for moral as well as self-interested reasons, each would prefer being subject in a three-person state to being ruler in a two-person state.

So, once again, we have battle-of-the-sexes preferences, although these preferences are a function of the moral, religious, and self-regarding interests of the people. The game-theoretic situation underlying the creation of the Lockean state is therefore the same as that which underlies the creation of the Hobbesian state.[16] Locke also believes that there can be reasonable disagreements over the form that government should take, as well as over who should be ruler in it (although he himself argues for a government with divided powers and legislative dominance). But again, note that as long as each party does not prefer a continuation of war to

---

[16] Only if considerable numbers of people believe that there is *no* candidate (outside of their favorite) to whom it is better to be subjugated than to remain in a total or partial state of war is the conflict so great that the battle-of-the-sexes character of the game is destroyed. But given the way in which Locke believes government secures peace, such radical preferences are not defensible on his view on either moral or self-interested grounds, and he does not take seriously in his political writings the possibility that people could come to have them.

compromise on a non-favorite form of government, their disagreement will have a battle-of-the-sexes structure, and thus present them only with a conflict-ridden coordination game.

So we have actually discovered the two common threads running through the Lockean and Hobbesian arguments. First, both assume that the preferences of people regarding the creation of government in the state of nature give rise to a series of coordination games (most likely conflict-ridden) which must be solved and maintained to generate and sustain that institution. So in answer to the causal question, "How is a state created and maintained?" both say, "Through the generation and maintenance of conventions." Second, both see the state's role as primarily that of resolving, preventing, or punishing conflict among the people (although they disagree about exactly what reasons people have for desiring to create an institution that plays this role). And it is this role which they would regard as fundamental to understanding what a state is.

Granted that coordination games underlie the state's creation, and not prisoner's dilemmas, how are games of this kind solved and a desirable coordination equilibrium reached? Are contracts necessary to do so?

II. Creating Leadership Conventions

Although the word 'contract' is sometimes used loosely to mean any sort of agreement, it is generally understood to be a certain kind of agreement, one in which one or more promises figure. The American Law Institute defines a contract as "a promise or set of promises for the breach of which the law gives a remedy, or the performance of which the law in some way recognizes a duty."[17] The species of contract which the traditional contractarian invokes is known as a bilateral contract, in which a promise or set of promises by one side is exchanged for a promise or set of promises by the other side.[18] Contracts are made when parties to an agreement believe that the performance of the actions to be agreed upon is only collectively and not individually rational for each of them, such that an exchange of promises among them (i.e., a contract) to perform the actions seems necessary to secure performance. The prisoner's dilemma nicely represents the game-theoretic structure of this situation, and is depicted in Table 2. In circumstances such as the state of nature,

---

[17] From the Institute's *American Restatement of Contracts,* discussed by P. S. Atiyah, in *An Introduction to the Law of Contract,* 3rd ed. (Oxford, 1981), p. 28.

[18] From ibid., p. 32. There is also a species of contract which involves unilateral and not bilateral promising, but that species is not relevant to our concerns here.

TABLE 2. *Prisoner's dilemma*

		B	
		Action x	Action y
A	Action x	2, 2	1, 4
	Action y	4, 1	3, 3

in which no law exists to enforce the contract, performance would occur only if the parties to it were able and willing to keep their contractual promises.

So if people in a state of nature needed a contract to institute the state, this would be because there were one or more prisoner's dilemmas associated with its institution, and that institution would occur only if people had the ability to keep a contractual promise to perform collectively rational but individually irrational actions. But we have seen that prisoner's dilemmas do not underlie the institution of the state in Hobbes's or Locke's theory. Although they are the sort of problem *precipitating* conflict for which the state is supposed to be a solution, they are not the problem which must be solved to create that solution. Another and more easily solved problem underlies the state's creation – that is, the conflict-ridden coordination game. Might contracts, nonetheless, be necessary to solve these games?[19]

---

[19] In his book *Hobbesian Moral and Political Theory*, Gregory Kavka sends conflicting messages about how this question ought to be answered. He agrees that the battle-of-the-sexes game characterizes the problem people face when they want to create a commonwealth, but he characterizes Hobbes's theory of the social contract as follows:

commonwealths are formed by institution, when a number of independent individuals create a common power over themselves by mutual agreement. This state-creating pact, or social contract, is pictured by Hobbes as having a complex structure. It is not really a single agreement, but a set of bilateral agreements linking each contractor with every other. Hence, a single party can rightly demand fulfillment of the agreement by each of the others. Each of these bilateral agreements surrenders the individual's right of self-rule to, and authorizes all the actions of, a sovereign person or assembly to be elected later by the parties by majority vote. In this two-stage process, the actual sovereign is selected only after the parties are joined into a social union by overlapping mutual agreements. The parties bind one another to confer on whoever is elected their combined power and authority, in hopes thereby of achieving protection against foreigners and one another. The sovereign is not, qua sovereign, a party to the social contract and is therefore not constrained by it. (p. 181)

Kavka's language here clearly signals that he sees this contract as not just an agreement but a promissorial agreement – one which binds and constrains.

The idea that a promissorial agreement is necessary for the state's creation is puzzling, because promises are not usually taken to be either necessary or desirable for the solution of any coordination dilemma – even those with conflict. Consider that the task of the participants of such a dilemma is to realize only one coordination equilibrium. An effective way of doing so, if circumstances permit, is to communicate with one another so as to *reach an agreement* to pursue only one of the equilibria (e.g., players in a traffic coordination dilemma might specifically agree with one another to drive on the right rather than the left). Such agreements work as solutions to these problems because they give each party the "common knowledge that each prefers to conform to [the equilibrium chosen] conditionally upon conformity by others involved with him in [the game]."[20] How does that common knowledge help to effect a solution to this dilemma? I propose the following answer.[21] The fact that the agreement is commonly known causes each player to make a high assessment of the likelihood that the other player(s) will choose the agreed-upon equilibrium, such that an expected utility calculation performed by each of the players will dictate the action realizing that equilibrium by each player. Henceforth I will call such agreements "self-interested," or SI, agreements, because self-interested rational calculation, rather than the sense of "duty" arising out of a promise or fear of a coercive power, is the motive for each person's performance of the act agreed upon.

But as David Lewis explores,[22] SI agreements might not be necessary for the resolution of a coordination problem. What is needed for its resolution is the generation of a *convention* governing which equilibrium to realize, and that convention can be generated even without agreement if there is an obviously salient equilibrium, one that stands out from the rest by its uniqueness in some conspicuous respect. If it is common knowledge that this equilibrium stands out in an obvious way, each will estimate the probability that they will perform the action leading to that equilibrium as higher than the probability that they will perform any other action, so that an expected utility calculation will dictate the pursuit of that equilibrium. In such situations it is "as if" there were an agreement on the pursuit of that salient outcome; hence it is common to hear people

[20] Lewis, *Convention*, p. 83.
[21] Lewis does not answer this question. My general answer to it in this essay is given in more precise form in my *Hobbes and the Social Contract Tradition*, ch. 6, pp. 142–45.
[22] See Lewis, *Convention*, p. 35.

speak of there being a "tacit agreement" in these situations. Literally, of course, no one explicitly agreed with anyone on anything, but each did act by making reference to the beliefs and preferences of the others in the pursuit of this particular outcome, just as she would have done if there had been an explicit agreement among them to pursue it. If this coordination problem persists and is repeatedly solved in this way, the participants have developed (without explicit agreement) a *convention* to solve their coordination problem.

So in order to solve their leadership problem, people who want to create a state must generate a leadership convention. As we shall discuss, either of the strategies involved, or some combination of the two, could be used to do so. Moreover, *something like* a contractual process *could* produce it. If each member had explicitly agreed with the others on who should rule and how, where that agreement involved a compromise by members of the group whose favorite outcome was not selected, then the conflict in the situation would be resolved and coordination achieved. However, notice that this compromise agreement *would not literally be a contract* because promises would not be necessary to keep it. Once the agreement was made, it would already be in each party's interest to realize the coordination equilibrium agreed upon. This agreement would only be more difficult to make, requiring capitulation or compromise by some or all of the parties.

Another more historically plausible scenario used by Hobbes to explain the institution of a sovereign involves voting,[23] a method that is actually used by democratically organized states to select their rulers (although they use it in a situation where there is already a convention on how these leaders will rule, what powers they will have, and how long their term of office will be). Consider the problem facing any political party of selecting a viable candidate to represent the party in a general election. All members of the party realize that it is overwhelmingly in their interest to select someone from among their ranks to represent them, but there is often considerable disagreement as to who shall do so. Political parties such as the Democratic Party in the United States or the Labour Party in Britain resolve this controversy by holding successive elections (either in different geographical areas at different times or successively at one

---

[23] Explicit mention of voting and democratic choice procedures occurs in *Elements of Law,* ed. F. Tonnies (Cambridge: Cambridge University Press, 1928), pp. 198–99. Kavka thinks it is also suggested in *Leviathan,* chs. 18 and 20, but I do not see the idea explicitly present there.

national party convention), with those who get the majority of the votes staying in contention, and those who get small percentages of support dropping out. As the process continues, there is a gradual "snowball" or "bandwagon" effect, with one person usually emerging as the clear-cut favorite. The snowball effect in these elections is a clear indication that they are tactics for effecting a solution to a conflict-ridden coordination problem. The results of each successive election give people a way to determine the probability that their favorite leader will be able to receive support from the rest of the electorate, and thus allow them to calculate whether or not it is rational for them to hold out for that leader's selection. Those people who find themselves supporting candidates with little or no support from the rest of the electorate will find it rational to switch to a more popular candidate they prefer less in the interest of getting a resolution to this coordination problem.

If this election technique ever fails to effect a solution to a leadership selection problem, it is because a significant number of those whose favorite candidates lose refuse to accept that their candidates are effectively out of contention for selection, in just the same way that the loser of a coin flip might repudiate that coin flip as a strategy for solving this sort of problem. Such a refusal in a political context can produce stalemate and even civil war, but Hobbes would insist that this refusal is generally irrational. Holding out for a better deal means risking no solution to the problem, and thus a return to the state of war; it is a risk that an expected utility calculation in the state of nature would likely tell one not to take (unless, of course, the winning candidate posed a threat to one's life).

Historically, people have not been so rational or so moral, and have frequently resorted to warfare to choose their leaders and their governmental structures. But warfare is another device for achieving a resolution to a battle-of-the-sexes problem relying on natural saliency rather than SI agreements. To see this, imagine a pre-political situation in which war has gone on for some time and consider the plight of a very unsuccessful inhabitant. Unless he is badly vainglorious, such a person knows that he will never score a complete win over all the others in this state. Such a person is ripe for the following offer by a more successful inhabitant whom I will call a "sovereign-entrepreneur." This entrepreneur says, "Look, you are getting nowhere on your own. But if you join forces with me and *do my bidding* (so that I am your ruler), then you will have more security than you now have." If this person does not accept this rather attractive-looking positive incentive by the sovereign-entrepreneur, he might be "offered" the following negative incentive: "Do my bidding or else I will harm you!"

And this threat will be real since, as we said, the sovereign-entrepreneur is a better warrior.

In general, both of these incentives are important tools for successful warriors to use in attracting subjects. The advantages of submission to this sovereign entrepreneur are substantial: the subject will receive greater protection from other members of the confederacy, he will have a greater chance of warding off attacks from outsiders if he is allied with this leader than he would have on his own, and he might receive a share of the spoils of any victory achieved over the forces of these outsiders. However, negative incentives are useful as a method of encouraging some reluctant members of the state of nature to "give in" and accept the sovereign-entrepreneur as leader. Hence, the threats help to resolve the battle-of-the-sexes problem over who should be declared ruler.

As entrepreneurs attract subjects in these ways, a certain number of powerful confederacies may emerge. But with their emergence comes a real market choice for the people in this state, as Robert Nozick actually noticed in his own attempt to construct a scenario of the creation of government.[24] In Nozick's scenario the forces of the two competing "protection agencies" do battle. One of these agencies will emerge as the usual or continual winner of these battles. And since the clients of the losing agency are ill-protected in conflicts with clients of the winning agency, they leave their losing agency to "do business" with the winner. Eventually one confederacy emerges as winner over all others and is thus the "best buy" in protection for everyone in this state. So the inhabitants of the state of nature looking for a protection agency are in a market. Heads of different confederacies essentially say to them: "Buy me if you want protection." And the confederacy that wins more often than any other will be the best buy for the people in that state.

There are two important points to notice about this scenario. First, coordination on who should be leader is being achieved *not* via explicit agreement among the inhabitants of the state of nature, but via a series of independent choices of a salient sovereign candidate by each inhabitant. Second, the negative incentives in this scenario are particularly useful in solving the *sort* of coordination problem which leadership selection presents: in particular, it breaks the conflict over who should rule (and how). Nor does the sovereign-entrepreneur have to threaten *everyone* in

---

[24] See Robert Nozick, *Anarchy, State and Utopia* (New York, 1974), p. 16ff. Nozick actually constructs three scenarios, but the second and third are not sufficiently different from the first to merit discussion here.

the state of nature. He need only threaten enough people to get a cadre of support enabling his confederacy to dominate in the state of war. Thereafter his confederacy will be the "best buy" in the state of nature and, as such, the salient choice for subjugation by everyone else.

The fact that warfare is not generally regarded as a *legitimate* way to solve this type of conflict-ridden coordination problem does not alter the fact that it can succeed in effecting a solution to it. Nonetheless, most social contract theorists have not used this warfare scenario in their arguments because it does not serve their justificatory interests. Any theorist interested in showing what kind of state we *should* create and maintain does not want to use stories of state creation such as the warfare scenario in which the mightiest, but not necessarily the most just, leadership faction would prevail. It is natural to present a just government, which takes account of the rights of each individual subject, as the product of an agreement process in which those rights are respected. But Nozick's scenario has other advantages. In my restatement of his scenario I attributed to people the intention to leave the state of nature and create a government. But I needed to attribute to them at each moment only the intention to subjugate themselves to the best confederacy leader at that moment, and given the structure of the situation, this intention on the part of each of them would more than likely lead to the creation of a confederacy leader with a monopoly of power. Insofar as this "invisible hand" explanation need only make use of this limited intention, it not only has certain desirable explanatory features,[25] but may also be closer to what actually occurred in the generation of existing political conventions than explicit-agreement scenarios.

The fact that traditional contractarians all resorted to the notion of an explicit agreement to construct a scenario of the state's creation has obscured the two causal explanations of the state that their arguments are making, namely, that states are created via the generation of a leadership convention, and second, that states persist through time for as long as this convention is maintained. As we noted above, this convention can be generated without the people having the explicit intention to create a

---

[25] In Nozick's words:

Invisible-hand explanations minimize the use of notions constituting the phenomena to be explained; in contrast to the straightforward explanations, they don't explain complicated patterns by including the full-blown pattern-notions as objects of people's desires or beliefs. Invisible-hand explanations of phenomena thus yield greater understanding than do explanations of them as brought about by design as the object of people's intentions. It is therefore no surprise that they are more satisfying. (Ibid., p. 19)

state. So despite what Nozick himself says, he is not any less of a "contractarian" because he uses in his argument a story in which the leadership convention is not generated by explicit agreement; instead, his successful use of a nonagreement story simply points up the fact that creating and maintaining a government involves the generation and maintenance of a conventional solution to a (probably conflict-ridden) coordination problem.

III. Empowerment

Thus far, this model makes the creation and maintenance of government a result of people's participation in a convention empowering rulers in a certain form of government. But we still do not know what participation in a leadership convention involves, such that the state is created and maintained. What actions must people take such that someone becomes their ruler?

Consider that a person is only a ruler – that is, only has *power* – when his subjects do what he says, so people presumably make someone a ruler when they (or at least most of them) obey his commands. According to the contractarians, each subject gives the ruler the power of command over him: in Locke's words, "the first *Power, viz. of doing whatsoever he thought fit for the Preservation of himself,* and the rest of Mankind, *he gives up* to be regulated by Laws made by the Society."[26] But what does it mean to be "regulated by laws made by the society"?

At the very least, it means being subject to the ruler's power to punish violations of these laws. Hobbes suggests that a subject grants the ruler punishment power when he does three things:[27]

1. The subject must be disposed to obey the punishment orders of the person or group chosen as ruler.
2. The subject must surrender his right to come to the aid of another who is being punished by the ruler (although not, some might think, his right to defend himself).
3. The subject must oblige himself to assist the ruler in punishing others (but not, some might say, himself).

Regarding the first action: if we assume that the situation underlying the creation of a ruler is a battle-of-the-sexes dilemma, then once the subjects have agreed (implicitly or explicitly) that a certain person or group will

---

[26] Locke, *Second Treatise,* sec. 129, pp. 397–98.
[27] See *Leviathan,* ch. 28.

be their ruler, obeying that person's punishment commands is identified as the way to achieve coordination in this situation; hence to the extent that obeying the punishment commands of any other person or group would disrupt this coordination, they have good reason not to do so.[28] Regarding the second action, it would seem that, in general, people are able to refrain from interfering with their government's punishment of people other than friends and relatives. Hobbes would point out that such punishment does not threaten their own well-being and insofar as allowing it to happen is a way of instituting a remedy to the warfare in that natural state, it is desirable to let it occur. Locke would point out that people are generally supportive, for moral as well as self-regarding reasons, of punishment of those who do not live by the law of reason and hence deserve the infliction of pain (indeed they support such punishment in the state of nature). Thus, any problems generated by those who do attempt to intervene on behalf of criminals for whom they care are small enough to be easily handled by a ruler who has sufficient police force to help him carry out the punishments.

But this brings us to the third action. In a community of any significant size the government will need help enforcing its edicts: police, judges, and jailers will all be required to make effective enforcement of the laws possible. Therefore, some percentage of persons in the community must be willing to carry out these jobs in order that the government have power. If (as Locke contends) people have the capacity to act in other-interested ways even at some cost to themselves, the ruler could appeal to them to volunteer their services. If (as Hobbes contends) they have no such capacity, a natural way for the government to receive their services would be to make individual contracts with each of them to become part of that cadre, giving them goods in exchange for service. Moreover, such a contract would not require either the ruler(s) or the members of the cadre to be fine, upstanding promise keepers: it would only require that they be self-interested and smart enough to see the repetitive prisoner's dilemma nature of the agreement.[29] That is, because the government will stay in power only for as long as this cadre functions, it is in its interest to

---

[28] Of course the state is continually threatened by those who claim to be a higher authority than the ruler, e.g., religious figures. Hobbes was particularly contemptuous and hostile toward the Christians of his day who maintained their right to disregard the commands of their ruler because a higher authority (e.g., the Pope, a Protestant leader, even their own consciences informed by God through prayer and biblical revelation) permitted them to do so.

[29] The literature on iterated prisoner's dilemma arguments is voluminous, but for a well-known discussion, see Robert Axelrod, *The Evolution of Cooperation* (New York, 1984).

pay cadre members in order to ensure their future service. And because members of the cadre will get that pay only if they do what the government wants, it is in their interest to follow its orders. So we can expect these cadres to develop, and it is in the other subjects' interest not to interfere with their formation. The upshot of this discussion is that *no general social contract* is necessary for a government's empowerment.

But is this all that is necessary for a state to exist? Some legal theorists have argued it is not; on their view the state not only has the power to punish but also the authority to rule.[30] What is state authority? Philosophers such as Raz or Anscombe understand it to be that which a state has, such that members of it believe they are obligated to obey its directives.[31] So on this view, if I am a subject of a political system, then I obey a command of the state not only because I am fearful of the sanction if I do not and I am caught, but also (and more importantly) because the command is authoritative for me. "I have to do this because it is the law!" I think to myself. The exact definition of state authority is the subject of controversy, but one recent philosopher argues for the following definition: "α has authority over β if and only if the fact that α required β to ϕ (i) gives β a content-independent reason to ϕ, and (ii) excludes some of β's reasons for not-ϕ-ing."[32]

Students of positivist legal theory know that it is important not to mistake a claim of authority for a claim of justification. As Hart was at pains to stress, to say that states have authority over their citizens is to make a purely descriptive statement, not a normative one. Whether or not a subject is right to obey the state, and whether or not a state deserves to have the obedience of its subjects, Hart claims that a coercive regime is only a state (as opposed to a group of gunmen coercing a population through the use of physical power) if the people accept a rule granting the regime the right to issue commands they will regard as binding upon them (i.e., that they will believe give them a content-independent reason for following them simply because they are issued by this regime).[33]

---

[30] In *Hobbes and the Social Contract Tradition* I failed to emphasize sufficiently the extent to which states have authority, and not merely coercive power, over the ruled. This discussion aims to correct that oversight.

[31] See E. Anscombe, "On the Source of the Authority of the State," *Collected Papers*, vol. 3: *Ethics, Religion and Politics* (Minneapolis, 1981), pp. 130–55; Joseph Raz, *The Authority of Law* (Oxford, 1979); and Leslie Green, *The Authority of the State* (Oxford, 1988).

[32] Green, *Authority of the State*, pp. 41–42.

[33] Indeed, one might believe that a state can be properly said to have punishment power (as opposed to the mere physical power to coerce) only if it is the authoritative command-giver in the society. I will not take up here to what purpose a state ought to punish; this

Now there are some who deny that states possess authority, even when this is understood in a purely positivist sense. But for those who believe it exists, the traditional, explicitly contractarian interpretation of the social contract argument might seem to promise an analysis of it. In the same way that my doctor has authority to take out my appendix if we have contractually agreed that she should do so, so too does it seem that my state has authority to dictate how I should behave in certain areas if we have contractually agreed for it to do so. Locke's appeal to promissorial consent is therefore explanatorily useful if one reads it as part of an explanation of how the state comes to have authority to command me. Someone who believes this may therefore want to supplement or replace any convention-based model of the state with an explicit appeal to an authority-giving contract between the ruler and the people.

But is this explanation of authority any good? Over and over again, from David Hume to Ronald Dworkin, the contract tradition has been ridiculed for failing to provide anything like a plausible explanation of the state's authority using the idea of a promissorial contract. Just when, asks Hume, have most of the world's population undertaken this contractual obligation? People, he notes, generally obey the state because they think they are "born to it," not because they have promised to do so. What about the notion of tacit consent? If tacit consent is understood simply as the acceptance of benefits, then it is hard to know why it obliges us (it certainly would not do so normally in a court of law – acceptance of benefits rarely, if ever, counts as making a promise), or why it obliges us members any more than it obliges any foreign traveller who enjoys the benefits of the state while she is here. And if we interpret this kind of consent such that it is more explicitly made and more explicitly promissorial, then it becomes increasingly difficult to argue that all or even most citizens of regimes around the world have ever given it.

Well then, might political authority be explained contractually if the contract explaining it is hypothetical rather than actual in nature? But here Dworkin has the appropriate rejoinder: "A hypothetical contract is

would be part of a moral theory of the state's legitimate role. Notice how much Hobbes suggests the idea that states have (and ought to have) not merely power but authority of this kind in the following passage:

And when men that think themselves wiser than all others, clamor and demand right Reason for judge; yet seek no more, but that things should be determined, by no other men's reason but their own, it is as intolerable in the society of men, as it is in play after trump is turned, to use for trump on every occasion, that suite whereof they have most in their hand. (*Leviathan*, ch. 5, para. 3 [pp. 18–19 in 1651 pagination])

not simply a pale form of contract; it is no contract at all."[34] We are obliged
not by make-believe contracts, but by real ones. Hence, whatever excellent
use a hypothetical contract has in defining justice or legitimating the state,
a contract that never really took place cannot explain real authority.

I still think that there is something about a contractarian approach
to state authority that is right, but I want to argue that this "something"
can be best captured only by using the convention explanation of the
state. The reason why explicitly contract-based explanations of the state's
authority invariably fail is that they rest on a false history of the state.[35]
But one can use the more plausible convention analysis to explain the
state's authority by arguing that the process of generating a leadership
convention involves not only the creation of rulers who have a virtual
monopoly on force, but also (and perhaps more importantly) rulers who
have authority to command. As Anscombe suggests, to create the state is
to create *an authoritative office*.[36] An umpire in baseball has his authority
by virtue of holding that authoritative office (required if the game is
to be played), and not by virtue of any contract between him and the
players that explicitly gives him the right to command them. Similarly, it
is the nature of their office, and not any real or make-believe contract,
which explains why our rulers have authoritative power. But that office is
nonetheless one that, on the convention model, the people create and
maintain through their participation in a certain kind of convention.

Now perhaps that participation is unwitting. A people who decide to
regard a certain person as their queen because they believe that God has
authorized her to rule and thus obey her are in fact giving her both power
and authority through their obedience as a result of their interdependent
acceptance of her as leader, so that God does not authorize her, they do.
The fact that their consent to her rule is unwitting, that is, that they
do not know that it is they who are responsible for her holding that
particular kind of office which exists because of their need for it, might
be greatly to her advantage. In particular, it might give her more security
of reign because her subjects would not see that they in fact have the
ability and indeed good reason to strip her of her authority to command

[34] Ronald Dworkin, "The Original Position," in *Reading Rawls,* ed. N. Daniels (New York,
1974), pp. 17–18.

[35] For this way of seeing the issue I am indebted to Alan Nelson, "Explanation and Justification in Political Philosophy," *Ethics* 97, no. 1. (Oct. 1986): 154–76.

[36] "Authority arises from the necessity of a task whose performance requires a certain sort
and extent of obedience on the part of those for whom the task is supposed to be done."
Anscombe, "On the Source of the Authority of the State," p. 134.

them if her performance as ruler were poor. Nonetheless, she gets both her power and her authority by virtue of their unwitting convention-generating activity.

If one adds to one's analysis of the state the idea that the state is an institution whose rule is ultimately authoritative in the community ("the final court of appeal" as Rawls puts it),[37] one is accepting a Hartian approach to the nature of a legal system rather than an Austinian approach.[38] Insisting that Austin was wrong to suppose that a legal rule could be binding simply because the rulegiver has the physical power to coerce people to obey it, Hart maintained that a binding rule can be created only by one who has the authority to give the people such a rule. And this authority, he argues, can come only from another rule accepted by the people which he calls the "Rule of Recognition."[39]

I want to argue that if the contractarian chooses to do so, she can give an account of the state that dovetails nicely with the Hartian legal theory.[40] On the convention analysis, the leadership convention created by the people generates rules which together constitute the Hartian Rule of Recognition. First, the convention defines governmental offices and establishes limits on the powers and duties of these offices. These powers and duties constitute what I will call the "operational" rules of government. Second, the convention bestows on some of these offices the authority to command, which involves giving the office-holder the power to make a command that the people will believe they have a prima facie reason to obey simply because these office-holders have made it. Call these "authority-bestowing" rules; they entitle the office-holder to make directives that are binding on the people, and making them is actually part of the process of defining the offices of government. (What kind of authoritative directives a particular office-holder can make is determined by the leadership convention.) And finally, there are rules which specify the process of filling these offices, such that the person selected by the process is entitled to the office.

---

[37] Rawls uses this phrase to describe the authority of the principles of justice upon which he believes rulers should act. See *A Theory of Justice* (Cambridge, Mass.: Harvard University Press, 1971), p. 135.

[38] Hart's legal theory is set forward in his *The Concept of Law* (Oxford, 1961).

[39] For a discussion of Hart's approach to authority, see Ronald Dworkin, "Model of Rules I," in his *Taking Rights Seriously* (Cambridge, Mass.: Harvard Univesity Press, 1977).

[40] The relationship between political analyses of the state and positivist and natural law theories of jurisprudence is badly underanalyzed. The discussion here is merely a start at such an analysis.

Creating the leadership convention involves generating these sorts of rules. Together they constitute an *impersonal* authority in the legal system, and I would argue that it is part of the conceptual analysis of the state that this impersonal authority exists. These rules are obligating not because they are themselves dictated by an authoritative office-holder (this puts the cart before the horse – these rules define what counts as an authoritative office-holder), but because they are accepted, via convention, by the people. Indeed, as Hart points out, these rules can exist and operate effectively even when there are many who are not terribly clear about the details of the authority of different offices of the government which the convention establishes. As long as there are some people who know the details, and these few are trusted by the rest to monitor the performance of any office-holder on the basis of these details, the convention can be said to be accepted by everyone.[41]

Let me stress again that on this approach to understanding the state's authority, the issue of whether the state is morally justifiable is irrelevant. This model offers an explanation of what the institution is, not a normative defense of it. If a moral theorist desires to pursue the justification of this institution, she will morally evaluate at the very least its use of negative sanctions to enforce its dictates, and perhaps also the moral legitimacy of the authority the state has over its subjects. If she believes the institution is morally justifiable, how would she defend it? She would do so using her favorite moral theory. Utilitarians, Kantians, and divine rights theorists will have different ways of defending (or attacking, if they choose) the state's legitimacy. And, of course, there are also contractarian ways of doing so. Contemporary philosophy has seen the rise of what I call contractarian moral theory, in which the notion of "what we could agree to" is understood to be central to evaluating actions, policies, and social institutions. There are a variety of contractarian moral theories that have been developed, and all of them are controversial. Embracing the convention analysis of the state commits one to *none* of these views, because it is a non-normative analysis. So, of course, if one wants to legitimate the state, one must supplement that analysis. Which theory one should choose, however, is a matter of independent philosophical assessment; there is no more reason to choose a contractarian defense of the state than to choose a contractarian defense of any institution or policy. One would do so only if one thought, on independent grounds, that this was the right moral theory to choose.

---

[41] See Hart's discussion in *The Concept of Law,* p. 111.

IV. Summary

The contractarian explanation of the state can therefore be summarized as follows:

The state is an institution whose primary role is to deter, prevent, and forestall conflict among people through the use of legislators, adjudicators, and coercive enforcers, and it is maintained by convention in which people are "in agreement" about what their government will be and who will rule within it; specifically, it establishes the offices of government and procedures for filling those offices, and it grants punishment power to some of these office-holders. Participating in that convention means, at the very least, not interfering with, and perhaps actively assisting in, the state's punishment activities – especially its formation and maintenance of punishment cadres. Hartian positivists will also argue that this convention is itself a complex set of rules entitling those selected by the procedures to hold office, obligating them to respect the terms of the office, and entitling them to make rules that are binding upon the people, so that it is an impersonal authority in the society by virtue of being accepted by the people.

The convention, once instituted, exists only for as long as the people maintain it, which involves their participation in the three punishment activities, and their continued acceptance and enforcement of the rules constituting it.

Note that the convention model presents the state as an institution whose primary role is to encourage cooperation and discourage conflict. For many this will be too limited a conception of the role of this institution, ignoring the way it may properly be engaged in the redistribution of assets in the name of justice, or in the education of its citizens, or in the promotion of cultural opportunities and endeavors. Contractarians can always argue for the addition of these duties to the state's agenda, but they would also argue that such additions do not change the fact that the state's power and authority to wield sanctions and issue binding commands are fundamental to understanding what it is, and how it is created and maintained.

What kind of relationship exists between the rulers and the ruled when the rulers' power is generated and maintained by convention? This is actually a complicated question, whose answer requires that we recognize that there is a hierarchy of what I will call (following Wittgenstein) "games" in a political society. First, there is the "political" game, in which the people are subordinated to government office-holders, who have the power to obligate them and to inflict sanctions upon them. So the relationship between people and ruler in this game is the relationship of a subordinate to a commander.

TABLE 3. *Ruler-subject relationship (preferences for the outcome created after the people's second move, 1 = highest, 4 = lowest)*

Ruler	People	Ruler	People
Govern according to terms of empowerment	Keep in power	2	1
	Depose	4	3
Ignore terms of empowerment	Depose	3	2
	Keep in power	1	4

But second, there is the meta-game that creates and maintains this object game, in which the people define and control the power of these offices and office-holders through their participation in the leadership convention. To understand the people's relationship with the rulers of this meta-game, let me use some of Locke's metaphors for a moment. Locke argued that creating the state involves the people becoming, after making contracts with one another, one unified entity – what he called a "political community." He then argued that the people, so understood, enter into contractual relations with the ruler. Of course literally there is rarely if ever such an explicit promissorial agreement between ruler and ruled, but if this language is metaphorical, it can be successfully cashed out using the convention model. That model places these parties in what I call an "agency" relationship, which is not contractual either in nature or origin, but which is similar enough to actual agency relationships, which are initiated by contract, to make any metaphorical talk of a social contract between ruler and ruled forgivable. Just as a principal gives (usually via contract) a person known as her 'agent' power to act by allowing her to wield a right belonging to the principal, so too do the subjects give a ruler political power through their generation of a leadership convention. And just as a principal can supervise the performance of her agent, and control the agent, by threatening to fire her if she does not use the principal's rights as the principal wished, so too can the people supervise the performance of the ruler-agent by threatening to depose him if he does not perform as the people wish. In Table 3 I give the game-theoretic structure of the ruler-subject relationship. Because the subjects in this game are able to make their move contingent upon how the ruler has moved, their possible moves, which are represented in the second column, are understood to be temporally posterior to the ruler's move. The two columns of numbers correspond to the players' preferences for outcomes created by the combination of their possible moves.

This game is not a prisoner's dilemma, and hence does not require promises to bind ruler and people effectively. The ruler knows that if she rules against the people's wishes, they will fire her: their keeping her in power when she rules badly ranks lowest for them, while their firing her when she rules badly ranks second highest for them. She also knows that if she rules well they will keep her "employed": their keeping her employed when she rules well ranks highest for them; their firing her when she rules well ranks second lowest for them. So she has a choice between ruling well and staying in power (ranked second) or ruling poorly and being deposed (ranked last). So her best move is to rule well. But this is exactly the move by her that the people most want her to make. Their preferences and power in this situation force her to make a first move which allows them to achieve their favorite outcome, but the game is also such that she is able to retain power (a highly desirable outcome for her as long as she pleases them). However, note that she is not completely powerless in this situation. Because the people need her to rule, she can be assured that her least favorite outcome (i.e., her doing the job and their deposing her) is also one of their least preferred outcomes. So she has enough power over them (at least for the time being) *because they need her* to secure a desirable outcome for herself (although not her most desirable outcome). Indeed, how well the agent needs to work is a matter of degree: to stay employed she must work just well enough to make it more advantageous to the principal to keep her rather than incur the costs of firing her. (So, in the end, the people who are the principal in this relationship will be unlikely to be able to demand and get exactly the performance from their ruler-agent that they would like.)

As I shall discuss in the next section, this analysis of the relationship between ruler and ruled is too simplistic, and I shall be discussing how to make it more sophisticated. However, one correction is easy to make, and making it allows us to cash out another Lockean metaphor. Insofar as the ruler's power is created through the generation of a convention, her power is the result of many individuals determining that obeying the commands of only this ruler (in particular, her punishment commands) is rational. Hence a single entity called "the people" do not literally bestow or withdraw power; instead, whether or not a person rules depends upon many individuals determining whether or not obedience or rebellion is in their best interest (where that interest is defined either by a moral or religious law or by their desires). Nonetheless, there is this much truth to the idea that "the people" institute and depose rulers: in order for individuals to institute a ruler, *each must coordinate (either explicitly or implicitly) with one another* on who the ruler shall be and what the scope of her legitimate areas of command are; and in order for individuals to depose a ruler, they must, once again, coordinate (either explicitly or implicitly) with one another on the idea that an alternative state of affairs would be better than the present state. So although Locke is saying something literally false when he says that the people contract with one another to form a unified political community which contracts with the ruler, nonetheless a state exists only when the individuals composing it are "in agreement" with one another, coordinating such that a leadership convention is established and maintained, and thereby becoming, collectively, the principal in an agency relationship with the office-holders.

One of the difficulties of coming to understand the state is that it is an enterprise constituted by two distinct games, in one of which the people are the controllers of the rulers, and in the other of which the people are controlled by them. We are indebted to the social contract theorists for trying, albeit with metaphors, to make that double relationship clear.

V. Criticizing the Convention Model

How successful is this model? In this section I want to evaluate two criticisms someone could make of my claim that the social contract tradition generates a historically plausible, convention-based model of the state's creation and maintenance. First, one might object that the model, regardless of its success as an explanatory theory, is simply not generated by the social contract tradition; second, one might argue that it cannot be successful as an explanation because it is not historically plausible. I will discuss each of these criticisms in turn.

The Convention Model and the Social Contract Tradition

To build the convention model out of Hobbes's and Locke's political writings using the resources of contemporary game theory strikes many as anachronistic at best, deeply distorting at worst. Are the language and tools that I use to state the model too dissimilar to the language and tools of the traditional contractarians to allow me to claim that it is nonetheless their model?

I do not believe so. We must resist the temptation to treat philosophical figures as museum pieces. Instead we should dissect, analyze, explicate, and respond to their arguments in order to see how far those arguments are right. Of course, it is anachronistic to read game theory back into traditional contractarian writings – that is not the point. The issue to be decided is whether or not we learn anything of value about Locke's and Hobbes's understanding of the state if we do so, and I think we do. These philosophers were groping for ways of understanding the state, not as the creation of God, not as ordained by nature, but as a human creation. The convention model explains how this is possible, and in the process, preserves two central ideas in the tradition: first, that there is a kind of agreement among the people that explains why the state exists, and second (although this point was contested by Hobbes), that there is an agreement between the people and the ruler setting out the terms of his rule. The first agreement is, on this model, a convention rather than an explicit promissorial agreement, whose generation could take many forms. The second agreement, on this model, is really an agency relationship between the people (who create and maintain the ruler's power for certain purposes) and the ruler (who must use that power to satisfy them or be deposed).

Still, I have made substantial revisions in the traditional contract argument by replacing talk of contracts with talk of conventions and agency relationships. I have argued that these revisions are consistent with and even required by the presuppositions of the traditional contractarians' arguments. By making these revisions have I vindicated the contractarian argument as an explication of the state, or have I refuted it?

Perhaps it really does not matter how one answers this question; what is important is the model itself and not its philosophical pedigree. Nonetheless, I tend to regard my analysis as a vindication of the contractarian argument. If one shows that the premises of a political argument require a different conceptual representation of the state than the representation given by the original users of that argument, then it is appropriate to say that the revisionist conceptual representation has been implicit in the argument all along (albeit unacknowledged by its previous users). It is because the preferences of the people in the traditional contractarians' state of nature establish battle-of-the-sexes dilemmas rather than prisoner's dilemmas that it becomes right to say that, on the contractarian's view, the creation of government requires the generation of a convention.

Hume saw himself as an opponent of the social contract argument because he endorsed ideas which this analysis incorporates. But I would argue that he should be seen only as an opponent of the traditional contractarian's persistent use of the idea of contract, an idea which my analysis shows is not implicit in the argument itself and which, if inserted into it, damages the argument's operation as an explanation of a ruler's political power. Indeed, I would argue that both Hume and I are "revisionists" only in the sense that we are revising, and improving upon, the standard interpretation of the social contract argument.

Is the Model Right?

Critics may worry about the extent to which the model can be empirically verified. I think such worries have merit, but before I explain why, I want to show that it does have some real explanatory power.

First, do the preferences of real people match the coordination-game preferences of Locke's or Hobbes's people on the question of whether or not to enter civil society? This is an empirical question to be answered by empirical study, but given that these philosophers show why moral, religious, and self-interested motivations give rise either to pure or to conflict-ridden coordination-game preferences on the question of instituting the state, this suggests that a wide range of real people, with any of these motivations, would nonetheless have preferences that fit the convention model.

This model can also be used to illuminate the actual reasoning processes of people who are considering whether or not to rebel against their government. Consider Gregory Kavka's intriguing discussion of what he calls the paradox of revolution. In Kavka's words, the paradox goes as follows:

> Exploited citizenry are apparently in a multiparty prisoner's dilemma situation with respect to participating in a mass revolt. Collectively they have the power to overthrow their oppressors, and would probably be better off if they did so. But an individual's participation in a revolt is dangerous and will have only a minute effect on the prospect of the revolt succeeding, while the individual can expect to reap most of the benefits of a successful revolt (should one occur) without participating. Hence, rational individuals will not participate, and mass revolts of rational citizens will never occur even against tyrannical, repressive, or exploitive regimes. This odd conclusion – that the rationality of the members of a society prevents them from overthrowing a despised government – is called *the paradox of revolution.*[42]

Kavka contends that the paradox shows that people are in a multiparty prisoner's dilemma with respect to the question of revolution, and as all students of this dilemma know, rational actions by rational people will lead to a suboptimal outcome in a prisoner's dilemma – in this

---

[42] See Kavka, *Hobbesian Moral and Political Theory*, p. 267, who cites the work of Olson, Tullock, and Buchanan in his development of the paradox.

case, the outcome of continued submission. But in stating the paradox in argument form, Kavka does not explicitly mention any game-theoretic situation. He presents it as follows:

1. Rational individuals act so as to maximize expected payoffs.
2. In a potentially revolutionary situation, the expected costs of participation are higher than the expected costs of non-participation, and there are no sufficiently compensating expected benefits of participation.
3. Therefore, rational individuals in a potentially revolutionary situation will not participate in a revolution.[43]

Of course, the argument cannot establish that revolution will never occur, because, as Kavka notes, people sometimes act irrationally, and thus irrational motives might explain revolutionary activity throughout history. Moreover, "the possibility of others irrationally joining a revolt may influence the cost-benefit analysis of *rational* potential revolutionaries."[44] With this in mind, Kavka proposes what he calls the "dynamic-maximizing" solution:

Rational agents' expected utility calculations about participation in revolution will *change* as they observe others joining the revolutionary struggle. In particular, as a first approximation we would expect agents' estimates of the probability of the revolution succeeding to go up, and their estimates of the probability of being punished for taking part in the revolt to go down, as the number of people they observe taking part in the revolt increases. These changes in probability will in turn raise the expected benefits associated with participation (since the receipt of many such benefits is contingent upon the revolt succeeding) and decrease the expected costs (e.g., the risk of being punished for participating). It is also possible that the intrinsic payoffs of participation, such as the pleasure of taking part in a mass enterprise, and the intrinsic costs of nonparticipation, such as the guilt one may feel over being a free-rider, will increase as the number of others participating increases.[45]

So the idea is that as confederacies enlarge, more and more people will find it rational to participate. In particular, any individual will join the revolution when his or her "revolution-participation threshold" is reached. "Whether a revolution will occur will depend upon the distribution

---

43 Ibid., p. 268.
44 Ibid.
45 See ibid., pp. 273–74. Kavka proposes three possible solutions to the paradox. The first two are in Kavka's eyes problematic, and he is most pleased with the third. Hence this is the one I concentrate on here.

of revolution-participating thresholds among the members of a population."[46] It is possible that a population will have thresholds distributed such that revolution is essentially impossible, but it may also have thresholds distributed such that it is inevitable.

I like Kavka's solution to this paradox, but I want to argue that it is a solution only because, in fact, the citizenry are *not* in a multiparty prisoner's dilemma with respect to the question of revolution. This should be evident because, in a real prisoner's dilemma, it does not matter how many of my fellow players are disposed to choose the cooperative action – I am still rational to refrain from cooperation. The fact that Kavka's solution has it that people will find cooperation in the revolution rational with increasing numbers of rebels shows that they are in a different kind of game.

As I have argued at length elsewhere, problems can seem "prisoner's dilemma-like" even though they have a different game-theoretic structure,[47] and that is what is going on here. In fact, parties are in a coordination game with respect to the question of revolution. Just as creating a state involves solving a host of potentially conflict-ridden coordination problems, so, too, does changing it. Imagine that I am a disgruntled citizen who would like a new ruler. What reasons do I have for maintaining what I take to be a bad convention? Consider the reasons I have for maintaining any convention, for example, the convention to drive on the right. If there is no law requiring me to respect this convention, I will respect it anyway if I believe (a) that I am in a coordination dilemma, (b) that in fact driving on the right is the conventional solution to that dilemma, (c) that it is a convention that enables the community to achieve a desirable coordination equilibrium, so that it furthers the interest of those in the coordination dilemma, and most importantly (d) there is no other convention on a different coordination equilibrium which it is rational for me to pursue (given the costs and benefits of doing so) by (in part) not obeying the convention. Note (d) presupposes that by acting so as to respect a convention, I also help in a very small way to maintain it through my respect for it.

These four considerations are also central to explaining why and when a citizen has reason to obey her ruler. I have reason to respect a leadership convention about who should rule, and thus obey the ruler, when (a') I

[46] Ibid., p. 274.
[47] See my "Free Rider Problems in the Production of Collective Goods," *Economics and Philosophy* 3 (1987): 245–73.

am in a (conflict-ridden) coordination dilemma about who should rule; (b′) in fact this ruler is the conventional solution to that problem; (c′) it is a convention that enables us to realize a coordination equilibrium, so that it furthers the interests of those in the coordination dilemma; and (d′) there is no other leadership convention that would realize a different coordination equilibrium whose adoption I believe it rational for me to pursue (given the costs and benefits of doing so) by (in part) not respecting this convention. Again, this last point presupposes that when I act so as to respect the leadership convention and obey the ruler's commands, particularly his punishment orders, I help in a small way to maintain this convention and keep him in power.

Now what happens when a subject believes (a′) and (b′), but denies (c′) – judging the convention to be bad either because it fails to realize a coordination equilibrium at all (so that, barring exorbitant costs, changing should be pareto efficient for everyone) or because there is a better coordination equilibrium available to the group (although perhaps not better for everyone). In either case he concludes that people have made a mistake, and would be better off, on the whole, deposing the present leader and replacing her with another ruler. He therefore wishes to take from her the authority to rule which this bad convention grants her. If they come to agree that they have a better alternative (so that for each of them [d′] is no longer true), then (as we discussed above) neither he nor they will believe they should obey her, and will rebel. But if they do not agree with him, then his unilateral action in support of another candidate will be useless. *In fact*, in this situation, a convention, albeit a bad one, does exist. And it is this fact which he is forced to take into account in his calculations. He might still draw the conclusion that he should obey the ruler if, for moral or self-interested reasons, the consequences of acting to change the convention will be worse than the consequences of acquiescing in the bad convention. He may make this judgment when he finds the present government bad but believes (given what he knows) that so few others agree with him that an attempt to change the convention by refusing to obey the ruler would be futile, or when he believes that they do agree with him that the present ruler is bad but disagree among themselves about what convention should replace it.[48]

---

[48] Hobbes argued that it was against reason for a subject to rebel against her government, but I have argued (in *Hobbes and the Social Contract Tradition*, chs. 8 and 9) that the premises of his argument commit him to the rationality of rebellion in certain circumstances. That discussion runs along roughly the same lines as the discussion here.

However, there is one other reason why someone might obey a convention even when he judges it to be bad, and that is when there is no
common knowledge of how the government is evaluated by the citizenry
generally. Kavka gives a model for how this kind of situation inhibits revolution in his paradox of perfect tyranny. As Kavka explains, a tyrant who
is universally disliked can, paradoxically, remain in power, when the situation is such that the people obey the tyrant out of fear of one another.
That is, each citizen is obedient

out of fear that some of his fellow citizens would answer the ruler's call to punish
him if he were not. So citizen A obeys out of fear of citizens B, C, et al., B obeys
out of fear of A, C, et al., and so on. In this situation, the beliefs of rational citizens
that their fellows will punish them for not following the ruler's orders constitute
a network of interlocking mutual expectations, a "net of fear," that provides each
citizen with a sufficient motive of obedience.[49]

Kavka's remarks here fit with my analysis, given earlier, of sovereign
empowerment through the citizenry's decision to obey and/or respect
his punishment commands. This is, in effect, the decision by which people generate the leadership convention. Once in place, that convention
yields considerable power for the ruler. But it is always power that, in
the last analysis, can be traceable to the decisions of the individuals who
are participating in the punishment process. Thus, if the frail and universally disliked ruler can inhibit the passing of information among the
disgruntled citizenry, their knowledge of the convention's existence and
their uncertainty about receiving support from others will likely make it
irrational for them to risk opposing the ruler.

In this situation the people are "mastered" by their ruler, despite the
fact that they empower him by their obedience to him. To be *mastered is
to be subject to the use of coercion in a way that disables one from participating in
the process of creating or changing a leadership convention.* Because there are
degrees of disablement, there are degrees of mastery. The use of coercion against blacks in South Africa, against left-wing Chileans by Pinochet,
and against Tibetans in China is substantial enough to inhibit such activity severely, rendering these people mastered to an extreme degree. But
techniques of mastery are present in all Western democracies, as anyone whose name is on file at the FBI knows. A ruler has, and must have,
significant coercive power over her citizens. That power makes her disproportionately more powerful than any of her subjects (or even fairly

49 Kavka, *Hobbesian Moral and Political Theory*, p. 257.

large groups of those subjects), and she may be able to use this power to disable, partially or totally, one or more of them from participating in or changing the leadership convention. And it is so tempting for rulers to do so that there probably never has been (nor ever will be) a regime in which such disabling does not go on to some degree or other.

Even worse, a portion of the population may approve of the mastery of the rest of the population and actively support their ruler's use of power to disable that portion from participation in the leadership convention. Those who are disabled may even be in the majority if the ruler and his supporters are clever enough to keep important technology from them, rendering them badly unequal (e.g., in South Africa).

So there are really two forms of political domination which our discussion has revealed: the domination of a master, and the domination of a "hired" protection agency. The contractarian story, which presupposes that every person involved in the creation of the state is the equal of every other, results only in the creation of the second form of domination. But if, as seems true in the real world, equality cannot be presupposed because of technological (if not natural) superiority, then mastery can and does exist. Indeed, insofar as the very empowerment of a ruler destroys equality by making her more powerful than those who are ruled by her, the seeds of political mastery are planted in the very act of generating a leadership convention.

A pure form of mastery in a human community is very unlikely. Given human frailty and technological limitations (Superman and James Bond movies to the contrary), no ruler can hope to master people all by himself: he needs supporters to do so, and this means there must be at least an agency relationship between him and his supporters. In this sense Pinochet, Stalin, and Idi Amin, despite their mastery of subject populations, have all been agents; the power relationship within the ruling clique supporting them fits the contractarian's agency analysis of a political regime.

On the other hand, a pure form of agency seems just as unlikely. Aside from the fact that a portion of the population may approve of the mastery of others and actively support their ruler's use of power to disable the rest from participating in the leadership convention, a ruler is always able to take advantage of the fact that the punishment power granted to him makes him disproportionately more powerful than any of his subjects (or even fairly large groups of those subjects) in order partially or totally to disable one or more of them from participating in or changing the leadership convention. For better or worse, when people create a state, they create a monster, over which it may not be easy to maintain control.[50]

Given both the reality and the limitations of technological dominance, the explanatory truth about political regimes would seem to be that they are mixtures, to various degrees, of the agency and mastery forms of domination. So what the contractarian "explains" with his convention model is only one aspect of our political reality: that is, the extent to which rulers have power, and perhaps also authority, through some or all of the subjects' participation in a leadership convention. The convention model fails to accommodate the reality of the nonagency aspects of subjects' relationships with the regimes that rule them.

But even if contractarians have overemphasized the agency aspect of our political life, this may be because they have intuitively sensed that probably only the agency aspect can be morally justified. The convention model gives us the form of domination we would create if we were and always remained equal, and even as that state of equality is more ideal than fact, so too is the kind of political regime it generates.

---

[50] Thus many polities (e.g., the United States) rely on separation of powers to prevent any one individual or office from achieving significant degrees of mastery.

Selected Bibliography

Books

The Authority of Reason. Cambridge: Cambridge University Press, 1998.
Forgiveness and Mercy (with Jeffrey Murphy). Cambridge: Cambridge University Press, 1988.
Hobbes and the Social Contract Tradition. Cambridge: Cambridge University Press, 1986.
Political Philosophy. Boulder, Colo.: Westview Press, 1996.

Articles

"Contracts and Choices: Does Rawls Have a Social Contract Theory?" *Journal of Philosophy* 77 (1980): 315–38.
"The Failure of Expected Utility as a Theory of Reason." *Economics and Philosophy* 10 (October 1994): 195–242.
"The Hobbesian Side of Hume." In *Reclaiming the History of Ethics: Essays for John Rawls,* ed. B. Herman, C. Korsgaard, and A. Reath. Cambridge: Cambridge University Press, 1997.
"Immigration, Identity, and Justice." In *Justice in Immigration,* ed. W. Schwartz. Cambridge: Cambridge University Press, 1995.
"The Moral Education Theory of Punishment." *Philosophy and Public Affairs* 13 (1984): 208–38.
"On Instrumental Rationality." In *Reason, Ethics, and Society: Essays in Honor of Kurt Baier,* ed. J. Schneewind. Chicago: Open Court, 1996.
"Should Political Philosophy Be Done without Metaphysics?" *Ethics* 99 (1989): 791–814.
"Two Faces of Contractarian Thought." In *Contractarianism and Rational Choice: Essays on Gauthier,* ed. P. Vallentyne. Cambridge: Cambridge University Press, 1990. Pp. 31–55.

Index

abortion, 176
agency relationship, 208
agreement: in convention model, 211; promissorial, 195; self-interested, 195; tacit, *see* convention
Anscombe, G. E. M., 202, 204n36
Archimedean point, 16n33
Aristotle: on culpable ignorance, 98; on friendship and justice, 2; on self-hatred stemming from vice, 58
authority, 204n36; installing one's own, 78; legal, 103–5; political, 202–6; of reason, 77

Badhwar, Neera, 65
Baier, Annette, 1, 7n18, 33n51, 43; on Gilligan's moral voices, 4–5
Battle-of-the-Sexes game, 189, 192n16
beneficence: authentic, 62–63; self-serving commendation of, 64; thought never immoral, 47; as a vice, 53–54
Bentham, Jeremy, 7n18
Book of Esther, 144
Brontë, Charlotte, 6–7
burdens of judgment, 171

Calabresi, Guido, 112n8
Cicero, 72
Coleman, Jules, 112n8, 112n9; on corrective justice, 110–11
communitarian critique of contractarianism, 35–37
comprehensive moral doctrine, 152n2, 161

consensus, on process, 179, 181
contract, 193; justificational use of, i, 11, 13–14
contract image: Hampton's use of, 25–26; Rawls's use of, 23–24
contract test: animated by conception of human worth, 23; applied to family, 21, 22; applied to relationships, 20–21; rejects commodization, 26; reveals exploitation, 30–32; used to evaluate response to beneficence, 34; when inappropriate, 32–33
contractarian approach to morality, 1, 8–9, 24–25; communitarian critique of, 35–37; feminist critique of, 9
contractarian explanation of the state: obscured by explicit agreement narratives, 199; summarized, 207
convention, 195
coordination equilibria, 189
culpability: includes knowledge of authoritative command, 89; legal, 102; moral, 85; rational, 74
culpable ignorance, 99

Dante, 89
defiance: beliefs involved in, 94; mental act of, 83; of practical reason, 79–80; of reason, 78; renders irrationality intelligible, 83; value of, 106–7
defiance account of immorality: degrees of defiance, 96; limits of, 92; stated, 91
degradation, 121–22

221

For EU product safety concerns, contact us at Calle de José Abascal, 56–1°,
28003 Madrid, Spain or eugpsr@cambridge.org.